Caring for Children in School-Age Programs

Volume I
A Competency-Based
Training Program

Derry G. Koralek
Roberta L. Newman
Laura J. Colker

TEACHING
STRATEGIES
INC.

Washington, DC

Updates to Module 1 (Safe), Module 2 (Healthy), and Bibliography © 1999

Updates to Bibliography, learning activities, and Module 13 (Professionalism) © 2000
Printed and bound in the United States.

Editor: Diane Trister Dodge
Layout Design: John Fay
Illustrations: Jennifer Barrett O'Connell
Cover Design: Margaret C. Pallas
Production: Douglas Gritzmacher

Published by:
Teaching Strategies, Inc.
P.O. Box 42243
Washington, DC 20015

4th Printing: 2000

Two Volume Set, ISBN: 1-879537-13-3
Volume I ISBN: 1-879537-14-1

Library of Congress Catalog Card Number: 95-060465

ACKNOWLEDGMENTS

Caring for Children in School-Age Programs is based on a set of training materials originally developed for the U.S. Army Child and Youth Services. It is the last in Teaching Strategies' series of competency-based training programs that includes: *Caring for Infants and Toddlers, Caring for Preschool Children,* and *Caring for Children in Family Child Care.* All of these materials are organized into 13 modules that address the competencies required to provide a quality program.

Many individuals contributed to the development of these training materials. M.-A. Lucas, Chief of Army Child and Youth Services, recognized the important role school-age programs play in the lives of children and initiated the development of this training. Dr. Victoria Moss, Program Manager, Supplemental Programs and Services, Department of Army, guided the development of the training modules and provided us with constructive and helpful suggestions that greatly improved the program. We are grateful to P. K. Tomlinson and Linda Harwanko, Education Program Specialists, Department of Army, who reviewed and gave extensive feedback on the modules. The following Service representatives also reviewed and provided input that enriched these training materials: Keith Painter, Recreation Specialist, Department of Army; Carolee Van Horn, Community Recreation Specialist, Department of Navy; Madeline Wagner, Communication Recreation Specialist, The Marine Corps; and Maryalice Howe, Child Development and Youth Specialist, Department of Air Force. Dr. Charles H. Flatter, Professor, Institute for Child Study, University of Maryland, provided us with initial guidance on the development of the modules.

Caring for Children in School-Age Programs was reviewed by Ellen Gannett, Associate Director, and Susan O'Connor, Research Associate, School-Age Child Care Project at the Center for Research on Women at Wellesley College. Their critique of each module and suggestions for enhancing the content were invaluable. Ellen and Susan also verified the linkages between this training program and the criteria outlined in *Advancing School-Age Child Care Quality.* We are indebted to each of them for taking a strong interest in this project and sharing their expertise so generously.

In 1999, we updated Modules 1 (Safe) and 2 (Healthy) to reflect current guidelines. We thank Karen Sokal-Gutierrez, M.D. for reviewing and revising these modules. We thank Caitlin Pike for updating the resources and she and Toni Bickart for editing the 1999 reprint.

In 2000, we again updated resource information, including web sites, and revised learning activities to incorporate the *National School-Age Care Alliance (NSACA) Standards for Quality School-Age Care.*

It is our hope that as school-age staff undertake this training program they will gain knowledge and develop new skills that will allow them to offer the highest quality of programming. We also hope this training will lead to greater understanding of how school-age programs encourage and support children's development, allow them to explore and build on their interests, and help them grow into competent, independent, and productive citizens.

ORIENTATION

OVERVIEW

You are about to begin a unique and personalized training program designed to help you acquire the skills and knowledge to provide a high-quality program for school-age children. Whether you are new to the profession or have years of experience, this training program offers practical information on topics central to working with school-age children.

Working in a school-age program is more than a job. You are part of an important profession, one with an established body of knowledge and nationally-recognized standards. You can take pride in the important role you play in the lives of children. High quality school-age programs can benefit children now and in the future. Skilled staff can help children learn to get along with others and communicate ideas and feelings. By participating in a wide variety of recreational activities children develop skills, interests, and talents they can pursue throughout their lives.

How the Training Program Can Help You

As an adult, you bring years of experience that will help you to provide a quality program for children during their out-of-school hours. Once you begin this training program, you will find you already have many skills addressed in the modules. Completing the modules will enable you to extend and expand on the skills and knowledge you already have. The training will help you meet the profession's standards. As a result, you will find working with school-age children to be more and more rewarding.

One of the major factors in achieving a high-quality program is the specialized training available for staff. *Caring for Children in School-Age Programs* is designed to provide this specialized training. Children change every day as they grow and develop new skills and interests. Therefore, information is provided on the typical developmental stages of children in three age groups: 5 to 7, 8 to 10, and 11 to 12. The modules include many examples of how you can apply this knowledge to plan and implement your program. The more you know about children, the more effective you can be in developing a positive relationship with each child.

The Content Addressed in the Training Program

Training designed to improve knowledge and skills is called "competency-based" training. The knowledge and skills for working with children under five years of age have been defined as 13 "functional areas" by the Council for Early Childhood Professional Recognition. They are known as the Child Development Associate (CDA) Competency Standards.

To develop *Caring for Children in School-Age Programs*, we used these same 13 areas to define the content. Experts in school-age care helped us identify the most important skills in each of the 13 functional areas. We applied their input to define the topics you will study as you go through the training program.

Additionally, we reviewed standards for school-age programs as defined in the following publications:

> *Advancing School-Age Child Care Quality* (School-Age Child Care Project,[1] Center for Research on Women at Wellesley College, 1991)

> *Developmentally Appropriate Practice in School-Age Child Care Programs* and *Quality Criteria for School-Age Child Care Programs* (Project Home Safe, American Home Economics Association, 1991)

> *Standards for Quality School-Age Child Care*.[2] (National Association of Elementary School Principals, 1993)

The National School-Age Care Alliance (NSACA) and the National Institute on Out-of-School Time (NIOST) used *Advancing School-Age Child Care Quality* while developing the *NSACA Standards for Quality School-Age Care* and a system for school-age program improvement and accreditation, *Advancing and Recognizing Quality (ARQ)*. *Caring for Children in School-Age Programs* reflects both the original and new national standards and allows staff to gain the skills and knowledge used to implement quality programs.

How the Training Program Works

Your first step in this training program will be to take a self-assessment. This self-assessment is **not** a test. It is designed to introduce you to the major topics covered in each module and help you identify which topics you want to learn about first.

---

[1] Now called the National Institute on Out-of-School-Time (NIOST).
[2] Reissued in 1993 as *After-School Programs and the K-8 Principal: Standards for Quality School-Age Child Care*, Revised edition.

Before you begin the training program your trainer will observe you working with children. Observation is an important training tool. Trainers use observations throughout the training program to give you feedback on your progress in applying the skills and knowledge gained as you work on the modules. Together with your trainer you will review the observation notes and the results of the self-assessment and develop a plan that will work for you.

Some people are concerned when they see the size of the training program. Do not be alarmed. You can take one module at a time and pace yourself. Once you finish one module, you will be familiar with the approach. This will help you work through and apply what you learn in the remaining modules.

While the modules are designed to be self-instructional, it is best if you can work with an experienced trainer. A trainer can review and discuss your responses to the learning activities, answer your questions, and discuss your plans for applying new skills and knowledge.

There are five steps you will follow for each of the modules. These steps are described below.

The **overview** introduces and defines the topic addressed in the module. You learn why the topic is important and review concrete examples of how school-age staff demonstrate their competence in that functional area. Three short situations demonstrate how school-age staff apply skills in this area. After reading these, you answer questions to help you learn more about the topic. The last activity in the overview asks you to relate the topic to your own experiences as an adult.

Complete the overview.

The **pre-training assessment** is a list of the key skills competent staff should possess in each area. You indicate whether you use a skill regularly, sometimes, or not enough. After completing the assessment, you identify three to five skills to improve or topics you wish to learn more about. Before beginning the learning activities you discuss the overview and the pre-training assessment with your trainer.

Do the pre-training assessment.

Each module has four to six **learning activities**. The activities begin with objectives—what you will learn—and several pages of information about the topic. After completing the reading, you apply what you learned to work with the children in your program. This may involve answering questions, completing a checklist, trying out suggestions you have read, planning an activity, or taking notes and thinking about your observations of children.

Complete each learning activity.

When you have completed each learning activity, arrange a time to meet with your trainer to discuss the activity and to receive feedback. For some activities, you also meet with colleagues to discuss what you did and what you learned.

Summarize your progress.

After you have completed all the learning activities in the module, you review the pre-training assessment and **summarize your progress**. You then meet with your trainer to discuss your progress and to determine whether you are ready to be assessed.

Complete the assessment process.

Your trainer will give you the **knowledge and competency assessments**. On the knowledge assessment, you must achieve a score of 80 percent before going on to a new module. For the competency assessment, your trainer observes you working with children to assess your competence in the functional area. Some competency assessments must take place at a specific time. For example, the competency assessment for Module 11, Families, should take place at drop-off or pick-up time, when parents are present. After you have completed both assessments you and your trainer discuss whether you have successfully completed the module. If you need to spend more time on the module, your trainer may suggest activities to help you gain the skills needed to demonstrate competence.

You can expect to spend about four to six weeks on each module. Generally, it takes 12 to 18 months to thoroughly complete the training program.

What Makes the Training Program Unique

Several features of the training program make it unique.

- The materials are appropriate for new as well as experienced staff.
- You will receive your own set of materials that become your personal resource and journal for working with children.
- You take responsibility for your progress through the training program with guidance and feedback provided by a trainer.
- The information presented in the modules is practical and of immediate use in your daily work with children.
- Many of the learning activities ask you to observe children to learn about their skills and interests. Observation is a key way to get to know children and to plan ways to respond to each child as an individual.

When you have completed the training program, you will have the skills and knowledge to plan and implement a program designed for school-age children. You will be able to:

- create an environment and plan activities that complement children's experiences in school;
- give children opportunities to make choices;
- involve children in planning the program;
- offer a balance of education and recreation activities to meet different interests, skills, and needs.

Before You Begin

Take a few minutes to review the **glossary** on the following page. It defines the words and phrases used throughout the training program. The glossary is followed by a bibliography of suggested resources on school-age programs and a list of publishers and distributors of resources. You may find the recommended resources in your program's library, or you may want to collect some for your own professional library. The self-assessment comes after the list of publishers and distributors of resources.

When you are ready, take the self-assessment and begin planning your training.

Please Note: Throughout the modules we use stories and examples to clarify and illustrate the content. While in many school-age programs, children call the staff by their first names, in these modules we refer to them by their last names to distinguish them from the children in the stories. When the children address staff members, they use their first names.

GLOSSARY

Competencies Those tasks, skills, attitudes, and values needed to provide a high-quality school-age program. Competencies differ from knowledge in that competencies describe a staff member's actions and performance.

Competency assessments The performance-based section of the assessment process. For the competency assessments, staff demonstrate their skills while working with children.

Developmentally appropriate practice Program environment, activities, and adult interactions with children reflect children's individual characteristics and stages of social, emotional, physical, and cognitive development. Developmentally appropriate practice is age, individually, and culturally appropriate.

Developmental stages All the stages a child passes through as he or she gains social, emotional, physical, and cognitive skills.

Environment The indoor and outdoor space regularly available for the program. It includes furniture, materials, equipment, the schedule and routines followed, and the interactions of children and adults.

Functional areas The 13 major categories of tasks or functions used as the framework for this training program. Each module addresses a functional area in which a staff member must demonstrate competence in order to complete the training program.

Knowledge assessment The paper-and-pencil exercises of the assessment process, testing knowledge of the concepts presented in the module.

Observation The act of systematically watching and objectively taking notes on what a child says and does. Staff use observation notes to learn more about a child in order to offer a program that reflects the child's current needs, strengths, and interests.

Pre-training assessment A tool used at the beginning of each module by a staff member and a trainer to identify what skills the staff member has and where more training is needed.

School-age children Children from 5 (kindergarten) to 12 (sixth grade) years old.

BIBLIOGRAPHY

It would be impossible to list all of the excellent resources for school-age professionals. Here are some favorites—old and new. Under "General Topics" we list materials relevant to all modules. There are additional materials listed for specific modules. Many could be listed in more than one category. You can purchase items marked with an asterisk (*) and review additional books and videos at the Teaching Strategies web site (www.teachingstrategies.com).

Activities for School-Age Child Care, Barbara Blakley, et. al. (Washington, DC: National Association for the Education of Young Children, 1989). This resource includes hundreds of activities for children ages 5 through 10. Suggestions for working with parents are included.

Anti-Bias Curriculum: Tools for Empowering Young Children, Louise Derman-Sparks and the A.B.C. Task Force (Washington, DC: National Association for the Education of Young Children, 1989). This book has suggestions to help adults minimize, deal with, and eliminate biases unintentionally conveyed to children.

Caring for School-Age Children, 2nd edition, Phyllis Click (Albany, NY: Delmar Publishers Inc., 1998). This book is directed to front-line staff who work with school-age children. There are chapters on how children grow and develop, budgeting, planning, and the environment. Section II addresses all aspects of the curriculum. The final section of the book discusses the community and how to involve representatives in the program.

*Developmentally Appropriate Practice in Early Childhood Programs, Revised edition, Sue Bredekamp and Carol Copple, eds. (Washington, DC: National Association for the Education of Young Children, 1997). This publication defines standards for quality in programs for children up to age eight and strategies to support growth and development.

Half a Childhood: Quality Programs for Out-of-School Hours, 2nd edition, Judith Bender, Charles H. Flatter, and Jeanette Sorrentino (Nashville, TN: School-Age NOTES, 2000). This completely revised book describes best practices in programs serving school-age children during out-of-school time. It includes information on children and families, staff requirements, and more than 1000 activity ideas.

How to Play With Kids: A Powerful Field-Tested Nuts and Bolts Condensed Guide to Unleash and Improve Your 'Kid-Relating' Skills, Revised edition, Jim Therrell (Pacifica, CA: Play Today Press, 1992). This resource presents strategies for leading children's play and stresses the importance of leaders becoming actively involved in playing games with children.

MegaSkills, 3rd edition, Dorothy Rich (Boston, MA: Houghton-Mifflin, 1998). MegaSkills are the 11 basic values, attitudes, and behaviors used by successful individuals in school, on the job, at home, in the family, and in the community. Though written for parents, there are many strategies school-age

General Topics

staff can use to help children develop skills such as confidence, motivation, initiative, and focus.

The New York Times/KIDS FIRST! Guide to the Best Children's Videos, Ranny Levy (New York, NY: Pocket Books, 1999). Written with The Coalition for Quality Children's Media (CQCM), this book features reviews of over 1,000 children's videos, 500 recommended family feature films, and more than 100 CD-ROMs, organized by age and subject matter. Selections were reviewed by child development and media specialists, librarians, teachers, and over 3,000 children from diverse backgrounds. Listings are organized by age group—from infancy to the teen years—as recommended by child development specialists.

School-Age Children With Special Needs: What Do They Do When School Is Out? Dale Fink (Boston, MA: Exceptional Parent Press, 1988). This book discusses the child care needs of school-age children with disabilities and offers suggestions for meeting these needs.

School-Age Ideas and Activities for After School Programs, Karen Haas-Foletta and Michele Cogley (Nashville, TN: School-Age NOTES, 1990). This book includes helpful hints and strategies along with over 140 program-tested activities and games. There are ideas on shared space, scheduling, programming for older children, clubs, summer themes, and field trips.

The Smart Parent's Guide to KIDS' TV, Milton Chen, Ph.D. (San Francisco, CA: KQED Books, 1994). Although written for parents, this book will give school-age staff information about the effects and benefits of children's television programming. As informed consumers, they can decide when and how to use the medium to support children's development and learning.

Working for Children and Families: Safe and Smart After-School Programs, (Washington, DC: Partnership for Family Involvement in Education, U. S. Department of Education, 2000). This report presents positive research and examples showing the potential of quality after-school activities to keep children safe, engaged, and learning. Examples of successful approaches and programs are highlighted throughout the publication. The report includes an extensive bibliography and list of resources for after-school programs. Download at www.ed.gov/pubs/parents/SafeSmart or call 1-877-4-ED-PUBS to order a copy.

Yardsticks, Children in the Classroom, Ages 4-14, A Resource for Parents and Teachers, Chip Wood (Greenfield, MA: Northeast Foundation for Children, 1997). This easy-to-read book describes growth and development of children ages 4 to 14. Staff can use it as a handy reference when planning activities and trying to understand children's behavior.

Health and Safety

Caring for Our Children, National Health and Safety Standards: Guidelines for Out-of-Home Child Care Programs, 2nd edition (Washington, DC: American Public Health Association and Elk Grove Village, IL: American Academy of Pediatrics, in press 2000). This comprehensive volume defines the standards and rationale for ensuring children's health and safety in child care programs.

Cup Cooking: Individual Child-Portion Picture Recipes, Barbara Johnsonn (Beltsville, MD: Gryphon House, 1998). *Cup Cooking* offers step-by-step instructions children can follow to make their own snacks. Each of the 40 recipes provides a single serving.

Model Child Care Health Policies, Revised, Early Childhood Education Linkage System, Pennsylvania Chapter of the American Academy of Pediatrics, (Washington, DC: National Association for the Education of Young Children, 1997). These model policies provide an excellent starting point for writing health policies. Programs can order the policies on a computer disk so they can adapt and reproduce them.

Program Environment

The Complete Learning Center Book, Rebecca Isbell (Beltsville, MD: Gryphon House, 1995). This illustrated guide gives layouts and suggestions for setting up and using 32 learning centers. Staff can adapt these ideas for school-age programs.

The Outside Play and Learning Book, Karen Miller (Beltsville, MD: Gryphon House, 1989). A comprehensive and creative collection of outdoor activities that includes many suggestions for making good use of the outdoor environment in all seasons.

School-Age Care Environment Rating Scale, Thelma Harms, Ellen Vineberg Jacobs, and Donna Romano White (New York, NY: Teachers College Press, 1995). School-age staff can use this 49-item rating scale to assess program quality in seven areas: space and furnishings; health and safety; activities; interactions; program structure; staff development; and supplementary items. Training guides and score sheets are available.

Physical

Beyond Winning: Sports and Games All Kids Want to Play, Lawrence Rowen (Carthage, IL: Fearon Teacher Aids, 1989). This book describes 40 fun games for athletes and non-athletes. The games emphasize teamwork and creativity. Included are techniques for helping children overcome fears related to sports and strategies for reducing aggression.

The Cooperative Sports and Games Book and *The Second Cooperative Games Book*, Terry Orlick (New York, NY: Pantheon Books, 1978 and 1982). Both books provide directions for cooperative games aimed at helping adults and children work together rather than compete against each other. The games are new, adapted versions of familiar games, and games borrowed from other cultures.

Fit Kids. Kenneth H. Cooper, M.D., M.P.H. (Nashville, TN: Broadman and Holman, 1999). This book on the physical development of school-age children has tips for encouraging children to participate in fitness activities and follow nutritious diets. Menus and recipes are included. Although written for parents, this resource includes useful information for school-age program staff.

Cognitive, Communication, and Creative

Growing Up Creative, 2nd edition, Teresa Amabile (Buffalo, NY: Creative Education Foundation, 1992). Written for parents, this book explains Amabile's theories about creativity and offers strategies for keeping children's creativity alive. Suggested practices are applicable to school-age program settings.

Intelligence Reframed: Multiple Intelligences for the 21st Century, Howard Gardner (New York, NY: Basic Books, 1999). In this book, Gardner explains his theory of multiple intelligences and describes how to apply the theories to help children develop to their full potential.

Making Make Believe: Fun Props, Costumes, and Creative Play Ideas, MaryAnn F. Kohl (Beltsville, MD: Gryphon House, Inc., 1999). Read this book to learn how to use inexpensive and throw-away items to create a life-size igloo, build a stage, and make a variety of props and dress-up costumes. The ideas in this book will take children's imaginative play to new heights.

101 Drama Games for Children: Fun and Learning with Acting and Make Believe, Paul Plooyackers (Alameda, CA: Hunter House, 1997). The playful ideas in this book are designed to encourage everyone to get involved in different kinds of drama games—sensory, pantomime, story, and sound. There are also chapters devoted to games with props, masks, puppets, and costumes.

101 Music Games for Children: Fun and Learning with Rhythm and Song, Jerry Storms (Alameda, CA: Hunter House, 1995) The music games in this collection encourage cooperation rather than competition. Each game indicates recommended ages and group size, how much time it takes to play, and necessary props.

Starting Out Right: A Guide to Promoting Children's Reading Success, National Research Council, M. Susan Burns, Peg Griffin, and Catherine E. Snow, Editors (Washington, DC: National Academy Press, 1999). This book offers practical suggestions for supporting children's literacy development that are based on the published findings of a national research panel, *Preventing Reading Difficulties in Young Children*. Of interest to school-age staff are sections on children in kindergarten through grade three and preventing reading difficulties. The appendixes include a glossary and list of recommended Internet sites on reading and related issues.

Story S-t-r-e-t-c-h-e-r-s for the Primary Grades and *450 More Story S-t-r-e-t-c-h-e-r-s for the Primary Grades*, Shirley C. Raines and Robert J. Canady (Beltsville, MD: Gryphon House, 1992 and 1994). Each volume includes activities to expand children's enjoyment and understanding of 90 favorite books. The suggestions in these resources are a great way to support children's reading and writing skills.

*Your Child's Growing Mind: A Guide to Learning and Brain Development from Birth to Adolescence, Jane M. Healy (New York, NY: Main Street Books, Bantam Doubleday Dell Publishing Group, Inc., 1994). This reliable, clearly written guide to learning skills for children translates the most current scientific research on brain development into practical information. The author explains in detail how children develop

language and memory, and addresses academic learning—reading, writing, spelling, and mathematics. This book provides solid advice for parents, and others who support children's learning, including how to promote (not push) children's readiness, motivation, and problem-solving skills.

Adventures in Peacemaking: A Conflict Resolution Activity Guide for School-Age Programs, William J. Kreidler and Lisa Furlong (Hamilton, MA: Project Adventure, 1996). The authors of this book explain how to implement a school-age program based on mutual respect and use of creative conflict resolution strategies. Children gain conflict resolution skills through drama, problem solving, and art activities.

Alike and Different: Exploring Our Humanity with Young Children, Bonnie Neugebauer, Ed. (Washington, DC: National Association for the Education of Young Children, 1992). A series of articles offering thoughtful advice and approaches to meeting the needs of all children. Also addresses diversity issues related to staffing, living in a changing world, and resources.

Creative Conflict Resolution, William J. Kreidler (Glenview, IL: Scott, Foresman, and Company, 1984). This book describes conflict resolution techniques, activities, and cooperative games for school-age children. There are practical strategies children can use to improve their communication skills, understand and settle their own disputes, and deal with strong feelings in useful ways.

The Difficult Child, Stanley Turecki, M.D. and Leslie Tonner (New York, NY: Bantam Books, 1989). Written primarily for parents, this book describes the inborn behavioral characteristics of children. It offers help in identifying and understanding specific difficulties at each stage of development. There are practical suggestions for responding to conflicts and tips for reducing stress in adults and children.

Discipline in School-Age Care: Control the Climate, Not the Children, Dale Borman Fink (Nashville, TN: School-Age NOTES, 1995). The author of this book focuses on preventing behavior problems by planning six key elements of a school-age care program. It is a useful resource for analyzing the causes of chronic problem behaviors.

*Emotional Intelligence, Daniel Goleman (New York, NY: Bantam Books, 1995). Is IQ destiny? Not nearly as much as we think. This fascinating and persuasive book argues that a narrow view of human intelligence ignores a crucial range of abilities that contribute to success in life. Drawing on brain and behavioral research, he shows the importance of nurturing children's emotional intelligence—that is, their self-awareness, impulse control, persistence, self-motivation, empathy, and social deftness.

Greater Expectations: Overcoming the Culture of Indulgence in America's Homes and Schools, William Damon (New York, NY: The Free Press, 1995.) Written in response to what the author believes has been an overemphasis on misguided efforts to promote self-esteem, Damon advocates providing children with meaningful challenges, moral guidance, and

Self, Social, and Guidance

opportunities to serve others. He stresses the importance of the quality of interactions between adults and children.

The Kid's Guide to Social Action, Barbara A. Lewis (Minneapolis, MN: Free Spirit Publishers, 1998). This book includes step-by-step instructions for letter-writing, fundraising, interviewing, making speeches, and getting media coverage. The resource section includes addresses and phone numbers of government offices and national organizations. Stories about children's accomplishments are included.

Parents, Please Don't Sit on the Kids, Clare Cherry (Belmont, CA: David S. Lake Publishers, 1985). Contains many practical suggestions for guiding children's behavior, explaining techniques that work with children and those that don't.

Playground Politics, Stanley Greenspan (Reading, MA: Addison-Wesley Publishing Company, 1993). Dr. Greenspan, child psychiatrist and author, reviews the stages of normal emotional development for school-age children and offers suggestions for parents on how to assist their children in handling typical problems and challenges. These strategies can be adapted by school-age program staff as they help children master social skills.

Families, Program Management, and Professionalism

After-School Programs and the K-8 Principal: Standards for Quality School-Age Child Care, Revised edition, National Association of Elementary School Principals and the National Institute on Out-of-School Time (Alexandria, VA: National Association of Elementary School Principals, 1993). Although directed to elementary school principals, this revised edition is a valuable resource for school-age staff. The publication reflects the latest research on school-age care, describes elements of high quality programs, and provides checklists for starting and improving programs. (This document is available through the Department of Education On-Line Ordering System. Call 1-877-4-ED-PUBS to obtain a copy via fax-back service.)

Bringing Education to After-School Programs, Office of Educational Research and Improvement (Washington, DC: U. S. Department of Education, 1999). A wide range of topics are addressed in this publication, from reading and mathematics to parent involvement in after-school programs. The on-line version has links to other sites and sources of information. Download at www.ed.gov/pubs/After_School_Programs or call 1-877-4-ED-PUBS to order a copy.

Building Relationships with Parents and Families in School-Age Programs, Roberta L. Newman (Nashville, TN: School-Age NOTES, 1998). This training resource focuses on building positive relationships with parents and families of school-age children. It includes staff training activities, assessment tools, and tips for reaching out to parents.

The NSACA Standards for Quality School-Age Care, National School-Age Care Alliance (NSACA) (Boston, MA: National School-Age Care Alliance, 1998). The 144 standards in this publication, describe 36 keys of quality for school-age programs. Developed with the National Institute on Out of School Time (NIOST), school-age experts, and practitioners, the standards are organized in six categories: human relationships, indoor environment, outdoor environment, activities, safety, health, and nutrition, and administration. Also included are specific examples that illustrate the standards, a glossary, and a questionnaire programs can use to assess readiness for a self-study process. View the standards at the NSACA web site, www.nsaca.org and/or purchase a copy from NSACA.

The Power of Observation, Judy R. Jablon, Amy Laura Dombro, and Margo L. Dichtelmiller (Washington, DC: Teaching Strategies, 1999). The authors present observation as more than a set of skills. Observation is a mindset of openness and wonder that helps staff get to know more about each child and build strong relationships. There are also guidelines for effective observation.

Activity and Resource Books for School-Age Children and Staff

Adventures in Art, Susan Milord (Charlotte, VT: Williamson Publishing, 1997). This book includes 100 projects children can carry out alone or with friends. Although directed to children, staff will find it a rich resource for planning arts and crafts activities. Information on art history and the cultural source of different techniques and types of art are provided for each activity. Many activities are adaptations of crafts representative of different cultures.

The Big Messy Art Book: But Easy to Clean Up, MaryAnn F. Kohl (Beltsville, MD: Gryphon House, 2000). The activities in this book allow children to express themselves in new and exciting ways. For example, an artist might paint a hanging ball as it swings back and forth.

Creative Resources for Elementary Classrooms and School-Age Programs, Ron Wheeler, PhD. (Albany, NY: Delmar Publishers Inc., 1997). This book includes writing, science, math, social studies, and music activities for over 50 interesting themes such as inventions and inventors. In addition to goals and instructions for 800 activities, there are parent letters, lists of print and computer resources for children and adults.

Discovering Great Artists: Hands-on Art for Children In the Styles of the Great Masters, MaryAnn F. Kohl (Bellingham, WA: Bright Ring Publishing, Inc., 1997). After reading a short biography of a great master, children can make their own creation, using the style and technique of the artist. For example, they might make a collage in the style of Matisse, use dots as did Lichtenstein, or paint a close-up of a flower, similar to the work of O'Keefe.

Everyone Wins! Cooperative Games and Activities, Sambhava and Josette Luvmour (Stony Creek, CT: New Society Publishers, 1990). This book contains directions for a wide variety of cooperative games and activities. School-age staff will especially appreciate that each game is accompanied by a suggested age level and group size, as well as an expected activity level.

Games, Games, Games, Creating Hundreds of Group Games and Sports, David L. Whitaker (Nashville, TN: School Age NOTES, 1996). The games and sports in this book can be played indoors and outdoors. In addition to the basic rules and instructions, there are suggested variations for each game and sport. Children are encouraged to initiate and play games and sports on their own, with little adult direction.

Global Art: Activities, Projects, and Inventions from Around the World, MaryAnn F. Kohl and Jean Potter (Beltsville, MD: Gryphon House, 1998). Children gain an understanding of the geography and culture around the world through collage, painting, drawing, construction, and sculpture. There are clear instructions and illustrations for each project.

Great Games to Play With Groups, Frank W. Harris (Carthage, IL: Fearon Teacher Aids, 1990). A wide selection of games from around the world are featured in this book. Instructions are provided for more than 70 games.

Hands Around the World, Susan Milord (Charlotte, VT: Williamson Publishing, 1992). The introduction to this book describes how the book includes 365 activities, one for each day in the Gregorian calendar. It goes on to explain, however, that other calendars are also used throughout the world—for example, the 4,690-year-old Chinese calendar and the Islamic calendar. This approach and level of detail is typical of the entire book—a collection of activities that introduce and celebrate cultural diversity.

Hopscotch, Hangman, Hot Potato, and Ha, Ha, Ha: A Rulebook of Children's Games, Jack Maguire (New York, NY: Simon and Schuster, 1990). There are rules and guidelines for playing more than 250 games and sports with children of all ages and skill levels. Diagrams and drawings make the instructions easy to understand.

Incredible Indoor Games Book and *Outrageous Outdoor Games Book*, Bob Gregson (Cortnagel, IL: Fearon Teacher Aids, 1983 and 1984). These books are excellent resources on games to play when everyone is tired of the old standbys. Soon the games described in these books will become the children's new favorites.

Indoor Action Games for Elementary Children, James M. Foster and David L. Overholt (Upper Saddle River, NJ: Prentice Hall, 1989). The games in this book encourage children to be actively involved, even when space is limited. This is a good resource for rainy or cold days when children can't play outdoors.

Juba This and Juba That: 100 African-American Games for Children, Darlene Powell Hopson, Derek S. Hopson, and Thomas Clavin (New York, NY: Simon and Schuster, 1995). This collection includes indoor, outdoor, board, and musical games, and sections on crafts and Kwanzaa. Many of the games were passed down from one generation to the next and celebrate the wealth and diversity of African-American heritage.

The Kid's Address Book, Michael Levine (New York, NY: Perigee Books, 1999). Place this book in the quiet area with some paper, pens, and envelopes, and soon children will be writing letters to their favorite authors or athletes and to learn more about the world beyond their local community. Mailing and e-mail addresses are provided for individual actors, singers, sports figures, and cartoon characters. There are also addresses for recording companies, sports teams, T.V. networks, businesses, clubs and organizations for children, publishers, and government and world leaders.

Kids Around the World Create! The Best Crafts and Activities from Many Lands, Arlette N. Braman, Ariette Braman, and Jo-Ellen

Bosson (New York, NY: John Wiley & Sons, 1999). Children can learn about dozens of cultures from around the world while enjoying the projects in this book. For example, they might create an Italian carnival mask, weave a bookmark with a Guatemalan design, or string an Egyptian necklace using hand-made beads.

Kids Create, Laurie Carlson (Charlotte, VT: Williamson Publishing, 1991). Art and craft projects for children ages 3 through 9 are included in this book. Illustrated instructions are provided for a variety of activities that allow younger school-age children to exercise their creativity while making something "real."

A Kid's Guide to Building Forts, Tom Birdseye (Tucson, AZ: Harbinger House, 1993). This book includes illustrated instructions for building indoor and outdoor forts of many kinds. The outdoor forts described include a lean-to, teepee, and igloo. Indoors, children can make forts with furniture and coverings or with appliance boxes.

The Kids' Nature Book, Susan Milord (Charlotte, VT: Williamson Publishing, 1996). This book includes suggestions for crafts, experiments, and games that make use of or encourage involvement with nature. Included are 365 separate activities, one for each day of the year, organized by weekly themes. The appendices list sources for supplies, nature conservancy groups, and additional resources for children and staff.

Making Things: The Handbook of Creative Discovery, Ann Sayre Wiseman (Boston, MA: Little Brown & Company, 1997). This revised edition of a classic crafts book shows children how to make 125 different projects from everyday materials and recycled items. Techniques include weaving, tie-dying, batik, and more.

More Free Stuff for Kids, 23rd edition, Free Stuff Editors (Deephaven, MN: Meadowbrook Press, 1999). This book taps into several prime interests of school-age children—"collecting," learning more about the world beyond home and family, and receiving their own mail. Most items described are free or cost no more than a dollar. Children can write away for stickers, buttons, postcards, stamps, craft kits, or to learn more about another country.

Mudworks, Creative Clay, Dough, and Modeling Experiences, Mary Ann Kohl (Bellingham, WA: Bright Ring Publishing, 1991). Over 100 open-ended ways to engage children in modeling experiences; includes clearly written recipes in a format that gives appropriate guidance to adults.

Readers Digest Great Big Book of Children's Games, Debra Wise (Pleasantville, NY: Readers Digest Association, Inc., 1999) A great resource for learning how to play more than 450 indoor and outdoor games. Included are both competitive and non-competitive games for children of different ages.

Science Crafts for Kids: 50 Fantastic Things to Invent and Create, Gwen Diehn and Terry Krautwurst (New York, NY: Sterling Publishing Company, 1997). This book invites children to take part in hands-on science-related building and learning activities. For example, they might make clay-pot wind chimes, a xylophone, or a hypsometer—used to measure the height of tall objects. Each project is accompanied by simple explanations of related scientific principles.

Sportworks, Ontario Science Centre (Reading, MA: Addison Wesley Publishing Company, Inc., 1989). This book encourages children to learn about science while exercising, burning calories, and developing physical skills. The activities allow children to explore topics such as gravity, muscles, warming up before exercising, and why curve balls curve.

Steven Caney's Play Book, Steven Caney (New York, NY: Workman Publishing Group, 1980). This classic publication includes a wide variety of indoor and outdoor projects, games, and activities children can undertake alone or with others. Most of the projects are appropriate for even the youngest school-age children and make use of materials and equipment a typical school-age program would have on hand.

The Victory Garden Kid's Book, Marjorie Waters (Old Saybrook, CT: Globe-Pequot Press, 1994). The first section of this book includes a step-by-step guide to starting a garden. Children learn how to test their soil for lead, make compost, start seeds in peat pots, plant seedlings, and care for their plants throughout the growing season. The second section includes instructions for growing a number of vegetables, fruits, and flowers.

The Web of Support, Providing Safe, Nurturing, Learning Environments During Out-of-School Time, Wendy R. Nadel (Westport, CT: Save the Children, 2000). This guidebook is designed to support school-age staff with checklists of program activities, worksheets, sample evaluation forms, and suggestions for recruiting volunteers as well as community partners. Download the content of the guidebook at www.wosguide@savechildren.org.

Some Safe Internet Sites for School-Age Children and Staff

American Library Association (ALA), www.ala.org
Children and adults can take on-line classes on using the Internet safely, read about award-winning books, and link to librarian reviewed web sites for children (for example, *ALA's 700+ Amazing, Spectacular, Mysterious, Wonderful Web Sites for Kids and the Adults Who Care About Them*).

Ask Jeeves for Kids, www.ajkids.com
Children can ask Jeeves questions. Responses are filtered to make sure they are appropriate for children. In addition, Jeeves gives advice on social issues such as what to do when friends gossip, and recommends television shows.

Berit's Best Sites for Kids, www.beritsbest.com
Visitors can explore 1000 sites on holidays, animals, art, homework helpers.

Children's Express, www.ce.org
This is the site for the award-winning new service staffed by young people who write and report on news of interest to children and youth.

Children's Web Surfing Alliance, www.CyberSurfari.org
At this web site visitors build their on-line navigation skills by playing CyberSurfari's World Wide Web treasure hunt. Children seek the answers to

specific questions by reading clues and clicking on links to safe sites such as the Air and Space Museum and the MIR Space Station.

Funology.com: The Science of Having Fun, www.funology.com/
At this site, children can explore science experiments, jokes, games, magic tricks, trivia, recipes, and crafts.

Information Please: Kids' Almanac, www.kids.infoplease.com/
Curious children can learn about world and United States history, geography, and current events; famous people; sports; science; and math.

KIDSNet, www.kidsnet.org
Since 1985, KIDSNET has helped children, families, and teachers identify quality media programming. A monthly *Media Guide* describes children's programs and gives air dates, curriculum connections, grade levels, and supplemental materials. The quarterly *KIDSNET Media News*, features updates of awards, events, resources, and more. Staff can download free *Study Guides*, covering science, literature, history, social studies, and health.

National Geographic, www.nationalgeographic.com
Children will find a variety of activities on this web site. The GeoBee Challenge, updated daily, is a fun way to gain geography skills. The Fun Science link has hands-on activities such as making an indoor rainbow or a bottled vortex. At the Tomb of Tutankhamen, another link, provides an almost first-hand view of the unearthing of the boy pharaoh's tomb.

New Moon, www.newmoon.org
A special site where girls can read an on-line version of New Moon magazine, chat with other readers, join reading and writing clubs, enter contests, celebrate women's history, and more.

Penpals for Kids, kidspenpals.about.com/kids/kidspenpals
This is a useful site for children under age 12 who want to find a penpal. There are links to all kinds of pen pal lists—international, girls only, specific ages.

Public Broadcasting Service (PBS), www.pbskids.org
PBSkids, the premier public television web site for children, includes links to PBS children's shows such as *Between the Lions, Zoom,* and *Wishbone.* In addition, there are book lists, coloring sheets, science activities, and much more.

The Rainforest Alliance, www.rainforestalliance.org/kids&teachers/
The children's section has interesting information, projects, stories, and resources. The teacher's section offers activities, book lists, and rain forest facts.

SmartZones, www.edview.com
This site links to teacher-reviewed web pages listed by grade level and topic.

Sports Illustrated for Kids, www.sikids.com
Sports enthusiasts—players and fans—will enjoy reading about their favorite sports stars, keeping up with current games and standings, and testing theirknowledge of sports trivia.

PUBLISHERS AND DISTRIBUTORS OF RESOURCES

Association for Childhood Education International (ACEI)
17904 Georgia Avenue, Suite 215
Olney, MD 20832
1-800-423-3563
www.udel.edu/bateman/acei
• Publishes and distributes inexpensive resources on working with children from infants through early adolescence.
• Distributes journal, *Childhood Education,* to members 6 times per year.
• Provides newsletters on topics related to elementary and middle school age groups.
• Holds annual conference in April.

Creative Educational Surplus
1000 Apollo Road
Eagen, MN 55121-2240
1-800-886-6428
www.creativesurplus.com
• Offers wide variety of surplus items (e.g., pompoms, stretchy fishnet, divided trays) for crafts and projects.
• Suggests uses for items on web site.

Education Resources Information Center (ERIC)
U. S. Department of Education
1-800-LET-ERIC
www.accesseric.org/sites (links to all ERIC Clearinghouses and Adjunct Clearinghouses)
• Operates 16 clearinghouses of up-to-date information on development and education of children and youth.
• Includes centers on specific age groups, settings, and/or topics (e.g., disabilities and gifted education, elementary and early childhood education, parents, reading, English, communication, urban education, and child care).

Federal Support to Communities Initiative
Housed at National Partnership for Reinventing Government and Government Services Administration (GSA)
www.afterschool.gov
• Connects to federal agency resources that can support school-age care.
• Maintains database of federal grant and loan programs.

• Shares community success stories and opportunities to network.
• Links to guides, reports, research, organizations, and safe web sites for children and youth.

Gryphon House
P. O. Box 207
Beltsville, MD 20704-0207
1-800-638-0928
www.ghbooks.com
• Publishes and distributes resources for child care professionals, including school-age staff.
• Provides sample activities on web site.

National Association for the Education of Young Children (NAEYC)
1509 16th Street, NW
Washington, DC 200326-1426
1-800-424-2460
www.naeyc.org
• Publishes numerous inexpensive resources on topics of interest to school-age staff.
• Distributes journal, *Young Children,* to members 6 times per year.
• Holds annual conference in November (separate track for school-age care).
• Provides position statements on web site.

National Child Care Information Center
243 Church Street, 2nd Floor
Vienna, VA 22180
1-800-616-2242
www.nccic.org
• Writes and distributes reports, handbooks, and newsletter, *Child Care Bulletin.*
• Provides up-to-date information and answers questions on child care topics.
• Manages web site linked to numerous child care groups and publications.

National Clearinghouse on Families and Youth
P. O. Box 13505
Silver Spring, MD 20911-3505
301-608-8098
www.ncfy.com
• Provides information and publications on youth development.
• Offers links to youth-serving organizations.

National Institute on Out-of-School Time (NIOST)
Center for Research on Women
Wellesley College
106 Central Street
Wellesley, MA 02481
781-283-2547
www.niost.org
• Offers fact sheets, books, videos, and reports on school-age care.
• Co-owns list serve, *SAC-L,* with ERIC Clearinghouse on Elementary and Early Childhood Education (ERIC/EECE).
• Provides training for school-age staff and administrators.

National Network for Child Care
Family Life Extension
Iowa State University
1322 Elm Hall, Suite 1085
Ames IA, 50011
515-294-5702
www.nncc.org
• Provides on-line publications on school-age programming, behavior, start-up, evaluation and assessment, and more.
• Manages e-mail list-serve.
• Offers support and assistance from regional experts.
• Publishes quarterly newsletter, *School-Age Connections* (available on line).

National School-Age Care Alliance
(NSACA)
1137 Washington Street
Boston, Massachusetts 02124
617-298-5012
www.nsaca.org
• Disseminates, with NIOST, national standards for school-age care and materials for program improvement and accreditation.
• Holds annual training conference.
• Publishes a professional journal, *School-Age Review.*

Redleaf Press
450 North Syndicate Avenue, Suite 5
St. Paul, MN 55104-4125
1-800-423-8309
• Publishes and distributes resources for school-age staff professionals.

School-Age NOTES
P. O. Box 40205
Nashville, TN 37204
1-800-410-8780
www.schoolagenotes.com
• Publishes and distributes resources for school-age care and summer programs for ages 5 through 14.
• Offers monthly newsletter, *School-Age NOTES,* with ideas and activities for working with school-age children.

Search Institute
700 South Third Street, Suite 210
Minneapolis, Minnesota 55415-1138
U.S.A.
612-376-8955
www.search.org
• Publishes quarterly magazine, *Assets: The Magazine of Ideas for Healthy Communities & Healthy Youth.*
• Offers resources based on 40 "developmental assets" needed by children and youth.
• Includes many articles on web site.

21st Century Schools
Charles Stewart Mott Foundation
503 S. Saginaw Street, Suite 1200
Flint, MI 48502
810-238-5651
www.mott.org/21stcentury
• Coordinates public, private, and nonprofit alliance to raise awareness and expand resources on school-age care.
• Links to resources for school-age staff.
• Operates a list-serv, MottAfterschool.

U. S. Department of Education
600 Independence Avenue, SW
Washington, DC 20202-8173
1-800-USA-LEARN
www.ed.gov
• Offers on-line and print resources on topics related to school-age care.
• Links to publications, clearinghouses, and web sites for school-age staff, families, children, and youth.

SELF-ASSESSMENT

	I Do This		
	Regularly	Sometimes	Not Enough

1. Safe

a. Maintaining indoor and outdoor environments that prevent injuries. ☐ ☐ ☐

b. Planning for and responding to injuries and emergencies. ☐ ☐ ☐

c. Helping children develop habits that will prevent injuries. ☐ ☐ ☐

2. Healthy

a. Maintaining indoor and outdoor environments that promote wellness and reduce the spread of disease. ☐ ☐ ☐

b. Encouraging children to develop habits that promote good hygiene and nutrition. ☐ ☐ ☐

c. Recognizing and reporting child abuse and neglect. ☐ ☐ ☐

3. Program Environment

a. Organizing indoor and outdoor areas to support a variety of activities. ☐ ☐ ☐

b. Selecting and arranging developmentally appropriate materials and equipment. ☐ ☐ ☐

c. Planning and implementing a schedule and routines to meet children's developmental and individual needs. ☐ ☐ ☐

	I Do This		
	Regularly	Sometimes	Not Enough

4. Physical

a. Reinforcing and encouraging physical development through an appropriate environment, activities, and interactions. ☐ ☐ ☐

b. Providing equipment and opportunities for gross motor development. ☐ ☐ ☐

c. Providing equipment and opportunities for fine motor development. ☐ ☐ ☐

5. Cognitive

a. Creating an interesting and varied environment that encourages children to experiment and make discoveries. ☐ ☐ ☐

b. Interacting with children in ways that build on their natural curiosity. ☐ ☐ ☐

c. Providing opportunities for children to use their growing skills. ☐ ☐ ☐

6. Communication

a. Creating a varied environment that encourages children to develop and use communication skills. ☐ ☐ ☐

b. Interacting with children in ways that encourage them to express their ideas and feelings. ☐ ☐ ☐

c. Providing opportunities for children to use their listening, speaking, reading, and writing skills. ☐ ☐ ☐

| | I Do This | | |
| | Regularly | Sometimes | Not Enough |

7. Creative

a. Providing a rich and varied environment that invites exploration and experimentation.

☐ ☐ ☐

b. Offering a variety of activities and experiences that promote self-expression.

☐ ☐ ☐

c. Interacting with children in ways that encourage and respect original ideas, thoughts, and expressions.

☐ ☐ ☐

8. Self

a. Developing a positive and supportive relationship with each child.

☐ ☐ ☐

b. Helping children accept and appreciate themselves and others.

☐ ☐ ☐

c. Providing children with opportunities to be successful and feel competent.

☐ ☐ ☐

9. Social

a. Encouraging children to develop friendships and enjoy being with their peers.

☐ ☐ ☐

b. Helping children understand and respect the feelings of others.

☐ ☐ ☐

c. Providing an environment and experiences that help children develop social skills.

☐ ☐ ☐

	I Do This		
	Regularly	Sometimes	Not Enough

10. Guidance

a. Providing an environment that encourages children's self-discipline. ☐ ☐ ☐

b. Using positive methods to guide individual children. ☐ ☐ ☐

c. Helping children understand and express their feelings in acceptable ways. ☐ ☐ ☐

11. Families

a. Communicating with parents often to exchange information about their child at home and at the program. ☐ ☐ ☐

b. Offering a variety of ways for parents to participate in their child's life at the program. ☐ ☐ ☐

c. Providing support to families. ☐ ☐ ☐

12. Program Management

a. Observing and recording information about each child's growth and development. ☐ ☐ ☐

b. Working as a member of a team to plan an individualized program. ☐ ☐ ☐

c. Following administrative policies and procedures. ☐ ☐ ☐

13. Professionalism

a. Continually assessing one's own performance. ☐ ☐ ☐

b. Continuing to learn about working with school-age children. ☐ ☐ ☐

c. Applying professional ethics at all times. ☐ ☐ ☐

INDIVIDUAL TRAINING PLAN

Review your responses to the self-assessment with your trainer. What do you feel are your strengths, interests, and needs? Decide which areas you would like to work on first. Select three modules to begin with and set target dates for their completion. (Your trainer can let you know how much work is involved for each module.) Record the module titles and target completion dates below. You may also wish to determine a tentative schedule for completing *Caring for Children in School-Age Programs*.

Module	Target Completion Date
1. _____	1. _____
2. _____	2. _____
3. _____	3. _____

Tentative schedule for completion of the *Caring for Children in School-Age Programs* Training Program:

Module	Date
_____	_____
_____	_____
_____	_____
_____	_____
_____	_____
_____	_____
_____	_____
_____	_____
_____	_____
_____	_____
_____	_____
_____	_____

_____	_____	_____	_____
Staff	Date	Trainer	Date

Module 1:
SAFE

OVERVIEW

> **KEEPING SCHOOL-AGE CHILDREN SAFE INVOLVES:**
>
> - maintaining indoor and outdoor environments that reduce and prevent injuries;
> - planning for and responding to injuries and emergencies; and
> - helping children develop habits that will prevent injuries.

Safety is freedom from danger, and danger is minimized by reducing hazards that might cause an injury or emergency. You feel safe when you know:

Adults feel safe when they are in control.

- no harm will come to you;
- you can do something to prevent dangerous situations; and
- those around you share your concern for safety and act in a cautious way.

Adults feel safe when they are in control of situations. They are in control when they prevent injuries and when they know what to do if emergencies occur.

To feel safe, children must trust the important adults in their lives to prevent or reduce hazardous situations. They rely on adults to know what to do when injuries or emergencies occur. As children become more independent, they can take steps to control their environment. They are better able to explore their world safely and to stay free from danger.

Although injuries are the leading cause of death among children, national studies indicate 95 percent of these injuries are preventable. Active and curious school-age children are often vulnerable to dangers in their environment. Risk-taking is common, especially for children who have entered the rapid growth period prior to adolescence. They are testing their new physical and mental abilities. Children may think, "Bad things happen to other people, not to me."

School-age children may take risks.

As a school-age staff member, you have a professional responsibility to protect children from harm. Your program has established procedures to ensure children's safety. As stated in

Staff are responsible for protecting children.

the *Code of Ethical Conduct* of the National Association for the Education of Young Children (Principal 1.1):[1]

> Above all we shall not harm children. We shall not participate in practices that are disrespectful, degrading, dangerous, exploitive, intimidating, psychologically damaging, or physically harmful to children.

A safe environment for school-age children has structure and clear limits but also encourages and supports exploration and risk-taking. Emergencies are handled calmly and effectively. Through your actions, you help children develop positive attitudes about safety and learn how to keep themselves safe.

Listed below are examples of how school-age staff demonstrate their competence in keeping children safe.

Maintaining Indoor And Outdoor Environments That Prevent Injuries[2]

Follow the program's security procedures that limit access to building entrances.

Monitor children's arrivals and departures.

Check indoor and outdoor areas daily and remove trash, hazardous materials, and sharp or broken objects.

Check the room daily to be sure all electrical cords are kept away from water and walkways.

Check materials and equipment daily for broken parts, loose bolts, or jagged edges, and make sure they are repaired or replaced.

Check monthly to see that safety equipment and supplies (for example, fire extinguishers, smoke detectors, and first-aid kits) are in place, easy to reach, and in good condition.

Use separate areas for active and quiet games and activities so children don't get in each other's way or bump into each other.

Arrange the room to allow for clear traffic paths and fire exits.

---

[1] Stephanie Feeney and Kenneth Kipnis, *Code of Ethical Conduct and Statement of Commitment* (Washington, DC: National Association for the Education of Young Children, 1990), p. 5.
[2] Playground and other equipment should be designed and installed with safety in mind. This means considering the appropriate height of equipment, placing shock-absorbing material underneath climbing equipment, and allowing for needed clearances around fixed and moving equipment. See Checklist pp. 45-47.

Follow the program's requirements for adult-child ratios and group sizes (recommended ratios are 1:8 for children under 6 and 1:10 - 1:12 for children 6 and older).

Supervise children and know where they are and what they are doing at all times.

Limit access to supplies and equipment that could be dangerous when used by children who do not know how to use them safely.

Clean and properly store equipment and supplies when not in use.

Make sure the telephone is easy to get to and is working properly.

Respond quickly to children in distress in a calm and reassuring manner.

Planning for and Responding to Injuries and Emergencies

Develop and post emergency procedures.

Post emergency telephone numbers and directions to the child care site next to the phone (e.g., Emergency Medical Services, police, fire, poison control, Child Protective Services). Since a child may make the emergency call, the information needs to be clear.

For children with special needs, know how to recognize and respond to a medical emergency. Have on hand an emergency plan, supplies, and medication needed.

Have an evacuation plan and a 3-day emergency supply of food, water, clothing, medications, etc., in case of tornado, flood, earthquake, etc.

During an emergency, have a plan for attending to the injured child(ren) and also supervising other children.

Maintain current emergency information on all children, including parents' telephone numbers.

Follow established procedures for leading children to safety during fire and other hazard drills and in real emergencies.

Helping Children Develop Habits That Will Prevent Injuries

Talk about potential hazards so children will learn how to prevent injuries. "Anne, the edge of this rug has loose strings. Will you help me trim them so nobody gets a foot caught and trips?"

Involve children in making safety rules. "Many of you are excited about using our new woodworking tools. What rules do we need to be sure no one gets hurt while using them?"

Encourage children to help each other remember the safety rules. "Bonnie, would you and Erica like to make a safety poster? We need a reminder to hang up backpacks or put them in cubbies. This can help keep the entry way clear so no one trips and falls."

Show children how to use materials properly, and model taking risks. Closely supervise children during potentially hazardous activities. "Diandre, this X-acto knife is very sharp. Always cut away from your body so it won't slip and cut you."

Invite community representatives (fire or police) to talk with the children about safe practices. "Let's begin by talking about what you should do in a dangerous situation. For example, if you heard gun fire while walking to the store, what would you do?"

Teach children to observe safety rules on walks and field trips. "Raise your hand with your buddy and join your group leader."

Explain rules and procedures for sports and games before play begins. "We've marked a safety zone where you can stand while you're waiting for your turn at bat. If you wait there, you won't be hit accidentally by the batter who's up before you."

Change the activity when children become too excited, angry, or tired to continue playing safely. "At the end of this inning, we'll stop the game for today and take a slow lap around the field. Then I'll help you find something else to do."

Respond immediately when children are playing unsafely. "Jose and Pam, please get off the table. Do you remember why we came up with the rule about not standing on the furniture?"

Teach children proper procedures for cleaning up and storing equipment and supplies. "Kisha, here is the key so you can lock the chemicals for the science experiment back in the cabinet."

Remind children of safety rules. "Mandy, you can ride a bike in the area marked with safety cones. Helmets are next to the bikes."

Help children develop habits that prevent injuries. Model safe practices such as always using a seat belt in the car, crossing at the crosswalk and with the light, and using a helmet when biking.

Keeping Children Safe

In the following situations, school-age staff are ensuring children's safety. As you read them, think about what the staff are doing and why. Then answer the questions that follow.

Mr. Sullivan and his colleagues arrive at the program before the children so they can do a safety check of the indoor and outdoor areas. Today he is scheduled to check the playground used by the program. He attaches a copy of the outdoor safety checklist to his clipboard and heads outdoors. Although it's a sunny day, last night's storm has left the playground littered with branches and twigs. He removes the branches and decides to ask the children to help pick up the twigs. Next, he runs his hands across the climber and feels underneath to make sure there are no splinters. The surface is a little rough under one timber so he makes a note to have it sanded before it becomes a potential hazard. The storm washed away some of the wood chips under the climber so he rakes them back in place. He sweeps away the standing water on the asphalt, checks the swings and slide, then sets up for the afternoon. Softball has been a favorite activity this week so he checks to make sure the field is dry enough for play. It is, so he uses the safety cones to mark a safe waiting area for the next batter. Before going back inside to greet the children he puts out more cones to mark a safety area at the bottom of the slide and around the swings.

Maintaining Indoor and Outdoor Environments That Prevent Injuries

1. **What did Mr. Sullivan do to create a safe outdoor environment?**

   _____

   _____

   _____

2. **What next steps does Mr. Sullivan need to take to make sure the outdoor environment is safe?**

   _____

   _____

   _____

Planning for and Responding to Injuries and Emergencies

Mr. Lopez and a group of children are playing T-ball. Cecelia is at bat. She hits the ball high over the heads of the shortstop and the second baseman and into the outfield. Tony and Gillian, the two outfielders, see the ball coming and run toward it shouting, "I've got it!" As the ball lands on the grass beside them, the two children crash into each other and fall down. Mr. Lopez calls a "time out" and walks to the crying children. He asks them how they feel. Gillian says her head hurts and Tony just keeps crying. Mr. Lopez calls over to the other children and says, "I need to take Tony and Gillian inside so they can get some ice. Ms. Kendrick, today's 'air traffic controller,'* will come out so you can continue the game." After telling Ms. Kendrick she needs to go outside, he gets some ice from the refrigerator for Tony and Gillian to hold on their sore heads. While waiting to see if the ice helps he completes an injury report. Soon Tony and Gillian are feeling better and eager to go back to the game. He sends them back outside. Because the children have recovered, Mr. Lopez decides it is not necessary to call their parents. He does, however, write two short notes explaining the injury and asking the parents to be sure to read and sign the injury report. After putting the notes in the children's cubbies where the parents will see them, he returns to the game. Ms. Kendrick gives him a quick update and goes back inside to see who might need her help.

1. What did Mr. Lopez do to keep all the children safe?

_____

_____

_____

2. What did Mr. Lopez do after taking care of the children's injuries?

_____

_____

_____

*An 'air traffic controller' is a floating staff member who steps in to help when needed.

Three sixth-grade girls, Stephanie, Rhonda, and Candy, have organized a Double Dutch Jump Rope Club. They are very excited about getting started. As soon as they arrive, they rush out to the asphalt area to begin jumping. Just as the girls are about to start twirling the jump ropes, Ms. Nelson notices something flickering on the asphalt. She goes over to Stephanie and says, "From where I was standing, I noticed something on the ground where you're going to be jumping. Now that I've had a closer look, I can see that it's broken glass. Before you begin jumping, you need to check the area for glass, loose gravel, or anything else that might make you fall or cut yourself." Stephanie responds, "We were so excited about the club, we didn't even notice!" Ms. Nelson tells the girls, "I can see this club is going to be a lot of fun. I know you want it to be safe, too. Why don't you make a list of safety rules for the club. The first one can be to check the jumping area every day before you begin, and sweep it if needed. When you think of others, you can add them to the list."

Helping Children Develop Habits That Will Prevent Injuries

1. **Why did Ms. Nelson think it was important for the girls to make safety rules for their club?**

   _____

   _____

   _____

2. **How did the children learn to keep themselves safe?**

   _____

   _____

   _____

Compare your answers with those on the answer sheet at the end of this module. If your answers are different, discuss them with your trainer. There can be more than one good answer.

Your Own Need for Safety

Safety is a basic human need.

Everyone needs to feel safe. We particularly want to feel safe where we live and work. When we know we are protected from harm, we can function well. Safe environments make us feel secure, relaxed, confident, and able to enjoy ourselves. When we do not feel protected, we are fearful and anxious.

With the increasing level of violence in many communities today, especially random violence, it's difficult for many of us to feel safe. Children have the same fears as adults. They see violence on television and too often experience it in their homes and neighborhoods. Safety is an important issue for everyone.

When you are in charge of your environment, you can make it a safer one. You probably have experienced times when you were doing something that was potentially dangerous, and you did things to make that activity safer. Do you remember times when you:

- climbed a ladder while someone held it to keep it stable;
- parked your car at night in a well-lit area of the shopping mall; or
- carefully unplugged a lamp with a frayed cord, then had the wiring replaced?

Learning about safety begins in childhood.

You have learned about safety through experience. When you were a child, the important adults in your life controlled your environment to keep it safe. They helped you develop an attitude and habits concerning safety. As you grew older, they helped you learn what you could do to minimize dangerous situations.

Think of a situation where you didn't feel safe and describe it below.

_____

_____

_____

What did you want to happen?

_____

_____

_____

What can you learn from this experience that will help you keep children safe?

_____

_____

_____

As you work through this module, you will learn how to set up and maintain a safe environment. Safety is important in all aspects of school-age care—whether you are guiding children's learning, building self-esteem, or promoting self-discipline. Keeping children safe is one of your most important responsibilities.

When you have finished this overview section, you should complete the pre-training assessment. Refer to the glossary at the end of this module if you need definitions of the terms used.

PRE-TRAINING ASSESSMENT

Listed below are the skills school-age staff use to keep children safe. Think about whether you do these things regularly, sometimes, or not enough. Place a check in one of the boxes on the right for each skill listed. Then discuss your answers with your trainer.

Maintaining Indoor and Outdoor Environments That Prevent Injuries

	I Do This		
	Regularly	Sometimes	Not Enough
1. Following the program's security procedures that limit access to building entrances.	☐	☐	☐
2. Monitoring children's arrivals and departures.	☐	☐	☐
3. Checking indoor and outdoor areas daily for safety hazards.	☐	☐	☐
4. Conducting monthly safety checks, indoors and outdoors, to find out what needs to be repaired.	☐	☐	☐
5. Repairing faulty equipment immediately or removing it until it can be repaired.	☐	☐	☐
6. Checking monthly to be sure safety equipment and supplies are in place, easy to reach, and in good condition.	☐	☐	☐
7. Checking daily to see that equipment and supplies are cleaned up and stored safely.	☐	☐	☐
8. Limiting access to supplies and equipment for children who do not yet have the skills or judgment to use the items safely.	☐	☐	☐
9. Designating separate areas for active and quiet games and activities to avoid congestion and collisions.	☐	☐	☐
10. Arranging the environment so children and staff are visible at all times.	☐	☐	☐
11. Arranging the room so traffic paths and fire exits are clear.	☐	☐	☐

Maintaining Indoor and Outdoor Environments That Prevent Injuries

(continued)

	I Do This		
	Regularly	Sometimes	Not Enough
12. Maintaining appropriate adult-child ratios and group sizes.	☐	☐	☐
13. Planning a daily schedule to include active and quiet play.	☐	☐	☐
14. Making sure the telephone is easy to get to and working properly.	☐	☐	☐

Planning for and Responding to Injuries and Emergencies

15. Responding quickly to children in distress in a calm and reassuring manner.	☐	☐	☐
16. Developing and posting emergency procedures, telephone numbers, directions to the site, and having a plan for attending to injured children as well as supervising other children.	☐	☐	☐
17. Knowing and following emergency procedures.	☐	☐	☐
18. Knowing where to find parents' emergency phone numbers and maintaining current emergency information on all children.	☐	☐	☐
19. Having a plan for children with special needs.	☐	☐	☐

Helping Children Develop Habits That Will Prevent Injuries

20. Involving children in making the safety rules.	☐	☐	☐
21. Explaining rules and procedures for sports and games before play begins.	☐	☐	☐
22. Responding immediately when children are playing unsafely.	☐	☐	☐

Helping Children Develop Habits That Will Prevent Injuries (continued)	**I Do This**		
	Regularly	Sometimes	Not Enough
23. Inviting community representatives to talk with children about safe practices.	☐	☐	☐
24. Talking calmly with children about potential hazards in the environment.	☐	☐	☐
25. Teaching children proper procedures for using, cleaning up, and storing equipment and supplies.	☐	☐	☐
26. Showing children how to use equipment and supplies properly and modeling taking risks.	☐	☐	☐
27. Teaching children to observe safety rules on walks and field trips.	☐	☐	☐
28. Reminding children of safety rules and encouraging them to remind each other.	☐	☐	☐
29. Changing the activities when children become too excited, angry, or tired to continue playing safely.	☐	☐	☐

Review your responses, then list three to five skills you would like to improve or topics you would like to learn more about. When you finish this module, you can list examples of your new or improved knowledge and skills.

_____

_____

_____

_____

_____

Begin the learning activities for Module 1, Safe.

LEARNING ACTIVITIES

Learning Activity I.
Creating and Maintaining a Safe Environment

IN THIS ACTIVITY YOU WILL LEARN TO:

- set up a safe learning environment for school-age children;

- take actions every day to help make the environment safe for children; and

- use a safety checklist to keep indoor and outdoor play areas safe.

Your choice of materials and equipment and the way you arrange your space can reduce and prevent injuries. When the indoor and outdoor areas are safe, you can focus on what the children are doing, confident that the playground is free of broken glass and that materials and equipment are appropriate, sturdy, and in good repair.

Creating a safe environment can prevent injuries.

During the school-age years, children gain many skills and learn to use sound judgment. However, as you work with these children, you will find that they can't always tell what is safe and what is dangerous. When children are excited, they can be impulsive. They may run around without noticing people or objects in their path, or grab and handle objects carelessly. They may be so anxious to try out new skills they forget to follow safety rules. Marty and Eduardo were so eager to have a bike race they forgot to wear their helmets. Emily and her friends were half-way through their gymnastic routines before remembering to put down a tumbling mat. You and your colleagues must observe closely and be prepared for the unexpected.

Here are some general rules to follow in setting up a safe environment for school-age children.

Try these suggestions.

- Set up interest areas using dividers low enough so you can easily see all children at all times.

- Secure or remove furniture that could fall or be pulled over.

- Use open shelves for storage; **not** chests with heavy lids that can fall on children.

- Store heavy items on bottom shelves of bookcases or cabinets so children don't pull heavy things down on themselves.

- Create a floor plan that allows children to move easily from one area to another and allows quick exiting in emergencies.

- Designate separate indoor and outdoor areas for different kinds of activities—quiet, active, noisy—so children don't bump into one another or get into physical disagreements.

- Inspect electrical cords and appliances to be sure they are in good condition.

- Know the location of fire extinguishers and how to use them.

- Examine materials and equipment regularly to make sure they are nonflammable, non-toxic, free of sharp edges or splinters, and in good repair.

- Keep dangerous substances such as cleansers and chemicals in covered, safe containers that are plainly labeled. Store them in locked cabinets and make them available only to children who know how to use them safely.

- Locate activities using hazardous materials and equipment (such as melted wax, chemicals, hot oil, woodworking tools) away from traffic. When heating oil, make sure the pot or pan is below the level of children's faces.

- Use newspapers, dropcloths, or towels to control spills from sand and water play and "messy" activities. Limit the number of children who can participate at one time.

- Play ball games far away from streets so balls don't roll into them.

- Include in your written schedule the time during which each staff member will supervise a particular activity or area.

Use safety checklists regularly.

Now that you have created a safe environment, the next step is to keep it that way. A safety checklist, used regularly, is a good tool for identifying potential hazards. Children's frequent use of materials and equipment can cause wear and tear that can make a once-safe item or area dangerous. Although you must assume full responsibility, children can help you identify problems. Some things are checked daily: unlocked cabinets, broken glass, and wet spots. Others are checked monthly: splintered baseball bats, loose table screws, and bolts that should be replaced.

Applying Your Knowledge

In this learning activity you will invite two children to help you assess your indoor and outdoor spaces using the safety checklists that follow this page. Together, identify items that need your attention and what precautions you can take to improve the safety of the environment.

Indoor Safety Checklist

Date: _____

Safety Checkers: _____

_____

Safety Conditions	Satisfactory or Not Applicable	Needs Attention
—CHECK DAILY—		
1. The schedule allows for supervision of children at all times.	☐	☐
2. The room is free of clutter.	☐	☐
3. Tables and chairs are in good repair.	☐	☐
4. Furniture is free of sharp edges and splinters.	☐	☐
5. Storage units are stable and secured; drawers and doors are closed.	☐	☐
6. Extension cords are not used near water or placed where someone might trip over them.	☐	☐
7. Steps, platforms, and lofts have padding underneath and protective railings.	☐	☐
8. The room contains no highly flammable furnishings or decorations.	☐	☐
9. Each area has enough space for children to work and play.	☐	☐
10. Hazardous chemicals and equipment (woodworking tools, specialized knives), cleaning materials, and other dangerous substances are stored only in locked cabinets and used by children only with adult supervision.	☐	☐
11. Floors are dry.	☐	☐
12. Rugs are in place and securely fastened.	☐	☐

Indoor Safety Checklist
(continued)

Safety Conditions	Satisfactory or Not Applicable	Needs Attention
—CHECK DAILY—		
13. Exit doors are clearly marked and free of clutter.	☐	☐
14. Exit signs are in working order.	☐	☐
15. Required adult-child ratios are maintained.	☐	☐
16. Staff interact with children rather than congregating with each other.	☐	☐
—CHECK MONTHLY—		
17. Blocks and other wooden items are smooth and splinter-free.	☐	☐
18. Moving parts (wheels, knobs) are securely fastened and working properly.	☐	☐
19. Scissors and knives used by children are sharp enough to cut with easily.	☐	☐
20. Hinges, screws, and bolts on furniture and equipment are securely fastened.	☐	☐
21. The smoke detector is working properly and the fire extinguishers are properly located and fully charged.	☐	☐
22. Electrical wires are not frayed.	☐	☐
23. Radiators and hot water pipes are covered or insulated.	☐	☐
24. All windows have closed, permanent screens and cannot be opened more than 6 inches from the bottom.	☐	☐

Outdoor Safety Checklist*

Safety Conditions	Satisfactory or Not Applicable	Needs Attention
—CHECK DAILY—		
1. Play equipment is free of splinters and rough surfaces and meets height limitation requirements.	☐	☐
2. There is sufficient cushioning under play equipment.	☐	☐
3. No objects or obstructions are under or around equipment where children might fall.	☐	☐
4. Play equipment is free of frayed cables, worn ropes, and chains that could pinch.	☐	☐
5. Play areas are free of broken glass, debris, standing water, and loose gravel (on asphalt).	☐	☐
6. Safety zones are marked around swings, slides, and in areas where active sports and games are played (for example, waiting areas for next batter).	☐	☐
7. Riding paths for bikes and skates are clearly marked and separate from other acivity areas.	☐	☐
—CHECK MONTHLY—		
8. Screws, nuts, and bolts on climbing and other equipment are securely fastened and do not stick out.	☐	☐
9. Bicycles and other equipment are in good repair (screws tight, chains oiled, and not rusted).	☐	☐
10. Metal equipment is free of rust or chipped paint.	☐	☐
11. Equipment is securely affixed to the ground.	☐	☐
12. Fences enclose the area, are in good repair, and splinter-free.	☐	☐

* For more information, see *ASTM Consumer Safety Performance Specifications for Playground Equipment for Public Use*, ASTM F1487-98 (West Conshohocken, PA: American Society for Testing and Materials, 1998).
Caring for Our Children, National Health and Safety Performance Standards: Guidelines for Out-of-Home Child Care Programs—Video Series (Elk Grove Village, IL: American Academy of Pediatrics, 1995, p. 50).
Handbook for Public Playground Safety Pub. No. 325 (Washington, DC: U.S. Consumer Product Safety Commission, 1997).

Review the items on each checklist you and the children have found in need of attention, and list them below. Then identify what steps you can take to improve the safety of your environment.

Items Needing Attention	Steps to Improve the Safety of the Environment	Date Completed

Discuss the steps for improvement with the children who helped you complete the checklist and with your trainer. Make these changes and ask the children to check them off when they have been completed. Schedule times for daily and monthly safety checks throughout the year, and ask other children to help you.

Learning Activity II.
Preventing Injuries Through Supervision and Planning

IN THIS ACTIVITY YOU WILL LEARN TO:

- use effective supervision to keep school-age children safe; and

- plan a program that prevents children from becoming over-tired and frustrated.

Although they are becoming more independent and responsible, school-age children need adult supervision. As they test their physical skills and try out ideas, they may act impulsively or take risks. Some children are easily frustrated or get over-excited. They can be careless and cause injuries. In addition, when there is too much noise or when activities are too long or too demanding, the potential for injuries increases.

Injuries can occur when children are tired or over-excited.

Although school-age children like to spend some time alone, they generally prefer to be with friends. Social activity takes energy just as physical activity does; both can be very tiring. Tired children don't pay attention. They lose control over their bodies and feelings, and in a moment they can hurt themselves or others.

When the program schedule is paced to include time for both active and quiet play, children are less likely to get over-tired. Here are some steps you can take to maintain a safe pace in your program.

Plan a safe pace in your program.

- Ask children what they would like to do and when.

- Follow a flexible schedule that includes time for active sports and games and time to relax, take a break during an activity, and cool off at the end.

- Be ready to stop or change an activity if one or more of the children seems tired, angry, frustrated, or over-heated.

- Introduce a variety of cooperative games. School-age children tend to add their own competitiveness into the play.

Being aware of the characteristics of individual children also helps you prevent injuries. For example, some children do not tire quickly; they remain even-tempered during physical activities. Others who are also active and energetic may tire quickly or become over-excited. Certain developmental characteristics may

Allow for individual differences.

increase children's risk of injuries. Consider whether you have children with unusual physical abilities, developmental delays, hearing or vision impairments, movement disorders, seizures, or relational difficulties. To maximize safety for everyone, some children may need activities tailored to their abilities, more guidance, and/or closer supervision.

Try these suggestions.

Try the following strategies so children can participate at appropriate levels.

- Offer a range of activity choices to accommodate different skill levels. Guide children to appropriate activities based on their abilities.

- Provide choices appropriate for children of different ages. This is especially important during active sports in which younger children could be injured in collisions with older children.

- Follow a flexible schedule so you can support and guide children who have short attention spans or who tend to be impulsive or easily distracted. Offer alternatives so children can choose another activity.

- Set limits for the number of children who may use a piece of equipment or interest area at a time. Discuss these limits at group meetings and make and post signs stating the limits.

Follow safe adult-child ratios.

The adult-child ratio followed by your program has a large impact on your ability to keep children safe. Standards set in the ASQ *Program Observation Questions for the Director* include set ratios for children under and over age 6. The standard for children under age 6 is 1 staff person for 8 children, and the standard for children age 6 and older is 1 staff person for 10 to 12 children. Group sizes may vary according to the activity, but generally do not exceed 20. These ratios allow staff to supervise children and offer a variety of interesting activities. If you don't know the ratios followed by your program, ask your director or trainer.

Monitor children's arrivals and departures.

School-age programs also need security procedures covering entrances to the building and children's arrivals and departures. The number of open entrances to the building should be limited to the absolute minimum to prevent access to adults or children who are not enrolled. Ideally, visitors to the building should sign in and out at a reception desk and wear name badges.

In addition, children's arrivals and departures must be monitored. Parents should sign their children in and out, and children should sign out and/or let a staff member know when leaving one area to go to another. If children are allowed to leave the program alone—either to go home or to go to an activity such as scouts or gymnastics—written permission from the parents should be on file. Before leaving, children should tell a staff member and sign out, indicating the time and where they are going. Procedures for handling such problems as an intoxicated parent or unauthorized pick-up by a non-custodial parent should also be clear.

You and your colleagues must plan and work together to make sure all indoor and outdoor areas are supervised. For example, if you are working with a group of children in the woodworking area, arrange to have colleagues keep an eye on other indoor and outdoor areas in use. Some programs find it helpful to have as a rotating staff assignment, an "air traffic controller," who does not monitor a specific area or activity, but instead keeps track of the big picture. The air traffic controller monitors children's arrivals and departures, steps in to help other staff when necessary (as in the vignette in the Overview), and focuses on where children are as they move from one area to another and outdoors.

Work with colleagues to supervise all indoor and outdoor areas.

The amount of supervision children require lessens as they get older and more responsible. Your program may have policies for supervision based on children's ages. For example:

Supervision of children may lessen as they get older.

- children under age 7 must always be visible to staff;

- children ages 8 to 10 can sign out when going to another room or the outdoor area as long as a staff member is on duty in the area; and

- children 10 to 12 can sign out and go to an area that is monitored by staff every 30 minutes.

The amount of supervision also varies according to the activity taking place. If children are conducting an experiment using potentially hazardous chemicals, they need your close and constant attention. Children painting a mural or holding a Chess Club meeting are less likely to cause injuries. You can watch them from a distance and periodically stop by to see if they need help.

Some other strategies for providing effective supervision follow.

Try these strategies for effective supervision.

- Stand near equipment when it is in use and pay attention to the children.

- Provide constant, close supervision over active sports and games and for activities using hazardous materials.

- Participate with the children, not in conversations with other staff members.

- If children are spread out in a large area, be sure one staff member can move from place to place to view the entire area and monitor what everyone is doing.

Even safe materials can become dangerous if used the wrong way.

You must be very alert to keep children safe and protected. Your well-trained eyes can protect a child from water spilled on the floor, sharp edges, loose parts, wood splinters, and broken toys. Anything, including the program's "safe" materials and equipment, can become dangerous if used the wrong way. For example, so-called safe items can be harmful if a child:

- uses a table as a step-ladder;

- tilts back in a chair;

- pushes the swing when no one is in it; or

- wraps a jump rope around her arms and neck.

When you see these or other unsafe practices, step in as quickly as possible. Explain to children why their behaviors are unsafe, and remind them of safe ways to use materials and equipment.

Follow-up and debrief with staff after injuries occur.

In the weeks after injuries occur, staff can think about the causes and what could be done to prevent future injuries. Review injury report forms periodically to look for patterns. Are there any particular children, activities, equipment, or times of day that seem to be involved with the injuries? What could be done to prevent them? Then you can make an action plan and take preventive steps.

Applying Your Knowledge

In this learning activity you try to identify hazards in your environment as you observe a child for five minutes. Take notes on all the things the child does (index cards are handy for this). Then use your observation notes to answer the questions that follow. Begin by reviewing the example on the next page.

Preventing Injuries
(Example)

Child: _Benjamin_   **Age:** _11 years_   **Date:** _April 12_

Setting: _Science Area_

What is the child doing?

Benjamin is setting up a new aquarium in science area. He gets out old pump from closet and sets it on floor under table. Next, he carries water back and forth from sink. With each trip some water drips on floor. An electrical cord lying on floor. He doesn't notice dripping water and some of the water starts trickling down towards the cord. Simon calls him from across the room. Benjamin goes to see what Simon wants. He leaves behind the half-filled aquarium, wet floor, and wet electrical cord.

What dangers did you observe in the environment?

The water on the floor could cause Benjamin and other children to slip and fall. The wet electrical cord is hazardous. It would be dangerous for Benjamin or any one else to plug it in because it is wet.

What can you do to prevent injuries?

Because this is an immediate hazard, I stopped writing my observations and immediately went to remove the electrical cord before it was covered with water. I then can help Benjamin move the table closer to the sink so less water will spill. Then I can remind him to cover the area under the aquarium with towels before he begins to fill it. Also, I can help him learn it is important to keep electrical cords away from water. Finally, I can remind him he needs to finish the job he started before going to play with Simon. It is unsafe to leave the aquarium half-filled and the floor and cord dripping wet.

Preventing Injuries

Child: _____ **Age:** _____ **Date:** _____

Setting: _____

What is the child doing?

_____

_____

_____

_____

_____

_____

What dangers did you observe in the environment?

_____

_____

_____

_____

_____

_____

_____

What can you do to prevent injuries?

_____

_____

_____

_____

_____

_____

_____

_____

_____

Discuss your answers with a colleague.

Learning Activity III.
Knowing and Following Emergency Procedures

IN THIS ACTIVITY YOU WILL LEARN TO:

- prepare for injuries and other emergencies; and

- follow the program's established procedures for dealing with emergencies.

Even the most safety-conscious and well-prepared staff member will face emergencies from time to time. How would you respond if a child fell off a bicycle, if the building lost power during a rainstorm, or if you smelled smoke?

Everyone needs to prepare for emergencies.

Emergencies often happen at the worst possible moments, so the time to get ready for them is before they happen. In fact, there are certain times that injuries are more likely to happen, for example, during transitions between activities and at the end of the day when children may be hungry and tired. These are times when staff need to pay close attention to children.

Participating in emergency drills helps everyone to be ready. Every program should have emergency procedures posted so all adults can cooperate to get the children to safety. It is helpful to know in advance who will be responsible for giving first aid, who will oversee the evacuation of the building if necessary, and how to act quickly and get help. Your program probably has specific forms for permission, injury reports, and emergency contacts. You may be asked to fill out these forms.

When a child is injured you must quickly assess how serious the injury is and respond correctly. Most injuries can be handled with soothing words. Others require first aid at the program. Rarely, a trip to the hospital may be necessary.

Responding to Children's Emergencies

If you must accompany a child in the ambulance, be sure to bring with you the child's signed medical history and emergency authorization forms.

Ask the parent to come right away and get medical help immediately when you observe any of the following:[3]

- The child acts unusually confused.

- The child has seizures for the first time or a seizure that lasts more than 15 minutes.

- The child has continuous clear drainage from the nose after a hard blow to the head.

- The child has uneven pupils (black centers of the eyes).

- The child breathes so fast or hard that he cannot play, talk, cry, or drink.

- The child has a severe stomachache that causes the child to double-up and scream; or a stomachache without vomiting or diarrhea after a recent injury, blow to the abdomen, or hard fall.

- The child has stools that are black or have blood mixed through them.

- The child has not urinated in more than 8 hours; the mouth and tongue look dry.

- A child has a temperature of 105° F or higher.

- The child has a severe headache, stiff neck, or neck pain when the head is moved or touched.

- The child looks or acts very ill or seems to be getting worse quickly.

- The child has a rash or blood-red or purple pinhead-sized spots or bruises that are not associated with injury; or a rash of hives or welts that appear quickly.

Call the parent and dentist immediately if a child knocks a permanent tooth loose. Have the child rinse out his or her mouth and bite down on a clean piece of gauze to stop the bleeding. Find the tooth, pick it up without touching the root and rinse it gently. Try to reinsert the tooth into its socket. If not possible, place the tooth in a cup of milk. Rush the child and tooth to the dentist within 90 minutes, if possible. This can increase the chance that the tooth might be successfully implanted.[4]

First-Aid Procedures

First aid is the immediate care you provide to a child who is injured or ill. It is a way to manage the patient's situation until further medical care can take place. CPR is used in situations such as drownings, electric shock, and smoke inhalation to clear the patient's airway, help him or her to breathe, and restart the heart if necessary. Remember to ensure that the other children are supervised adequately while tending to injured children.

---

[3] Based on American Academy of Pediatrics, PA Chapter, *Model Child Health Policies,* Revised (Washington, DC: National Association for the Education of Young Children, 1997).

[4] Based on American Academy of Pediatrics, *First Aid Guidelines* (1995) and American Red Cross (1993).

The program should maintain a well-stocked first-aid kit. Have one to take on field trips, as well as one to keep at the program. Supplies need to be accessible to where injuries occur. When supervising on the playground, staff should carry in their pocket or fanny pack a mini-kit (including a pair of latex gloves, gauze, bandages, and tissues) so they don't have to run back indoors leaving the injured child unattended or risk exposing themselves to blood to care for the child. Restock the kit after each use and check it every month to make sure all items are still in place. A basic first-aid kit contains at least the following items:[5]

Maintain a well-stocked first-aid kit.

- pen/pencil and note pad
- syrup of Ipecac
- cold pack
- current American Academy of Pediatrics (AAP) or American Red Cross standard first-aid chart or equivalent first-aid guide
- coins for use in pay phone
- poison control center phone number
- water
- small plastic or metal splints
- soap
- list of emergency phone numbers and parents' phone numbers
- disposable nonporous gloves
- scissors
- tweezers
- a non-glass thermometer to measure a child's temperature
- bandage tape
- sterile gauze pads
- flexible roller gauze
- triangular bandages
- safety pins
- eye dressing
- any emergency medication for a child with special needs (e.g., a bee sting kit or antihistamine for a child with severe allergy, honey or sugar for a child with diabetes, or an inhaler for a child with asthma)

It is also a good idea to keep on hand extra blankets, pillows, and ice packs.

While syrup of Ipecac should be in your first-aid kit, do not administer it until you have checked with the child's pediatrician or a physician at the poison control center in your community. After administering syrup of Ipecac, the child needs to go to a hospital for medical evaluation.

---

[5]Adapted by Karen Sokal-Gutierrez, M.D., from *Caring for Our Children, National Health and Safety Standards: Guidelines for Out-of-Home Child Care Programs*, 2nd edition (Washington, DC: American Public Health Association and Elk Grove Village, IL: American Academy of Pediatrics, in press 2000).

All staff need to be trained in using gloves for contact with blood to protect against the spread of bloodborne pathogens such as HIV/AIDS and hepatitis B.

When giving first aid, remember these important rules,

- **Do no harm.** (Harm might occur if you fail to treat the injury or if you make the injury worse.)

- **Do not move a child with serious head, neck, or back injury except to save a life.** (Moving the child might cause further injury.)

Follow these steps when evaluating an emergency situation and providing emergency care.

In an emergency, it is crucial to remain calm so you can think clearly and act appropriately. Remember the 3 C's: check, call, care. Check the scene, call for help, care for the injured.

- Survey the scene.

  Is the scene safe?

  Are the other children safe?

  How many children are injured?

  Are there bystanders who can help?

- Check for life-threatening problems.

  Is the child conscious and responsive?

  Do the A-B-C check: Is the airway open? Is the child breathing? Is circulation normal?

  Call 911 for help if you have any doubts about the situation. Then call the child's parents..

Follow these steps if a child is choking.

Begin the following if a child is choking and is unable to breathe. However, if the child is coughing, crying, or speaking, DO NOT do any of the following.

- Place thumbside of fist again middle of abdomen just above the navel. Grasp fist with the other hand.

- Give up to 5 quick upward thrusts.

- Repeat these steps until object is coughed up, or until the child starts to breathe or becomes unconscious.

Follow these steps if a child is unconscious and not breathing, but there is a pulse (heartbeat).

A child is breathing if the chest if moving and the air if coming out of the nose or mouth. Either phone 911 for help or have another staff person do so. Then begin rescue breathing. The following steps are a reminder of the procedure. Check your instruction manual for a detailed description of the process.

- With the victim's head tilted back, pinch the nose shut. Give 2 slow breaths.

- Check pulse. If pulse is present but child is still not breathing, give 1 slow breath about every 3 seconds.

- Do this for 1 minute (20 breaths).

- Recheck the pulse and breathing. Continue until help arrives.

The following steps are a reminder of the procedure. Check your instruction manual for a detailed description of the process.

Follow these steps if a child is unconscious and there is no breathing and pulse (heartbeat).

- With the victim's head tilted back, pinch the nose shut. Give 2 slow breaths. If the air won't go in, retilt the head and try again.

- If air still won't go in, place heel of one hand on child's abdomen above the middle of navel and below rib cage. Give up to 5 abdominal thrusts.

- If air still won't go in after repeating the abdominal thrusts, begin CPR.

CPR techniques include the following:

Follow these steps for CPR.

- Clear the throat with a finger sweep and wipe out any fluid, vomitus, mucus, or foreign body.

- Place the victim on his or her back.

- Find hand position on about the center of the breastbone. Position shoulders over hands. Compress chest 5 times.

- Give one slow breath.

- Repeat cycles of 5 compressions and 1 breath for about 1 minute.

- Recheck pulse and breathing for about 5 seconds.

- If there is still no pulse, continue sets of 5 compressions and 1 breath. Recheck pulse and breathing every few minutes until help arrives.

For minor burns, respond as follows:

Follow these procedures when responding to burns.

- Immerse the burned area in cool water or apply cool (50° to 60° F) compresses to burns on a child's trunk or face to relieve the pain.

- Do not break blisters.

- Call an ambulance for burns of any size on a child's face, hands, feet, or genitalia.

For extensive burns, call an ambulance; then respond as follows:

- Remove clothing from the burn area if it comes off easily; if not, leave it alone.
- Keep the patient flat and warm. Cover the child with a clean sheet and blanket.
- Do not use ointments, greases, or powders.

For electrical burns, respond as follows:

- Do not use your bare hands.
- Disconnect the power source if possible or pull the child away from the source using wood or cloth (these will not conduct electricity).
- Call an ambulance.
- Apply CPR if necessary.

Survey for specific injuries and treat as necessary.

Ask what happened and what hurts. Comfort the child and then check for injuries. Do a head-to-toe check: Head, scalp, face, ears, eyes, nose, mouth, neck, collar bones, chest, abdomen, arms, hands, legs (ask child to wiggle fingers and toes.)

Do first aid as needed.
- Stop bleeding.
- Immobilize injured bones, muscles, and tendons.
- Remove poisons, splinters, small objects.
- Clean and bandage wounds.

After you have performed necessary first aid, call the parent and explain what happened, what you did, and how the child is. Explain whether the child needs to be picked up or whether the child needs to be met at the hospital.

Talk with the other children and be reassuring. Later you can answer children's questions and talk about how future injuries might be prevented. Complete the injury report form and give a copy to the parent and keep a copy for your records.

Be prepared to respond to poison emergencies.

A poison emergency can happen when someone swallows or touches a toxic substance, gets chemicals in the eyes, or breathes toxic fumes. The following common substances might be poisonous: cleaners and laundry products; hair care products; prescription and over-the-counter drugs; hobby and craft supplies;

paint removal products; and workroom supplies. Whenever you suspect or know that a child has been poisoned, immediately call the poison control center or a medical clinic. Tell whoever answers the phone what product or chemical the child was exposed to (have the container with you when you make the call). Tell the person how much the child took or was exposed to and how long ago the incident took place.

Syrup of Ipecac is a substance that induces vomiting. Using it is not always advisable. Some poisons, such as drain cleaner or lye, can do serious damage to the esophagus if vomited. Do **not** use Ipecac unless told to do so by the poison control center.

Your calm and quick response to an emergency is important. Proper procedures include: notifying your supervisor that an incident has occurred; informing the child's parents (immediately for serious injuries or at the end of the day for minor ones); documenting, on the appropriate form, what happened.

Stay calm and follow proper procedures.

Handling Weather-Related Emergencies

Although you work hard to make your environment safe, emergencies may be caused by events outside your control. Floods, landslides, tornadoes, hurricanes, earthquakes, and other weather-related emergencies may happen with little or no warning. If you know what to do, you can act swiftly. Learn about those weather-related emergencies likely to happen in your area and review your program's plans for responding to these events.

The National Weather Service recommends the actions described below to keep safe in case of lightning storms, tornadoes, and earthquakes. Share this information with the children. Role-play how everyone should respond in a real emergency.

The best precaution is to avoid being outdoors in a lightning storm. Get weather information before traveling and carry a small transistor radio to get updates if the weather turns stormy. Move to shelter as quickly as possible. If you are caught in a lightning storm, take the following actions:

Take these precautions while outdoors during a lightning storm.

- Stay out of metal or wood sheds.

- Seek shelter in a vehicle or in a low area under **small** trees.

- Do not stand on a hilltop.

- Avoid being the tallest object in the area.

- Stay away from isolated trees and from items made of metal—pipes, rails, fences, and wire clotheslines.

- Do not touch or use metal sporting equipment (golf clubs or shoes, tennis rackets, bikes).

- If you are in a group, spread out and keep several yards apart.

- Stay away from water.

- If your hair stands on end, you are in **immediate danger**—crouch down and curl your head forward. Make your body as small as possible.

- When someone is struck, he or she carries no electrical charge and may be handled safely. Even if the person is feeling fine, immediate medical attention is recommended. Keep the person warm and elevate his or her legs.

During a tornado, take these actions.

In the event of a tornado, respond as follows:

If you are in a building:

- Move to a basement or storm shelter.

- Stay away from windows.

- If the building has no basement, go to a small room, closet, or bathroom in the center of the building.

- In a high-rise building, move to the center of the building, preferably to a stairwell. Do not open windows.

If you are in open country:

- Lie face down in a low area.

- Cover your head.

If you are in a vehicle:

- Stop the vehicle.

- Get out and lie down in a low area.

- Cover your head.

- **Do not try to outrun a tornado in a car.**

Take these precautions during an earthquake.

Earthquakes occur without warning. If you are in a location where earthquakes are likely, practice with the children what steps to take.

If **inside** during an earthquake, get under a table or desk. Try to stay away from windows. Cover your head. It helps to stand inside a strong doorway. If you are **outside** during an earthquake, stay there. Stay away from high buildings, walls, power poles, and similar objects.

After the earthquake, wait for additional shocks. Do not light matches or turn on any lights because you could cause a fire. Administer first aid if needed. Turn on a battery-powered radio and listen for emergency instructions.

Using a Fire Extinguisher

Knowing when and when not to use a fire extinguisher is an important part of being prepared for an emergency. Do not try to fight fires that spread beyond the spot where they started. For example, you will probably be able to put out a grease fire in a frying pan, but if it gets out of control, you and the children should get out of the building immediately. Also, if the fire could block your exit, evacuate the building immediately. Use an extinguisher only if the following is true:

• All the children are safely out of the building and in the care of a responsible person.

• You can get out fast if your efforts aren't working.

• You are nearby when the fire starts, or you discover the fire soon after it has started.

• The fire is small and confined to a space such as a trash can, cushion, or small appliance.

• You can fight the fire with your back to an exit.

• The extinguisher is in working order, and you can:

> stand back about 8 feet;
> aim at the base of the fire, not the flames or smoke; and
> squeeze or press the lever while sweeping from the
> sides to the middle.

If you have the slightest doubt about whether to fight the fire or get out, **get out of the building and call the fire department.** Your safety is most important.

Applying Your Knowledge

In this learning activity you review your program's established procedures for evacuating children and staff in case of fire or other emergencies. You also review your program's injury procedures. Then answer the questions on emergency procedures that follow.

Emergency and First-Aid Procedures

What is your emergency evacuation plan? What would you do if the planned route was blocked? What phone number would you use to call for assistance?

_____

_____

_____

_____

What would you do if a child cut his or her leg during outdoor play?

_____

_____

_____

_____

What would you do if a fire started during a cooking activity?

_____

_____

_____

_____

Who informs parents if their child has had a minor injury? When are the parents informed?

_____

_____

_____

Who calls for emergency medical assistance if a child has a serious injury or medical problem? What is the procedure for contacting the child's parents?

_____

_____

_____

What medical facility would you go to in an emergency? How would you get there?

_____

_____

_____

What emergencies (weather related or otherwise) might affect your program? What are the procedures for dealing with these emergencies?

_____

_____

_____

_____

When you are away from the program site, what are your emergency plans to notify parents and your supervisor of an injury?

_____

_____

_____

_____

Discuss your answers with your trainer. If you have questions about what to do in an emergency, review your program's emergency procedures and discuss them with your supervisor.

Learning Activity IV.
Ensuring Children's Safety Away From the Program

IN THIS ACTIVITY YOU WILL LEARN TO:

- teach children how to walk and cross streets safely; and

- take safe field trips and excursions with children.

School-age children are expanding their understanding of the world. Field trips and excursions in the neighborhood extend children's learning. However, taking children away from the program, crossing streets, or transporting them in vehicles to new and unfamiliar locations also involves an element of risk. You can minimize the risks by teaching children to walk and cross streets safely and planning safe field trips and excursions.

Walking Safely Near Traffic

There are many good reasons to walk in the neighborhood. For example, walking to a neighborhood park or going to a community facility (such as a bowling alley or a tennis court) could offer the children new and challenging experiences. You might plan walks to explore new concepts or skills: a listening walk, a walk to collect seeds in the fall, or a visit to local stores to purchase something the group needs. But children need to learn to walk safely near traffic.

Statistics indicate over 90 percent of all pedestrian-related injuries are the fault of the pedestrian, not the motorist. Police departments offer a simple slogan to children and adults when going into traffic: *Cross Wise*. Here are the guidelines offered by one police department for ensuring pedestrian safety.[6]

1. At crosswalks with signals, obey the **Walk/Don't Walk** signals. Where there are no signals, wait for a new green light in the direction you are walking before entering the intersection.

2. Always cross at the corner and stay within the crosswalk.

[6] Montgomery County Department of Police, Bethesda Traffic Squad, Pedestrian Safety Program, "Cross Wise" (funded by the Maryland Department of Transportation).

3. Do not walk out from between parked cars.

4. Always walk on the sidewalk. When there is no sidewalk, walk on the left side of the road, facing traffic.

5. Look in both directions for traffic before crossing, even if crossing on a **Walk** signal.

6. Wear or carry a reflective material when walking at night or at dusk.

7. Pay attention at all times.

Before taking a walk with children, review and discuss these safety guidelines. Think ahead about children who tend to act before thinking or who are easily distracted. Be sure one adult is assigned to be with these children at all times.

Planning Safe Field Trips and Excursions

School-age children often get excited about taking special trips away from the program. Their excitement is in part due to the fact the situation is unfamiliar. This may cause some children to be nervous and afraid. You too may be nervous about supervising the children in an unfamiliar location. You may be anxious about transporting children to and from a place where you have never been. By carefully planning ahead for these trips, you can reduce children's anxiety (and your own) and minimize the risks. Before taking a trip, it is important to establish procedures. The questions listed below can guide your planning.

- How will children be supervised?

- What should children do if they become separated from the group?

- What should children do if a stranger approaches them?

- What guidelines do children need for using public transportation and restrooms?

- How will children be kept safe while riding in program vehicles?

- What are the general guidelines for children's behavior?

Complete these steps before the trip.

Prior to each trip, take the following steps to ensure the children's safety. (Staff can divide up these tasks and then report back to each other.)

- Inform parents well in advance of the trip, and have them sign permission slips several days before the trip.

- If possible, travel to the site from the program using the same route you will follow on the trip. Look for potential problems such as road repairs or detours, traffic congestion, lane restrictions, one-way streets, or parking problems. Adjust the trip schedule accordingly.

- While at the site, locate the telephones, restrooms, food stands (or picnic tables), shelters for poor weather, and where to get emergency assistance. If you plan to separate into smaller groups, identify a convenient place to meet at the end of the visit. (On the trip, you may want to use "walkie-talkies" to communicate with each other.)

- Prepare a trip folder including the following information: emergency telephone numbers (the program, police); signed parent emergency forms (be sure information is correct and current); and signed permission slips.

- Check the first-aid kit and replace missing or outdated items.

- For children with special needs such as allergies, asthma, diabetes, or seizures, the driver/supervising adult needs to know how to recognize and respond to a medical emergency and have on hand an emergency plan, supplies, and any medications needed.

- Estimate how many children will go on the trip, and make sure the vehicle to be used has enough seats and seat belts. In cars with airbags, make sure children do not ride in the front seat.

- Plan for the unexpected. Bring a list of five to ten familiar games and activities that require no equipment or supplies in case there are delays or problems. Back-up activities such as guessing games, storytelling, and pantomimes will keep children calm and occupied in an emergency.

- Recruit volunteers—parents, senior citizens, college or high school students—to help supervise the children if your group is very big or if you are to visit a large or congested site. Be sure volunteers are always supervised by a staff member.

- Plan how members of the group can be identified (for example, program T-shirts or name tags). To protect children, name tags should include their first names only. Write the program's telephone number on the back.

Discuss safety procedures with children on the day of the trip.

On the day of the trip review the safety rules and emergency precautions with the children. Listed below are some things to discuss calmly and clearly, and without alarming the children:

- Where children should go if they become separated from the group. An emergency or first-aid area, the public telephone, or the main office of the building are good places to meet.

- Why it is important to remain on trails and with the group in wooded areas, and what children should do if they get lost:

  Stay in one place and let the group find you.

  Use the universal distress call—a signal such as a shout or a whistle repeated three times at frequent intervals—to let the group know where you are.

  Try to get as comfortable as possible. If necessary, find shelter for the night against a rock or under cover of trees or bushes. Use everything in your pack to stay warm and dry. If you can start a fire, collect as much wood as you will need before it gets too dark.

  Try not to worry! Lots of people will look for you.

- Where and when to go for snack, lunch, at the end of the visit.

- Why it's important to stay with a buddy at all times.

- How to use public bathrooms safely.

- Why it's important not to go into secluded areas (for example, behind buildings or into deserted areas of museums).

- How to be safe while riding to and from the site:

  Use seat belts.

  Keep arms and heads inside the windows.

  Stay seated while the vehicle is moving.

  Refrain from shoving, throwing things, or behaving in ways which could disturb and distract the driver.

- What children should do if a stranger approaches them: **try to get away**.

- Other rules related to strangers:

  Don't go near a stranger's car to give help or directions.

  Don't accept rides or gifts from strangers.

  Don't go into secluded areas with a stranger.

  Don't tell a stranger your name, address, or any other personal information.

  Do find a responsible adult and tell him or her a stranger approached you.

Follow your plans while on the field trip.

On the day of the trip, use a checklist of what to do at each stage. Include the following items and others relevant to your program.

- Before you leave the program:

    Gather all information and materials for the trip, including a list of who is going (check the list to be sure everyone is with you).

    Take the first-aid kit.

    Make sure vehicles do not have too many passengers.

    Make sure everyone is wearing seat belts.

    Remove any sharp or heavy objects from inside the vehicle—these become dangerous in a sudden stop.

    Review the rules for vehicle safety.

- On your way to and from the site:

    Be sure children observe safety rules.

    Ask the driver to pull off the road and stop if children are out of control; if you are the driver, stop before disciplining children.

    Never leave children without adult supervision.

- While you are at the site:

    Check prearranged procedures on arrival.

    Notify children and staff of changes in plans before small groups go in different directions.

- When you leave the site:

    Account for everyone and count at least twice.

    Give children the same reminders (vehicle safety) you used before leaving the program.

Ensuring children's safety is especially challenging when you are away from the program. Following the suggestions listed in this learning activity will help you meet the challenge.

Applying Your Knowledge

In this learning activity you review your program's policies and procedures for ensuring children's safety on field trips and when walking in your neighborhood. After recording them on the form that follows, you can compare them to the suggestions above and list safety precautions you want to add.

Protecting Children Away from the Program

What are your program's rules and procedures for taking children away from the program?

_____

_____

_____

_____

What does your program require you to do before a field trip?

_____

_____

_____

_____

What are the rules and procedures for keeping children safe on field trips?

_____

_____

_____

_____

What activities could you lead to keep children calm and safe during an emergency or unexpected delay?

_____

_____

_____

How can you improve the procedures and the planning process to more effectively ensure children's safety away from the program?

_____

_____

_____

_____

Discuss your answers with your trainer and your colleagues. Implement the ideas you feel are needed to ensure children's safety away from the program.

Learning Activity V.
Helping Children Keep Themselves Safe

IN THIS ACTIVITY YOU WILL LEARN TO:

- develop safety rules with children; and

- reinforce the rules so children learn them.

School-age children can understand how and why injuries happen and what they can do to prevent them. They can work with staff to complete safety checklists such as the one included in Learning Activity I and identify hazards or unsafe materials in the interest areas and outdoors. When children know what to look for, they can help prevent injuries and keep themselves safe.

Children learn about safety from watching adults.

The first step in teaching children safety is to show them, by your actions, how you prevent injuries. Children need to see you walking, not running, indoors; sitting, not standing, on chairs; and wearing goggles at the woodworking bench.

Children can help set program rules.

One of the best ways to teach children how to keep themselves safe is to include them in developing safety rules. Children can identify potential problems and hazards and help make a list of important rules. They can encourage others to learn and observe the rules. Even when they know the rules, however, they need constant supervision and frequent, firm reminders about the importance of safety.

Discuss potential dangers.

To develop safety rules, you might start a discussion by saying: "Tell me about . . . " or "What could happen if . . ." You can discuss the dangers of activities such as the following:

- pushing and shoving;

- crawling, climbing, or walking on furniture;

- carrying a pan full of hot liquid;

- sitting on furniture not intended for that purpose (for example, a Ping-Pong table);

- pushing an unoccupied swing, jumping from moving swings, or climbing on swing frames;

- using equipment designed for younger, smaller children, and therefore not strong enough to hold school-age children;

- using slides for standing, running up and down, or coming down backwards;

- throwing sand or gravel;

- climbing trees or fences;

- winding jump ropes around arms, legs, or necks;

- running while carrying sticks, shovels, or sharp objects; and

- throwing bats, hockey sticks, and other sports equipment.

Involve children in developing appropriate safety guidelines **before** they participate in a new activity. For example:

Set guidelines before a new activity.

- Show children how to use equipment properly (for example, how to hold a saw and where to place one's hands when sawing a board). Children who already know how can show others how to use the equipment.

- Emphasize the need for protective gear (helmets, pads, goggles, eyeglass guards) for active sports and games and potentially hazardous activities. Show children how to wear protective gear properly (for example, bicycle helmets need to be the right size, positioned properly on the head, and buckled).

- Set up safety zones for children waiting a turn in ball games.

- Plan cleanup routines so all equipment is safely put away and areas are free of clutter at the end of an activity.

When introducing children to a new sport or game, review the rules and explain how following them will prevent injuries. Follow these steps when introducing a sport or game:

Review the rules for a new sport or game.

- Describe the general goals of the game.

- Demonstrate new skills to be used. Have children practice the new skills.

- Explain the steps or rules clearly. If a game is complicated, break the directions into parts and let children learn one part of the game at a time. Minimize the potential for "horseplay" by keeping your explanations brief and to the point.

- Ask children to explain the rules to you, to make sure they understood your explanation.

- Answer children's questions to be sure everyone understands.

- Monitor the game once it has started to be sure everyone knows how to play.

Children need reminders of safety rules.

Even after rules are developed and communicated, children will still need occasional reminders. Try these suggestions to help children remember to follow the rules:

- Reinforce rules simply and often. "Amber, this is the bicycle riding area. You may kick your ball on the grass."

- Step in when necessary to help a child follow the rules. "J.T. and Gina, I reminded you several times you are not allowed to chase each other up and down the bleachers. One of you could fall and be hurt. If you need to burn off some energy, you may run laps around the gym."

- Remove a child from an activity if he or she continues to break a safety rule; explain the reason for your action. "Corey, the cue is only to be used for playing pool. I reminded you earlier it is dangerous to use it as a sword. Because you are still using it that way, you must put it away and leave the pool table. I'll help you find something else to do."

Safety slogans and posters can offer reminders.

Encourage children to write safety slogans and make posters to help everyone remember the program's rules. Posters might offer the following reminders:

- This area is reserved for bike riding (or jump roping).

- Wear goggles at the woodworking bench.

- Eating and running don't mix!

- Wear a helmet and protective gear when skating or bike riding.

- Stay clear of the batter's box.

Ask community representatives to teach children about safety.

Community resources are available to help children learn about safety. You might, for example, ask a community organizer or someone from the police department to come and talk about the issue of gun control and violence. They can help children learn ways to keep themselves safe in threatening situations. If an incident occurred near the program and children were witnesses or know the people involved, a counselor might be brought in to help everyone deal with their concerns and fears.

Applying Your Knowledge

In this learning activity you work with the children in your program to develop safety limits for an activity in an indoor or outdoor area. Review the example, then answer the questions that follow.

Developing Safety Rules With Children
(Example)

Area: _Asphalt Play Area_   **Age(s):** _8-10 years_   **Date:** _October 10_
Activity: _Relay Races_

What do you think are the safety hazards in this activity and area?

There could be loose gravel or trash on the playing surface that might make children fall.

There are several barriers near the area children could run into—a utility box, a large tree, and the brick wall of the building.

Children could run into each other if the relay teams run too close together.

Children also might fall if the bottoms of their shoes are too slippery for the asphalt surface or if their shoelaces are untied.

How did the children answer your "tell me about . . . " questions?

Joe said, "It takes a lot of energy."

Dennis said, "I like to run so fast nothing can stop me."

Kim said, "Sometimes it's hard to find the next person on your team when it's time to hand over the bean bag."

Julie said, "When you run really fast, sometimes you think you're going to fall."

How did the children answer your "what could happen if . . . " questions?

Kim said, "You could knock over other people if you're not careful."

Dennis said, "If I run too close to the wall, I might crash into it before I stop."

Julie said, "You could fall if you don't have your shoes on tight, especially if you trip on something."

What safety limits did you and the children develop for this activity and area?

Before you play, always check the playing area for loose gravel, glass, and trash.

Use orange cones to separate the relay teams and to mark a start line where the next player in line can stand.

Set up turning lanes so children won't collide with each other or run into the barriers.

Wear shoes that are good for running, and tie the shoelaces.

Developing Safety Rules With Children

Area: _____   Age(s): _____   Date: _____

Activity: _____

What do you think are the safety hazards in this activity and area?

_____

_____

_____

How did the children answer your "tell me about . . . " question?

_____

_____

_____

How did the children answer your "what could happen if . . . " questions?

_____

_____

_____

What safety limits did you and the children develop for this activity and area?

_____

_____

_____

_____

_____

Discuss your responses with your trainer.

SUMMARIZING YOUR PROGRESS

You have now completed all the learning activities for this module. Whether you are an experienced school-age staff member or a new one, this module has probably helped you develop new skills for keeping children safe. Before you go on, take a few minutes to review your responses to the pre-training assessment for this module. Write a summary of what you learned, and list the skills you developed or improved.

_____

_____

_____

_____

_____

_____

_____

_____

_____

_____

_____

_____

_____

If there are topics you would like to know more about, you will find recommended readings listed in the Orientation.

Your final step in this module is to complete the knowledge and competency assessments. Let your trainer know when you are ready to schedule the assessments. After you have successfully completed them, you will be ready to start a new module. Congratulations on your progress so far, and good luck with your next module.

ANSWER SHEETS

Keeping Children Safe

Maintaining Indoor and Outdoor Environments That Prevent Injuries

1. **What did Mr. Sullivan do to create a safe outdoor environment?**

   a. He completed the program's outdoor safety checklist.

   b. He removed the branches that fell during the storm.

   c. He checked the climber for splinters.

   d. He raked the wood chips back under the climber.

   e. He swept the water off the asphalt.

   f. He marked safety areas.

2. **What next steps does Mr. Sullivan need to take to make sure the outdoor environment is safe?**

   a. He needs to ask for volunteers to help pick up the twigs.

   b. He needs to report the rough surface under the timber on the climber and make sure it is sanded.

Planning for and Responding to Emergencies

1. **What did Mr. Lopez do to keep all the children safe?**

   a. He immediately stopped the game so he could check on Tony and Gillian.

   b. He asked Ms. Kendrick to take over for him while he got the ice for the injured children.

2. **What did Mr. Lopez do after taking care of the children's injuries?**

   a. He completed an injury report.

   b. He put a note in each child's cubby to let their parents know what happened and to ask them to review and sign the injury report.

1. **Why did Ms. Nelson think it was important for the girls to make safety rules for their club?**

   a. She knew the playground needed to be checked daily for loose gravel, glass, and trash.

   b. She realized the girls were so excited about their new club they hadn't stopped to think about safety before they began to play.

   c. She knew the girls were capable of thinking of ways to keep themselves safe.

2. **How did the children learn to keep themselves safe?**

   a. They learned it is important to think about safety and hazards in the environment before beginning to play.

   b. They wrote down some safety rules for their club.

Helping Children Develop Habits That Will Prevent Injuries

GLOSSARY

Emergency   Unplanned or unexpected situation in which children or adults are harmed or may be harmed.

Hazard   A source of danger; a condition that may cause an injury or emergency.

Precaution   Steps taken to prevent injuries or to ensure safety.

Safety   Freedom from danger.

Module 2:
HEALTHY

OVERVIEW

HELPING SCHOOL-AGE CHILDREN STAY HEALTHY INVOLVES:

- maintaining indoor and outdoor environments that promote wellness and reduce the spread of disease;

- encouraging children to develop habits that promote good hygiene and nutrition; and

- recognizing and reporting child abuse and neglect.

Good health is a state of well-being—physical, mental, and social—not simply the absence of disease. Adults who are healthy feel good about themselves. They:

Healthy people feel good about themselves.

- are well-rested, energetic, and strong;
- eat the right foods;
- avoid (or use moderately) alcohol, cigarettes, and caffeine;
- exercise regularly; and
- get along well with others;

Each of us has certain health and nutrition routines that are part of our daily lives. Some of these routines may be good for us, and some may not. Because most of us want to become and remain healthy, we try to increase the number of good routines, such as snacking on fruits and vegetables, and decrease the number of bad ones, such as smoking or failing to get enough exercise.

Most school-age children have the cognitive, socio-emotional, and physical skills they need to learn good health and nutrition routines. They can understand the consequences of eating foods high in fat or salt and failing to brush and floss their teeth, and may be motivated to adopt healthy eating and dental habits. Instead of keeping their feelings bottled up, children can learn how to express their emotions and manage their stress or anxiety. Children's physical skills are growing, too. Participating in a wide variety of fitness activities contributes to their overall health and well-being. (Promoting physical development is discussed in detail in Module 4, Physical.) The healthy habits children develop during these years usually continue throughout their lives.

School-age children can learn good health and nutrition routines.

School-age staff can model healthy practices.

One way children learn about good health and nutrition is by following the lead of adults. When you wash your hands and encourage children to wash theirs, you model an effective way to prevent diseases from spreading. When you eat breakfast family-style with the children, you model a healthy nutrition practice—starting the day with a balanced meal. In addition, you teach about good health and nutrition in the course of daily life at the program. You involve children in planning and serving nutritious snacks, encourage them to help keep the environment clean, and show them relaxation techniques to use after a stressful day.

Listed below are examples of how school-age staff demonstrate their competence in helping children stay healthy.

Maintaining Indoor and Outdoor Environments That Promote Wellness and Reduce the Spread of Disease

Check the facility daily for adequate ventilation and lighting, comfortable room temperature, and good sanitation.

Open windows daily to let in fresh air.

Provide tissues, paper towels, and soap in places children can reach; ask children to help keep these items stocked.

Complete daily health checks and be alert to symptoms of illness.

Recognize symptoms of common childhood illnesses (such as strep throat and chicken pox) and other health problems (such as obesity, anorexia, bulimia, and alcohol or drug abuse). Stay in regular contact with parents.

Wash their hands and encourage children to wash theirs at proper times.

Clean and disinfect surfaces before using them for food preparation.

Maintain a positive, relaxed, and pleasant program atmosphere to reduce tension and stress.

Encouraging Children to Develop Habits That Promote Good Hygiene and Nutrition

Help children learn to recognize, reduce, and handle stress. "Rochelle, you seem a little frustrated. How about taking a break from your computer game?"

Model healthy habits, such as washing hands, using tissues, eating nutritious foods, and sanitizing materials and surfaces. "Uh-oh, here comes a big sneeze! I'd better go get a tissue."

Provide resources on health and hygiene, such as magazines, books, pamphlets, clubs, and visiting health professionals. "I'm glad you signed up for the Fitness Club. A nutritionist is coming to our first meeting to talk about healthy snacks."

Involve children in planning and preparing nutritious meals and snacks for the program. "You collected some interesting recipes when you surveyed the other children."

Sit with children "family-style" during snack and meal times to encourage conversation and to model healthy habits. "I've never had tofu before, but I'm going to try some. Many people in Asia eat it. Joel, would you like to try some?"

Help children recognize when their bodies need a change—rest, some food or water, or movement. "Kegan, you've been working on your papier maché dinosaur all afternoon. How about coming down to the gym for a while? We're going to stretch our bodies and play a few games."

Offer self-service snack so children can determine when, what, and how much to eat. "The snack area will be open until 4 p.m. You can help yourself when you're hungry."

Plan a flexible daily schedule that includes time for outdoor activities and responds to children's physical needs.

Keep a supply of sanitary pads and tampons in the girls' bathroom and make sure girls know where they are in case they are too embarrassed to ask for them.

Recognizing and Reporting Child Abuse and Neglect

Learn the definitions of physical abuse, sexual abuse, emotional abuse or maltreatment, and neglect.

Recognize the physical and behavioral signs that a child might be a victim of abuse or neglect.

Follow required procedures to report suspected child abuse and neglect.

Maintain confidentiality after filing a report of suspected child maltreatment.

Protect children by reporting suspected abuse or neglect without waiting for proof.

Support families and help them get the services they need.

Helping Children Stay Healthy

In the following situations, school-age staff are helping children stay healthy. As you read them, think about what the staff are doing and why. Then answer the questions that follow.

Maintaining Indoor and Outdoor Environments That Promote Wellness and Reduce the Spread of Disease

Ms. Nunes enters the room and opens several windows. It is a cool day, so she raises them only a few inches. She checks the area around the sink and notices the soap dispenser is full but the towel supply is low. She makes a note to ask one of the children to put out some more paper towels. As the children arrive, she greets each one warmly, checking to see if anyone has signs of the flu that was running through the program. "You have a runny nose today, David. Please blow your nose with a tissue from the box next to the sink," she says. "Then wash your hands." Lacey, the last one to arrive, comes in with her father. "Hi Lacey," says Ms. Nunes. "Did you wake up late?" "Yeah," says Lacey, "I have a stomach ache, too." Ms. Nunes feels Lacey's head. "Hmm," she says to Lacey's father. "She feels a little warm. Let's take her temperature." Suddenly Lacey runs for the bathroom, yelling, "I'm going to be sick." Ms. Nunes follows Lacey to the bathroom. Lacey has already vomited, so Ms. Nunes helps her splash water on her face. She gives her a cup of water to rinse out her mouth. They both wash their hands. "There go some germs down the drain," says Lacey. "Good!" says Ms. Nunes. "You look very pale. Let's go tell your Dad you need to go home."

1. **What are three things Ms. Nunes did to maintain a healthy environment?**

   _____

   _____

   _____

2. **What did Ms. Nunes do to keep germs from spreading?**

   _____

   _____

   _____

Mr. Berry begins the first meeting of the Quick and Easy Cooking Club by asking children what are their favorite fast foods. Several children respond at once. "I love burgers; they're real juicy." "Yeah, big burgers!" "What makes the burgers so juicy?" asks Mr. Berry. "Well, the fat, I guess," says Tommy. Mr. Berry continues, "Do you know how much fat is in one burger?" "How much?" asks Tommy. "Well, about nine teaspoons of fat." "Is that a lot?" asks Julie. Mr. Berry offers Julie a measuring spoon, a tin of lard, and a plate. Horrified, the others watch Julie measure nine teaspoons of lard. "Do you want to taste it?" asks Mr. Berry . "Gross!" says Julie. "No way!" "Me neither!" says Tommy. "Let's not cook anything with fat in it!"

Mr. Berry suggests looking for recipes that don't use a lot of fat or other unhealthy ingredients, like salt and sugar. They talk about cooking techniques such as broiling, baking, and "frying" with water, which reduce the amount of fat in foods. "Today, we'll make bagel pizzas with tomato sauce, mozzarella cheese, and herbs and spices for flavor. The sauce is low-salt and the cheese is part-skim, which means it doesn't have as much fat as some other cheeses. It's one of my favorite snacks. Then you can look through the recipe books and find some healthy snacks to make next time. Before we handle the food, we all need to wash our hands."

Encouraging Children to Develop Health Habits That Promote Good Hygiene and Nutrition

1 . How did Mr. Berry help the children develop healthy habits?

_____

_____

_____

2 . How did Mr. Berry teach the children about good nutrition?

_____

_____

_____

Recognizing and Reporting Child Abuse and Neglect

Ms. Charles has worked at the school-age program for as long as Carolyn has been enrolled. They have a close relationship. Carolyn is usually friendly and outgoing and gets along well with children of all ages. Lately, she's been spending more time alone than usual. She's been reluctant to get involved in activities that used to be of interest, and she's been short-tempered with the younger children. Today, while they are walking back from the bowling alley, Carolyn says, "My big brother isn't nice. He made me do something really bad. I hate him." Ms. Charles asks Carolyn if she'd like to talk about it. "Yes," says Carolyn, her eyes full of tears. "I have to tell someone." Ms. Charles asks another staff member to take her place. She and Carolyn go to the director's office for a private conversation. After a few silent minutes, Carolyn begins talking. "My brother makes me touch him, you know, in his underpants," she says. They talk for a while, then Ms. Charles tells Carolyn she did the right thing by telling someone about her brother. Trying to respond without overstepping the bounds of her role she says, "Your brother's behavior is not okay. You haven't done anything wrong."

Ms. Charles immediately tells the director, Ms. Lee, about the changes she observed in Carolyn's behavior and what she said about her brother. They discuss the signs of possible child abuse. Ms. Lee says, "I'm glad you came to me with this situation." She is pleased Ms. Charles remembers it is her responsibility to file a report to the Child Protective Services (CPS). Ms. Lee suggests that Ms. Charles first write down her observations and concerns so this information will be available when she files the report to CPS. She reminds Ms. Charles to keep the information confidential. Together they brainstorm about how to talk with Carolyn's parents. Ms. Charles calls CPS; she then calls Carolyn's parents to let them know she has filed a report. CPS sends someone to the program to investigate.

1. **What are the clues to possible child abuse in this situation?**

_____

_____

_____

2. How did Ms. Lee support Ms. Charles?

_____

_____

_____

Compare your answers with those on the answer sheet at the end of this module. If your answers are different, discuss them with your trainer. There can be more than one good answer.

Your Own Health and Nutrition

Staying healthy can improve your life.

Most of us know good health and proper nutrition are important. The national focus on staying fit—which is stressed in the media, in schools, and at the workplace—has provided much useful information and has led to an increased motivation to stay healthy. We have learned that staying healthy improves the quality of life and can actually prolong life.

Most of us know what to do to stay healthy. We try to improve our health by doing the right things—and when we do, we tend to feel better about ourselves. Perhaps you have done some of the following things to improve your health:

- Began walking or jogging more often.
- Joined an aerobics class or exercise program.
- Quit smoking or vowed never to start.
- Increased the variety of foods in your diet to include more vegetables, fruits, and whole-grain products.
- Lost weight using a sensible diet.
- Began eating less sugar, fats, and salt.
- Decreased the amount of unnecessary stress in your life.
- Discovered the positive effects of relaxation techniques.

Improve your health and nutrition one step at a time.

You may have found, though, that changing too much too quickly led to failure. Have you found yourself saying these things?

- "I tried quitting smoking, but I felt like I was going crazy, and I couldn't stop eating!"
- "I don't have time to jog and still manage to go to work, cook for my family, and keep the lawn mowed."
- "Well, I'd like to cook healthier foods for my family, but it takes so long to plan and prepare. It's just easier to get fast food."

Changing our health and nutrition habits can be hard. It is one thing to know what to do; it is something quite different to actually do it. Being judgmental and critical of ourselves only makes us feel worse.

An old proverb states, "If we don't change our direction, we will very likely end up in the place we're headed." We might as well do all we can to ensure our own success by being gentle with ourselves and appreciating each step we take in our desired direction. Because doing everything "right" is very hard, you might think in terms of more and less. You want to do more of certain good things, such as:

- exercising;
- eating fruits, vegetables, and whole-grain products;
- getting enough sleep; and
- spending time with family and friends.

You want to do less of or stop doing certain unhealthy things, such as:

- smoking;
- eating foods high in fat, salt, or sugar;
- drinking alcohol; and
- letting stress build up.

Keeping in mind your whole state of well-being—physical, mental, and social—take time to answer the questions below. Your answers are personal and don't have to be shared with anyone.

What healthy habits do you want to maintain or improve?

_____

_____

_____

_____

What unhealthy habits do you want to decrease?

_____

_____

_____

_____

How do you feel your health affects your work?

_____

_____

_____

_____

List three concrete, specific steps you will take to maintain healthy habits or change unhealthy ones.

1. _____

   _____

   _____

   _____

2. _____

   _____

   _____

   _____

3. _____

   _____

   _____

   _____

Give yourself the positive support and appreciation you would give your best friend, and you are very likely to succeed!

As a reference, we have included a summary of the *Dietary Guidelines for Americans* from the U.S. Department of Agriculture and the U.S. Department of Health and Human Services and a copy of the "food pyramid." You will find these resources on the following pages.

When you have finished this overview section, you should complete the pre-training assessment. Refer to the glossary at the end of this module if you need definitions of the terms used.

Dietary Guidelines for Americans[1]

Eat a variety of foods daily in adequate amounts, including selections of the following:

>   fruits;
>   vegetables;
>   whole-grain and enriched breads, cereals, and other foods
>   made from grains;
>   milk, cheese, yogurt, and other products made from milk; and
>   meats, poultry, fish, eggs, and dried beans and peas.

Eat a variety of foods.

Eat calcium-rich foods, such as milk and milk products, for strong bones.

Eat iron-rich foods, such as beans, cereals, and grain products.

Eat a variety of foods that are low in calories and high in nutrients:

Maintain healthy weight.

>   more fruits, vegetables, and whole grains;
>   less fat and fatty foods;
>   less sugar and fewer sweets; and
>   for adults, fewer alcoholic beverages.

Increase your physical activity.

Eat slowly.

Drink lots of water.

Take smaller portions.

Avoid second helpings.

Choose lean meat, fish, poultry, and dried beans and peas as protein sources.

Choose a diet low in fat, saturated fat, and cholesterol.

Use skim or low-fat milk and milk products.

Moderate your intake of egg yolks and organ meats.

Limit your intake of fats and oils, especially those high in saturated fat, such as butter, cream, lard, heavily hydrogenated fats (some margarines), shortenings, and foods containing palm and coconut oils.

Trim fat off meats.

[1] Based on the U.S. Department of Agriculture and U.S. Department of Health and Human Services, *Dietary Guidelines for Americans*, 3rd edition (Washington, DC: U.S. Government Printing Office, 1990).

Broil, bake, or boil rather than fry.

Moderate your intake of foods that contain fat, such as breaded and deep-fried foods.

Read labels carefully to determine both the amount and type of fat present in foods.

Choose a diet with plenty of vegetables, fruits, and grain products.

Choose foods high in fiber and starch, such as whole-grain breads and cereals, fruits, vegetables, dry beans and peas.

Eat at least three servings of vegetables and two fruits daily.

Have six or more servings of grain products (breads, cereals, pasta, and rice) daily.

Substitute starchy foods for those with large amounts of fats and sugars.

Use sugar in moderation.

Use less of all sugars and foods containing large amounts of sugars, including white sugar, brown sugar, raw sugar, honey, and syrups (soft drinks, candies, cakes, and cookies).

Avoid eating sweets between meals. How often you eat sugar and sugar-containing food is even more important to the health of your teeth than how much sugar you eat.

Read food labels for clues on sugar content. If the word sugar, sucrose, glucose, maltose, dextrose, lactose, fructose, or syrup appears first, then the food contains a large amount of sugar.

Eat fresh fruits or fruits processed without syrup or with light rather than heavy syrup.

Brush with a fluoride toothpaste and floss regularly.

Use salt in moderation.

Limit your intake of salty foods such as potato chips, pretzels, salted nuts, popcorn, condiments (soy sauce, steak sauce, garlic salt), pickled foods, cured meats, some cheeses, and some canned vegetables and soups.

Learn to enjoy the flavors of unsalted foods.

Cook without salt or with only small amounts of added salt.

Try flavoring foods with herbs, spices, and lemon juice.

Add little or no salt to food at the table.

Read food labels carefully to determine the amounts of sodium they contain. Use lower-sodium products when available.

The Food Guide Pyramid

A Guide to Daily Food Choices

KEY
- • Fat (naturally occurring and added)
- ▾ Sugars (added)

These symbols show that fat and added sugars come mostly from the fats, oils, and sweets group. However, foods in other groups, like ice cream from the milk group or french fries from the vegetable group, can also be a source of fat and added sugars.

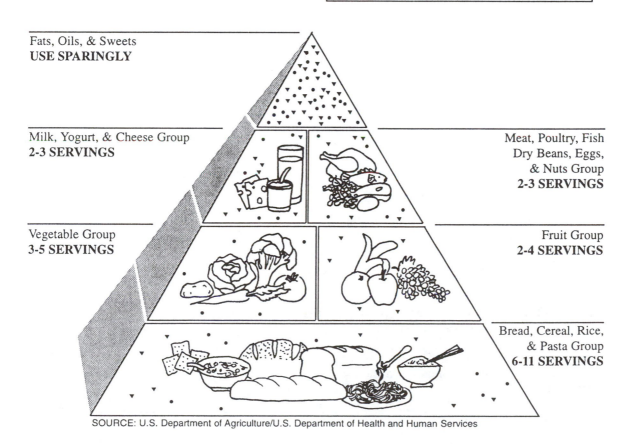

Fats, Oils, & Sweets
USE SPARINGLY

Milk, Yogurt, & Cheese Group
2-3 SERVINGS

Meat, Poultry, Fish
Dry Beans, Eggs,
& Nuts Group
2-3 SERVINGS

Vegetable Group
3-5 SERVINGS

Fruit Group
2-4 SERVINGS

Bread, Cereal, Rice,
& Pasta Group
6-11 SERVINGS

SOURCE: U.S. Department of Agriculture/U.S. Department of Health and Human Services

PRE-TRAINING ASSESSMENT

Listed below are the skills school-age staff use to help children stay healthy. Think about whether you do these things regularly, sometimes, or not enough. Place a check in one of the boxes on the right for each skill listed. Then discuss your answers with your trainer.

Maintaining Indoor and Outdoor Environments That Promote Wellness and Reduce the Spread of Disease

	I Do This		
	Regularly	Sometimes	Not Enough
1. Checking the facility daily for adequate ventilation and lighting, comfortable room temperature, and good sanitation.	☐	☐	☐
2. Opening windows daily to let in fresh air.	☐	☐	☐
3. Placing tissues, paper towels, and soap within children's reach; asking children to help keep them stocked.	☐	☐	☐
4. Washing hands and encouraging children to wash theirs at proper times.	☐	☐	☐
5. Maintaining a positive, relaxed, and pleasant program atmosphere to reduce tension and stress.	☐	☐	☐
6. Completing daily health checks and being alert to symptoms of illness.	☐	☐	☐
7. Recognizing symptoms of common childhood illnesses and other health problems.	☐	☐	☐
8. Clean and disinfect surfaces before using for food preparation.	☐	☐	☐

Encouraging Children to Develop Health Habits That Promote Good Hygiene and Nutrition

9. Planning a flexible schedule that includes time for outdoor activities and responds to children's physical needs.	☐	☐	☐
10. Serving family-style meals and eating with children in a relaxing manner.	☐	☐	☐
11. Offering self-service snack so children can determine when, what, and how much to eat.	☐	☐	☐

Encouraging Children to Develop Health Habits That Promote Good Hygiene and Nutrition
(continued)

	I Do This		
	Regularly	Sometimes	Not Enough
12. Providing opportunities for children to plan, prepare, and serve meals and snacks.	☐	☐	☐
13. Providing resources on health and hygiene, such as magazines, books, pamphlets, and visiting health professionals.	☐	☐	☐
14. Keeping a supply of sanitary pads and tampons in the girls' bathroom and making sure girls know where they are.	☐	☐	☐
15. Encouraging children to drink water and take breaks when exercising or outdoors on hot days.	☐	☐	☐
16. Modeling habits that promote good health and nutrition.	☐	☐	☐
17. Helping children learn to recognize, reduce, and cope with stress.	☐	☐	☐

Recognizing and Reporting Child Abuse and Neglect

	Regularly	Sometimes	Not Enough
18. Learning the definitions of different kinds of child abuse and neglect.	☐	☐	☐
19. Recognizing the physical and behavioral signs of possible physical, sexual, and emotional child abuse and neglect.	☐	☐	☐
20. Protecting children by reporting suspected abuse or neglect without waiting for proof.	☐	☐	☐
21. Knowing and following state laws and program regulations for reporting suspected abuse and neglect.	☐	☐	☐
22. Maintaining confidentiality after filing a report of suspected child maltreatment.	☐	☐	☐
23. Supporting families and helping them get the services they need.	☐	☐	☐

Review your responses, then list three to five skills you would like to improve or topics you would like to learn more about. When you finish this module, you can list examples of your new or improved knowledge and skills.

_____

_____

_____

_____

_____

Begin the learning activities for Module 2, Healthy.

LEARNING ACTIVITIES

Learning Activity I.
Maintaining a Hygienic Environment

IN THIS ACTIVITY YOU WILL LEARN TO:

- provide and maintain a hygienic environment, involving children when possible; and

- recognize symptoms of illness in school-age children.

What can you do to maintain a hygienic environment? First, you can check the environment daily to see it is clean and uncluttered. Even when custodial staff clean your facility, you should do a daily check. If you operate in shared space, you need to coordinate your efforts with others who use the space to ensure it is ready for each group each day. Report any problems to your supervisor. It is your job to be sure the space used by the program promotes wellness and minimizes or reduces the incidence of illness and disease.

It's important to maintain a hygienic environment.

It's important to keep your environment in good condition during the time the program is operating. You can do this by cleaning spills as they happen, disinfecting tables before and after eating, or after the program's pet gerbil has been for a walk; storing food properly; and throwing away garbage promptly. The children can assist with these chores. Keep tissues, soap, and paper towels within their reach.

In addition, you need to ensure your space is sanitary. Germs can be left by sick children on tables, materials, and equipment or can grow on perishable foods. Most childhood illnesses are contagious; therefore, it is very likely that when one child in the program gets sick, the germs can be passed on to the others. Germs can be spread from a child's saliva, mucus, and stool (when a child sneezes or coughs, when children share food or forget to wash their hands after going to the bathroom). You can't always tell who is contagious by whether they look sick. Sometimes children can be contagious even when they appear healthy. Most illnesses are contagious in the several days before symptoms appear (such as flu or chicken pox) and some diseases can be carried for a long time without any symptoms (such as giardia, hepatitis B, or HIV). That's why it's essential to follow Universal Precautions—handwashing, cleaning and disinfecting, and using gloves for contact with blood—to prevent the spread of diseases among all children and adults.

Germs can be passed from child to child.

Lice Happen!

Even when the school-age program practices good hygiene, you may experience an outbreak of head lice—tiny brown bugs about the size of a sesame seed that make themselves at home on people's hair. Adult lice lay eggs (nits) on human hair strands, about 3/4" from the scalp. Seven to ten days later the eggs hatch, and lice emerge and begin to bite the scalp. These bites make a person's head itch. If you see a child scratching his or her head repeatedly (or your head itches), lice may be the cause. You may see the tiny white nits attached to strands of hair, or the adult lice moving around. Nits, unlike dandruff, do not move when the hair is moved. Do not panic! Lice are quite common, do not carry diseases, and are not caused by unsanitary conditions. They are, however, extremely hardy and are easily transferred from one child to another—either from head to head or from pillows, rugs, seat backs, combs, bedding, hats, and so on. You need to respond immediately to rid the lice from children and the program environment. When lice and nits are off the body (on clothes or stuffed animals), they die within seven days.

Enlist the help of parents.

It's a good idea to have a letter about lice ready to be reproduced and distributed to parents. A similar letter can be sent to the elementary schools that the children attend so teachers and janitorial staff there can be alert to the problem. A joint home, school, and program campaign is needed to get rid of lice.

While it is important not to be judgmental or panicked by head lice, lice are an uncomfortable, annoying, and time-consuming problem for children, teachers, and parents. The tone of your letter should be informative and business-like.

- Explain the life cycle so parents know that they need to be thorough and vigorous in ridding their child and home of lice.

- Provide instructions on identifying lice and how to respond. Parents should call their pediatrician and ask about appropriate shampoos that will kill the lice and nits. The shampoo directions should be followed carefully. After shampooing, parents **must** remove the lice and nits from the child's hair, either with a fine-tooth comb or picking out by hand.

- Remind parents to check the whole family, children and adults, and use the same shampoo for all who are infested.

- Explain the importance of cleaning all items lice might have traveled to such as bedding, hats, clothes, scarves, stuffed animals, combs, brushes, pillows, carpets, and furniture. This involves sending things to the dry cleaner, washing them in water at least 140°F, drying them in a hot clothes dryer, or placing items in a plastic bag for 10-14 days. They can use the anti-lice shampoo to soak combs and brushes. Carpets, upholstery, and mattresses should be thoroughly vacuumed.

- Remind parents to continue checking their children for several weeks. Children who are free of lice today could still get them after the eggs hatch. That is why it is important to remove all nits with a comb.

- Ask parents to let you know if their child does have lice, so you can keep track of how widely it has spread.

An equally thorough response is needed at the program. Begin by checking all staff. You may also need to use a special shampoo. Let the children know that lice have been found and that you are beginning an all-out strategy to rid the program of these creatures. Explain that they are not caused by anyone's actions, and not the result of someone being dirty or careless. You can use the outbreak as a "teachable moment." Provide lots of information about lice and what we can do to remove them and prevent their spread. For example, this would be a good time to remind children not to share combs, brushes, or hats.

A comprehensive campaign is needed to get rid of lice.

Using one of the methods described above, you need to clean all items at the program to which lice may have attached. In addition to items such as those listed already, you must clean costumes, dress-up clothes (especially hats), carpet squares, wigs, beanbag chairs, the contents of the extra hats and gloves box, and so on. Lice are also commonly spread from children's backpacks and jackets touching on their hooks or cubbies. Try to separate them. For more information on handling head lice, see www.headlice.org (The National Pediculosis Association, Inc).

The program's materials and equipment should be cleaned and disinfected periodically. Begin by thoroughly washing surfaces with soap and water. Next, rinse with water to remove the soap solution. Then apply the appropriate bleach solution as described in the chart that follows, made fresh daily. The second solution is provided in case some of the younger children occasionally put things in their mouths.

Cleaning and Disinfecting Materials and Equipment

Finally, allow the surfaces or objects to air dry. Wash and disinfect surfaces children are likely to touch (floors, doorknobs, sinks, faucets, soap dispensers, toilet seats and handles, shelves) at least weekly.

Use This Bleach Solution	To Clean These Items

1/4 cup of bleach to 1 gallon of water
or
1 tablespoon of bleach to 1 quart of water
	All surfaces including:
	    tabletops and counters
	    bathroom
	    walls
	    door frames
	    mops, brooms, and dustpans used to wipe up body fluid spills
	    doorknobs
	    telephones
	    water fountains

1 tablespoon of bleach to 1 gallon of water or 1 teaspoon of bleach to 1 quart of water	All objects children have put in their mouths.

Bedding and bathrooms must be washed and disinfected and pets and their cages kept clean.

Children who attend a half-day kindergarten may nap or rest at the program. Each child should have a sheet and blanket for napping. These must be laundered at least once a week. Wash and disinfect mats and cots at least weekly if children use the same mat each day. If a different child uses the mat each day, it must be disinfected daily.

The bathroom is a major source of germs. You should check this room daily to make sure it is clean and stocked with enough soap and paper supplies. Report problems and missing items to the custodial staff or to your supervisor.

If your program has pets, cages must be cleaned frequently. Program pets need to be up-to-date on their shots and should be checked by a veterinarian monthly to ensure they are healthy and free from diseases. The animals need food and clean water daily to stay in good health. Children learn important health concepts by caring for pets.

Handwashing Procedures[2]

Health professionals state the most effective way to reduce illness is for staff and children to wash their hands properly throughout the day. Good handwashing techniques can reduce the spread of

---

[2] Adapted by Karen Sokal-Gutierrez, M.D., from *Caring for Our Children, National Health and Safety Standards: Guidelines for Out-of-Home Child Care Programs,* 2nd edition (Washington, DC: American Public Health Association and Elk Grove Village, IL: American Academy of Pediatrics, in press, 2000).

disease in child care by up to 50 percent and protect adults and children from serious illnesses. Wash your own hands:

- upon arrival for the day or when moving from one child care group to another;
- before and after eating, handling food, or feeding a child;
- before and after giving medication;
- before and after playing in water that is used by more than one person.
- after using the toilet or helping a child use the toilet;
- after handling body fluid (mucus, blood, vomit) from sneezing, from wiping and blowing noses, from mouths, or from sores;
- after handling uncooked food, especially raw meat, eggs, and poultry;
- after handling pets and other animals;
- after playing in sandboxes; and
- after cleaning or handling the garbage.

Make sure children wash their hands:

- when they arrive at the program;
- before and after food preparation activities;
- before and after eating;
- before and after playing in water that is used by more than one person;
- after using the toilet;
- after wiping their noses;
- after a nose bleed;
- after vomiting;
- after handling pets;
- after playing in sandboxes; and
- after outdoor play.

Use the following procedures for handwashing and teach them to the children so they can follow them each time they wash their hands. School-age children are not too old to need reminders to wash their hands. You can post signs in the bathrooms and next to sinks to remind children when and how to wash their hands:

- Check to be sure a clean paper towel is available.
- Use liquid soap and running water.
- Rub your hands vigorously as you wash them for at least 10 seconds.
- Wash all surfaces: backs of hands, wrists, between fingers, under fingernails.
- Rinse your hands well. Leave the water running.
- Dry your hands with a paper towel. Don't use the towel again.
- Turn off the water using a paper towel instead of bare hands.

Encourage children to wash their hands properly.

Symptoms of Common Childhood Illnesses

Even in an apparently spotless and sanitary environment, there will be germs. Children may come to the program with a variety of illnesses and may be contagious before they develop symptoms. You must be aware of the symptoms and incubation periods for common childhood illnesses. The chart on the next page summarizes this information.

If a child in your group has symptoms of an illness noted in the chart, he or she should not attend the program while ill. Parents need to inform you if their child has recently been exposed to one of these illnesses. Then you can ensure that all children and staff take necessary precautions to keep the illness from spreading.

Daily health checks help identify illness.

A daily health check upon arrival at the program will help you identify children who may be ill. As you take attendance and greet children, be alert for the following symptoms:

- difficulty breathing;
- yellowish skin or eyes;
- rashes;
- feverish appearance;
- severe coughing;
- pinkeye (tears, redness of eyelid lining, irritation, swelling, discharge of pus);
- infected skin patches or crusty, bright-yellow, dry, or gummy skin areas; and
- unusual behavior (child is cranky, less active than usual, or more irritable than usual; child feels general discomfort or just seems unwell).

During the program's operation, be alert for other signs that signify illness:

- frequent trips to the bathroom;
- complaints about difficulties going to the bathroom;
- sore throat or trouble swallowing;
- headache or stiff neck;
- nausea and vomiting;
- loss of appetite; and
- frequent scratching of the scalp or body.

Sometimes children need to be excluded from the program.

Most children with mild illnesses can safely attend your program. Because you know the children in your program, you are in a good position to evaluate if:

- the child can participate comfortably in activities; or

- the staff cannot adequately care for the sick child without affecting the care of other children.

For example, some children with mild colds can join in activities; others may not have the energy to do so. Other illnesses and their symptoms are listed below along with guidelines about exclusion. Check with a health provider as necessary.

Contagious Diseases[3]

Diseases spread through the intestinal tract	Symptoms	When child can return to the program
Diarrheal diseases	Increased liquid and number of stools in an 8-hour period.	The child no longer has diarrhea. If due to infection, 24 hours after treatment has begun.
Vomiting	Abdominal pain, digested/ undigested stomach contents, refusal to eat, headache, fever.	When vomiting has stopped.
Hepatitis A	Fever, loss of appetite, nausea, yellowish skin and whites of the eyes, dark brown urine, light-colored stool.	One week after illness begins, if fever is gone.
Diseases spread through the respiratory system	**Symptoms**	**When child can return to the program**
Bacterial meningitis	Younger children: fever, vomiting, unusual irritability, excessive crying with inability to be comforted, high-pitched crying, poor feeding, and activity levels below normal. Older children: fever, headache, neck pain or stiffness, vomiting (often without abdominal complaints), and a decrease in activity associated with not feeling well.	After fever gone and a closely supervised program of antibiotics. Health Department may recommend preventive medicine for exposed children and staff.
Strep throat	Red and painful throat, often accompanied by fever.	Generally when fever has subsided and child has been on antibiotics for at least 24 hours.

[3] Based on American Academy of Pediatrics, PA Chapter, *Model Child Health Policies,* Revised (Washington, DC: National Association for the Education of Young Children, 1997).
Adapted by Karen Sokal-Gutierrez, M.D., from *Caring for Our Children, National Health and Safety Standards: Guidelines for Out-of-Home Child Care Programs,* 2nd edition (Washington, DC: American Public Health Association and Elk Grove Village, IL: American Academy of Pediatrics, in press, 2000).

Contagious Diseases

(continued)

Diseases spread by direct contact (touching)	Symptoms	When child can return to the program
Chicken pox	Fever, runny nose, cough, rash (pink/red blisters).	Six days after onset of rash or when all sores have dried and crusted.
Head lice	Whitish-gray nits attached to hair shafts.	After treatment and removal of nits, and child's clothes and bedding are washed in hot water (140° F).
Herpes (mouth or cold sore)	Sores on lips or inside mouth.	No need for exclusion if lesions are covered.
Impetigo	Red oozing erosion capped with a golden yellow crust that appears stuck on.	After treatment has begun.
Measles	Fever, runny nose, cough, and red-brown blotchy rash on the face and body.	Six days after the rash appears.
Mumps	Swelling of the glands at the jaw angle accompanied by cold-like symptoms.	Nine days after swelling begins.
Pertussis (Whooping Cough)	Cold-like symptoms that develop into severe respiratory disease with repeated attacks of violent coughing.	Three weeks after intense coughing begins or five days after antibiotic treatment has begun.
Purulent Conjunctivitis (Pinkeye)	Eyes are pink/red, watery, itchy, lid swollen, sometimes painful, and pus is present.	Twenty-four hours after treatment is begun. (Not all pinkeye is contagious.)
Ring worm	Skin—reddish scaling, circular patches with raised edges and central clearing or light and dark patches on face and upper trunk or cracking peeling of skin between toes. Scalp—redness, scaling of scalp with broken hairs or patches of hair loss.	No need to exclude child. Advise parents about need for treatment.
Scabies	Crusty wavy ridges and tunnels in the webs of fingers, hand, wrist, and trunk.	After treatment has begun.
Shingles	Blisters in a band or patch.	No need for exclusion if lesions are covered.

Older school-age children may be self-conscious about bodily functions. For example, a child may find it embarrassing to tell someone he has diarrhea or that he feels constipated. Staff need to be especially aware of subtle mood or behavioral changes that may indicate a child is not feeling well.

If a child exhibits any of the above symptoms, separate him or her from the other children and contact the child's parents. Be sure to inform your supervisor. It is a good idea to designate an area where sick children can rest and be cared for until taken home.

What School-Age Staff Need to Know About HIV

HIV (Human Immunodeficiency Virus) is the virus that causes AIDS (Acquired Immune Deficiency Syndrome). HIV attacks the immune system that normally protects the body from viruses and bacteria. This makes it difficult for the body to fight off infection.

HIV is not transmitted through casual contact or from being around someone who is infected. It cannot be transmitted by mosquitoes or pets. The virus does not live by itself in the air. You cannot get it by:

- being in the same room with someone;
- sharing drinks or food;
- being near when someone coughs or sneezes;
- hugging, shaking hands, or kissing as friends do; or
- sharing a swimming pool, bath, or toilet.

HIV is transmitted in several ways.

HIV is transmitted through blood, semen, and vaginal secretions. A person can become infected:

From mother to child (perinatal). Most children under age 13 with HIV are infected this way. If the mother has HIV, her blood can transmit the virus to the baby during pregnancy or delivery. Because HIV has been found in breast milk, mothers with HIV infection are discouraged from breastfeeding.

Through sexual intercourse with a man or woman who has HIV. Sexually abused children are at risk for HIV infection.

By sharing intravenous needles that contain infected blood from a previous user.

From blood and blood product transfusions prior to 1985, before blood was tested for HIV infection. Many children were infected this way, including those with hemophilia.

Children with HIV infection can remain healthy for long periods of time. They have AIDS when the virus has severely damaged the immune system. Because children with HIV infection are more susceptible to germs, good hygiene is very important.

Because staff might not know whether or not a child has HIV and because HIV is carried in the blood, universal blood precautions should always be taken. You should **always** create a "barrier" between yourself and any person's blood when cleaning a cut or applying pressure to a bloody nose. This means wearing disposable and heavy duty gloves. In addition, if you have been exposed* to blood or other body fluids, federal regulations require the following measures:

- washing the exposed body part;

- cleaning and disinfecting spills;

- reporting to the supervisor;

- documenting the exposure;

- medical exam within 24 hours; and

- follow-up and treatment as necessary.

Children with HIV infection may have special nutrition and therapy needs. Encourage parents to share pertinent medical information in order to best care for the child. If a child has HIV or any other medical condition, programs should have a special care plan outlining measures to prevent and recognize illness, medications, and emergency procedures. If you are caring for a child with HIV infection, find out if specific training is available.

Applying Your Knowledge

In this learning activity you invite two children to help you assess the program's hygiene routines. Together, you use a health and hygiene checklist to identify items that need your attention. Next, you discuss routines that need to be improved and plan ways to improve them. Although it may be difficult for the children to assess some of the items (for example, number 17), this is a good opportunity to model the importance of good hygiene.

---

* A hazardous "exposure" to blood is defined as direct contact with blood or blood-containing body fluids onto the employee's eyes, mouth, or non-intact skin (OSHA 12/91).

Health and Hygiene Checklist

Date: _____

Health and Hygiene Checkers: _____

Routines to Maintain a Healthy Environment	Satisfactory	Needs Improvement
1. Let in fresh air daily by opening windows or doors.	☐	☐
2. Check the space daily to make sure it is clean.	☐	☐
3. Store toothbrushes so they don't touch each other and can air dry. (Children should brush their teeth after eating when the program operates for a full day.)	☐	☐
4. Ask children to wipe off tables after eating and messy activities.	☐	☐
5. Date, label, and store food so it does not spoil.	☐	☐
6. Put garbage in metal or plastic pails lined with plastic bags, with lids, and empty them daily.	☐	☐
7. Keep tissues, paper towels, and soap where children can reach them.	☐	☐
8. Check the bathroom daily to make sure it is clean and well stocked with toilet paper, soap, and paper towels.	☐	☐
9. Follow a flexible daily schedule to meet children's needs for activity and rest.	☐	☐
10. Call parents to ask them to pick up a sick child, and separate the child from others.	☐	☐
11. Ensure kindergarten children's sheets and blankets are laundered weekly.	☐	☐
12. Prepare fresh bleach solution daily.	☐	☐
13. Wash and disinfect play materials weekly.	☐	☐
14. Rinse brooms, dustpans, mops, and rags in a bleach solution after cleaning body fluid spills.	☐	☐

	Satisfactory	Needs Improvement
Routines to Maintain a Healthy Environment		

15. Wash your own hands:

- upon arrival for the day or when moving from one child care group to another ☐ ☐
- before and after eating, handling food, or feeding a child ☐ ☐
- before and after giving medication ☐ ☐
- before and after playing in water used by others ☐ ☐
- after using the toilet or helping a child use a toilet ☐ ☐
- after handling body fluids ☐ ☐
- after handling uncooked or raw meat, eggs, and poultry ☐ ☐
- after handling pets and other animals ☐ ☐
- after playing in sandboxes ☐ ☐
- after cleaning or handling the garbage ☐ ☐

16. Remind children to wash their hands:

- when they arrive at the program ☐ ☐
- before and after food preparation activities ☐ ☐
- before and after eating ☐ ☐
- before and after playing in water used by others ☐ ☐
- after using the toilet ☐ ☐
- after wiping their noses ☐ ☐
- after a nose bleed ☐ ☐
- after vomiting ☐ ☐
- after handling pets ☐ ☐
- after playing in sandboxes ☐ ☐
- after outdoor play ☐ ☐

17. Conduct a daily health check with children to be alert for:

- severe coughing, difficulty breathing, or sore throat ☐ ☐
- yellowish skin or eyes ☐ ☐
- pinkeye (tears, redness, irritation, swelling, or discharge) ☐ ☐
- infected skin patches, frequent scratching ☐ ☐
- nausea, vomiting, or diarrhea ☐ ☐
- loss of appetite ☐ ☐
- unusual behavior ☐ ☐

Review the items on the checklist you and the children have found in need of improvement, and list them on the blank chart that follows. Then identify the improvement strategies you plan to use.

Items Needing Improvement	Improvement Strategies

Discuss these improvement strategies with the children who helped you complete the checklist, your colleagues, and your trainer. Make the needed changes in your routines, and ask the children to check them off when they have been completed.

Learning Activity II.
Encouraging Healthy Habits

IN THIS ACTIVITY YOU WILL LEARN TO:

- teach children that healthy bodies need a variety of foods every day; and

- help children select and enjoy nutritious foods for snacks and meals.

School-age children tend to be concerned about body image.

Many school-age children tie their social success to looking and behaving just like their friends. As they develop and mature, body image becomes increasingly important, and the desire to have a certain kind of body may lead to unhealthy practices. Additional pressure to look or act a certain way comes from advertisements on television and in magazines. These pressures may cause school-age children to follow unhealthy diets or experiment with sex, drugs, or alcohol. In his book *Fit Kids,* Dr. Kenneth Cooper cites the following examples of what can happen when children have poor body images: "a 1989 study in *Pediatrics* revealed 45 percent of boys and girls in grades three through six wanted to be thinner, 37 percent had already tried to lose weight, and nearly seven percent were in the anorexia nervosa category." Anorexia nervosa, an eating disorder, can lead to starvation and death.

In addition to children who are overly concerned with body image, some of the children in your program may be overweight. Medical professionals define obesity as a child being 20 percent above the ideal weight for his or her age, sex, and height. This means much of their total body weight consists of fat. Obesity has been associated with high blood pressure, high cholesterol levels, heart disease, and numerous other medical problems. School-age staff should work with parents to help obese children learn healthy eating habits and to encourage their involvement in physical activities.

Growth spurts may lead to new concerns.

During growth spurts, children may be concerned about being taller, more awkward, or less attractive than their peers. They may worry about things like new body odors or pimples. Older girls may worry about getting their first menstrual period in school or at the school-age program. (It is a good idea to keep a supply of pads and tampons in the girls' bathroom. Be sure girls know where they are located, as some girls may be too embarrassed to ask for them.)

Children who are maturing at a slower pace than their peers also may worry about their body image. They may believe they are too short or look much younger compared to their friends. Both boys and girls are concerned about their bodies. Girls may worry they will never develop breasts or a slimmer figure. Boys may be concerned because their muscles seem less developed than those of their friends.

As discussed earlier, most school-age children have the cognitive skills needed to develop healthy habits. Education about AIDS and birth control, or to discourage children from experimenting with sex, drugs, and alcohol, may be provided at school. Before addressing these topics, school-age programs should consult with parents and the schools to find out what is already being done. Whether or not the program provides this education, it is important to remember these topics are of concern to children.

Teaching children good nutrition habits is a wise investment in their future. The food children eat affects their well-being, physical growth, ability to learn, and overall behavior. Attitudes about food develop early in life and are difficult to change.

School-age children need to learn about nutrition.

Yet it isn't always easy to help school-age children develop good nutrition habits. They are often in a hurry and find it easier to eat unhealthy foods on the run. Children who feel fat—whether or not they are—may attempt to diet without knowing healthy ways to monitor their fat intake. It is not uncommon for children who are overly concerned about their weight to starve themselves all day, only to fix themselves a double-fudge chocolate sundae before dinner. As a result of consuming these "empty calories," they put on additional unwanted weight and deprive themselves of nutrients that would support their healthy growth and development.

Even children who know the importance of eating well may have trouble doing so. It's one thing to know about good nutrition; it's quite another to be motivated enough to eat healthy foods every day. This is especially true if friends do not think good eating habits are important or when a hectic schedule leaves little time for eating right. Although school-age programs provide only a portion of the children's food intake, they can help children learn about the kinds of nutrients needed for healthy growth and development.

Much of the health and nutrition education that takes place in school-age programs is indirect. It occurs when you model healthy habits, serve a variety of healthy foods for snack, eat meals family-style, and offer cooking as a club, interest area, or special activity. These routines can be supplemented by activities such as talking with a visiting nutritionist, planting a vegetable garden, or conducting experiments to learn how the properties of foods change when dried, boiled, broiled, baked, or fried.

The USDA Child and Adult Care Food Program

The United States Department of Agriculture (USDA) Child and Adult Care Food Program (CACFP) provides funds which partially reimburse food costs to licensed public and nonprofit child care centers for nutritious meals and snacks served to children through age 12. For-profit child care centers can participate if they serve a certain percentage of income-eligible families. Meals and snacks served in programs enrolled in the CACFP must meet USDA guidelines for meal components and quantities. For example, breakfast for children 6 to 12 years must include 1 cup of milk, 1/2 cup of full-strength juice or a fruit or vegetable, 1 slice of bread, and 1/2 cup of hot or cold cereal. To ensure that children receive nutritious snacks and meals, some foods may not be claimed for reimbursement. This requirement encourages programs to serve low fat muffins rather than cakes, fresh vegetables rather than potato chips, and milk or juice rather than flavored drinks. The CACFP also provides training on topics such as nutrition, menu planing, family-style meals, sanitation, and using a variety of recipes. Ask the director if your program is enrolled in the CACFP. If not, suggest contacting your regional office of USDA to find out more about the benefits of enrolling in the CACFP.

Dental Health

An important topic related to nutrition is dental health. Almost everyone (98 percent of the population) gets cavities. Most children know sweet, sticky foods can cause cavities. They may not realize that to prevent tooth decay, the number of times sugar is consumed is more important than the amount.

Avoid serving sugary foods that stick to teeth.

Nutritious foods are good for both bodies and teeth. In general, it is best to serve foods without added sugars. Sweet and sticky foods should not be served as between-meal snacks. Examples of such foods include candy, cake, cookies, cupcakes, pie, jelly, jam, soft drinks, fruit punch, or fruit drinks. Encourage children to brush their teeth after eating.

Some children arrive at the program after school ravenously hungry. Perhaps they didn't eat enough lunch or ate hours ago. Or perhaps they are at a stage where they need to eat often to replenish their energy. Other children are not hungry when they arrive. They may need some time to unwind and relax, to make the transition from school to after school. To meet these varied needs, you may want to set up a self-service snack area that allows children to serve themselves over a period of time rather than all eating at a designated time.

A self-service snack area is recommended for a number of reasons.[4] Because children may have varied eating schedules outside the program, they may want to eat snack at different times. Children need different amounts of food during different developmental stages. Children of the same age often vary widely in the amount of food they require during the day. A self-service snack area allows children to prepare and serve their own snack and encourages them to eat as much or as little as they need.

The following tips can help you provide a self-service snack area:

- Discuss with children how long the area should be open, and procedures for serving, eating, and cleaning up.

- Assign a staff member to the area to assist children who request help, to visit with children and talk about the food being served, and to remind children to use safe, sanitary procedures as they serve, eat, and clean up.

- Have children make attractive signs to post in the area that include reminders of healthy eating habits and other guidelines about using the area.

- Have children plan, prepare, serve, and clean up.

Children often eat breakfast at the school-age program, and during full-day sessions they also eat lunch. One way to make meal times relaxed and pleasant is to serve and eat meals family-style. This means that a staff member sits with a group of children at each table. Everyone eats the same foods, serves themselves, and enjoys pleasant conversation. After experiencing family-style dining, children are more likely to try new foods because they serve themselves. They can decide for themselves whether to put

Implementing Self-Service Snack

Try these suggestions.

Serving and Eating Family-Style Meals

---

[4] Recommended in *Developmentally Appropriate Practice in School-Age Child Care Programs,* developed by Project Home Safe of the American Home Economics Association.

117

one pea on their plate or a spoonful. The following tips can help your program begin or enhance family-style dining.[5]

Try these suggestions before the meal.

- Provide or encourage food service staff to serve nutritious foods, including—fresh fruit, yogurt, applesauce, fruit juice, or cornbread.

- Arrange the furniture so tables are far enough apart to walk between but close enough for quiet conversation.

- Plan to seat five or six children and one adult at each table.

- Ask children who are assisting to set the tables.

- Serve the food in serving bowls or on platters.

- Serve drinks in pitchers so children can pour their own.

- Leave the salt and sugar off the table.

- Invite everyone to sit down after the tables are set.

- Suggest that everyone take a deep breath, relax, and think about how the food will make them strong and healthy.

Try these suggestions during the meal.

- Begin serving as soon as everyone is seated.

- Maintain a leisurely pace so children don't feel hurried.

- Allow children to refuse food, but encourage them to taste a little of everything.

- Encourage children to serve themselves only as much as they can eat. Don't force them to clean their plates.

- Model good hygiene, safety practices, and manners.

- Ask children to clean up their own spills.

- Encourage conversation about the foods served, the day's events, or other topics of interest to the children.

- Respect cultural traditions and beliefs regarding mealtime rituals. For example, in some cultures, a respectful silence is appropriate before the meal begins and talking during meals is considered inappropriate.

Try these suggestions after the meal.

- Remain relaxed.

- Allow children to leave the table when finished. They can clean their dishes, wash their hands, brush their teeth, then choose an activity.

- Ask children to clean up and wash the table.

[5] Based on Elaine McLaughlin, Nancy Goldsmith, and Peter Pizzolongo, *Living and Teaching Nutrition* (College Park, MD: Head Start Resource and Training Center, 1983), p. 5-D.

Cooking is one of the best ways to teach children about nutrition. When children prepare the snacks and meals they eat at the program, you help them develop good eating habits. Although some of the children may not know what vitamins or saturated fats are, spreading a vegetable cottage cheese dip on whole wheat crackers, and mashing bananas for muffins gives a much healthier message than opening a package of cookies or a bag of corn chips.

It is not necessary to plan special menus or use simplified versions of recipes to include children in cooking. The snacks and meals children cook can be part of the regular menu for the program. Through food preparation activities children develop self-help skills, improve small-muscle coordination, increase cognitive skills, socialize with friends, and share in the responsibilities of daily living. They will feel proud to help with the real work of snapping the ends off beans, cracking eggs, and stirring raisins and cinnamon into yogurt to make a dip. In addition, cooking is an activity that can be enjoyed by children of different ages. Each child can participate according to his or her interest and skill level. At times you can plan a more complex cooking activity for the older children; this is a time when they can feel special.

Here are some examples of the many learning opportunities that might take place during a cooking activity—making bread:

- learning what ingredients help make the bread nutritious (whole wheat flour, sunflower seeds, and nonfat dry milk);

- gaining a foundation in math (doubling the recipe to make two loaves);

- understanding scientific principles (observing how yeast makes the bread rise);

- expressing creativity (making braided loaves or loaves shaped like animals);

- working cooperatively (taking turns sifting the flour);

- developing responsibility (remembering to punch down the dough when the timer goes off);

- showing consideration for others (making room at the table for another baker);

- learning self-help skills (washing the dishes while the bread is rising);

- strengthening hand muscles (kneading the dough);

Cooking With Children[6]

Cooking provides many opportunities for learning.

[6] Adapted with permission from Diane T. Dodge and Laura J. Colker, *The Creative Curriculum® for Family Child Care* (Washington, DC: Teaching Strategies, Inc., 1998), pp. 204-208.

119

- coordinating eye and hand movements (carefully measuring the ingredients);

- having fun (enjoying cooking and eating as a group); and

- showing pride (taking some bread home).

Children might enjoy making these simple foods.

Here are some simple foods school-age children might enjoy preparing for snack or meals:

Mashed potatoes. Children can peel potatoes, cut them into pieces, drop them into the cooking pot, and mash them after they cool. They may be surprised at how much tastier "real" potatoes are than frozen or dried versions.

Fresh vegetables and fruit—cooked or served raw with dips. Children can grate carrots, slice apples, shell peas, wash grapes, break the flowerettes off cauliflower or broccoli, and snap the ends off beans.

Blender fruit smoothies. Use milk, yogurt, and fresh fruits such as bananas, strawberries, peaches, or whatever is in season.

French toast. It's fun to crack eggs, add the milk, and beat the mixture until it's smooth. Children can sprinkle some cinnamon in the mix, then dip pieces of bread into the mixture. An electric fry pan will hold four to six pieces of bread.

Lemonade. Have children roll fresh lemons on the table top, then twist them on the juicer. Add some sugar and water to taste. Slice a lemon to put in the pitcher.

Pizzas. Spoon tomato sauce and sprinkle grated cheese and spices on crusts made from English muffins, French bread, pita bread, bagels, or freshly made dough.

Try these suggestions.

Here are some suggestions to help make cooking a success:

- Use a work table near an electrical outlet so children can plug in cooking appliances, such as a blender or mixer. If this is not possible, block off the area where the cords are hanging so children do not trip over them.

- Use an electric frying pan or wok as a substitute for a stove. Children find these appliances easy to manage, especially if they are used on a low work table.

- Provide duplicates of favorite utensils so the children won't be frustrated or lose interest while waiting for a turn. Have more than one vegetable peeler, vegetable scrubber, knife, spoon, grater, sifter, hand beater, potato masher, and so on. Parents might be willing to donate their duplicates of these items.

- Ask children to make signs and posters on cooking safety.

- Keep cleaning supplies such as mops, sponges, and paper towels within children's reach.

- Provide aprons or smocks made of old shirts for all children. Much of the pleasure in cooking comes from rigorously stirring batter and enthusiastically beating eggs.

For younger children you can simplify recipes, and have them help you transfer the recipes to picture cards. On 5" x 8" pieces of cardboard, describe and illustrate each step in the recipe. Number each card so the steps in the recipe are easy to follow. Cover the cards with clear Contact paper to protect them. Children can lay out the picture cards left to right on the table so they can follow the recipe one step at a time. This will make them feel more independent and confident about what they're doing.

Children can make recipe cards.

Provide a variety of cookbooks (libraries usually have a good selection). Ask the children and their parents for suggestions for cooking projects. By cooking their favorite foods, you show respect for children and their families. This also allows you to introduce the concept of family traditions into your program.

The Centers for Disease Control has estimated that every year one in ten Americans has a bout of foodborne illness (usually vomiting, diarrhea, and fever). These can even be life-threatening for children and child care staff with certain medical conditions. Pay careful attention to food safety. That means remembering to:

Remember to think about food safety.

- refrigerate all perishable foods (meat, poultry, fish, milk products, eggs, mayonnaise) and don't leave them out for more than an hour;
- always wash hands well before preparing foods;
- don't return your tasting spoon to the bowl;
- don't eat raw eggs (e.g., in cookie/cake batter); and
- wash hands, utensils, and cutting boards after touching raw meat, poultry, and eggs.

Applying Your Knowledge

In this learning activity you plan and conduct a cooking activity. Ask interested children to help select a recipe, develop picture cards, gather ingredients and equipment, and prepare the food. After conducting the activity, complete the blank form that follows. Begin by reading the example on the next page.

Cooking Activity
(Example)

Children/ages: *Karen, Maria, Gregory, Carlos, Deena, Troy (7 to 10 years)*

What you made: *Cheese burritos*   **Date:** *April 23*

Describe what happened and how you involved the children.

We started a Cooking Club this week. For our first project, the children asked to make burritos. Deena said her dad made great cheese burritos. When Mr. Jansen, Deena's father, came to pick her up, I talked with him and he agreed to help. He gave me a list of ingredients and his recipe. Several children made recipe cards.

Today the children set up the recipe cards on the table next to the electric fry pan. Then they laid out the ingredients—wheat flour, shortening, salt, reduced fat cheese, onions, peppers, oil for the pan, salsa—and utensils—cheese graters, spatulas, spoons, pot holders, and knives. Troy asked why we were using shortening if it was bad for you. I explained, "We need some shortening so the tortillas will stay together when we cook them. It's all right to eat a little fat as long as we don't overdo it." Mr. Jansen brought his tortilla press.

The children followed the recipe cards to make the tortilla dough. After Deena demonstrated the technique, Mr. Jansen helped each child shape a tortilla and cook it in the fry pan. Children took turns making tortillas and grating cheese. Gregory explained how to hold the grater so they wouldn't scrape their fingers. We talked about how the calcium in cheese helps build strong bodies, and whether to make the burritos with cheese alone, with salsa, or with onions and peppers. I encouraged the children to taste the salsa and guess the ingredients. Gregory, Troy, and Maria said they wanted to chop up green peppers and onions for theirs and not have salsa. Carlos said he wanted the works—cheese, salsa, green and red peppers, and onions. I demonstrated how to use the knives safely. Once the burritos were assembled, we heated them in the broiler oven and had a feast.

What did the children learn from this activity?

How tortillas are made—most had only had store-bought tortillas.

How to make and appreciate a food from another culture.

Cheese helps develop strong bodies.

How to use graters and knives safely.

What a new food—salsa—tastes like.

When you repeat this activity, what changes (if any) would you make?

I'd suggest putting out other ingredients so children could make different kinds of burritos. I'd have two sessions of the club to accommodate more children. Once they smelled the burritos, everyone wanted a turn.

Cooking Activity

Children/ages : _____

What you made: _____ **Date:** _____

Describe what happened and how you involved the children.

_____

_____

_____

_____

_____

_____

What did the children learn from this activity?

_____

_____

_____

_____

_____

_____

_____

When you repeat this activity, what changes (if any) would you make?

_____

_____

_____

_____

_____

_____

_____

Discuss your answers with your trainer. Talk with other staff members about ways you can provide nutrition education activities in your program.

Learning Activity III.
Helping Children Cope With Stress

IN THIS ACTIVITY YOU WILL LEARN TO:

- help children handle stress in healthy ways; and

- reduce sources of stress within the program.

Staff can help children learn healthy ways to cope with stress.

Simply put, stress is any change to which a person must adjust. Extreme and continuous stress in children can have serious health consequences, such as tense muscles, a pounding heart, quickened breathing, and slowed digestion. Stress may also cause children to have injuries or experience frequent physical symptoms and complaints, such as stomachaches, strep throat, and respiratory ailments. Severe stress may cause some children to withdraw, become deeply depressed, and even consider suicide. It is important for school-age staff to understand what causes stress and help children cope with stress in healthy ways.

We all experience a certain level of stress in our lives. We are stressed when we perceive a threat, regardless of whether the threat is real or imaginary. For example, Toni has just found out her family is moving to a new city. She worries about fitting in at her new school. Will she like the new school and make friends easily? Will she miss her old friends and feel left out at her new school? The threat Toni perceives (she will be left out and will miss her friends) may be real or imaginary. Because Toni doesn't know how the move will turn out, she may respond by panicking: "Nobody will like me, my teacher will be mean, I won't be able to do the work." Even if the move goes smoothly, Toni will still have to recover from the effects of feeling stressed.

Sometimes feelings of stress give children extra energy.

What is stressful for one person may not be for another; and, not all stress is negative. Many occasions children find joyous can be sources of stress. For example, Jake is very excited about his upcoming birthday party—for the first time he's invited several girls. Laura is going on vacation with her cousins—she can hardly think of anything else. Sometimes, feelings of stress can give children the extra energy they need to complete a difficult math problem, handle a dangerous situation, or respond in an emergency. In the case of Toni, stress may lead her to discuss the move with her parents, or it might cause her to try to be as friendly as possible at her new school. Either response would help Toni relieve her stress and handle the move more effectively.

Although change can be perceived as a threat, it can also be experienced as a challenge; it does not always have to be bad. When we perceive a situation as threatening, it is difficult to use problem-solving skills. However, when the situation is viewed as challenging, problem-solving skills can be used to cope with it.

School-age children experience many kinds of stress. Some are related to common childhood fears. Others are related to conditions in society or within their families. Sensitivity to stress is as individual as each child. Some children can view a scary movie with no ill effects; others have nightmares for weeks after. Some children adjust easily to their parent's divorce; others respond by withdrawing or misbehaving.

Children vary in their responses to stress.

Certain sources of stress faced by children have relatively short-term effects:

• having trouble finding something to wear to school;
• arguing with a friend;
• misplacing a homework assignment;
• getting ready for a party;
• feeling bored; or
• losing a game.

Other sources of stress can have more long-term effects:

• serious illness (the child's own or a family member's);
• divorce;
• being a victim of child abuse or neglect;
• witnessing spouse abuse;
• living in a neighborhood where violence is prevalent;
• getting used to a parent going to work;
• death of a parent or sibling; or
• being pressured by peers to smoke, drink alcohol, use drugs, or have sex.

It's almost impossible to eliminate all the sources of stress in children's lives. Instead, children need to learn how to cope in healthy ways so the stress does not become overwhelming. Most people (adults and children) handle stress using a variety of healthy and unhealthy strategies. The "healthy" strategies generally are more effective and really do relieve tension.

There are healthy and unhealthy ways to handle stress.

The following are examples of unhealthy and healthy ways children may handle stress.

- **Unhealthy** ways to handle stress include:

  overeating (particularly foods high in salt, fat, sugar, or caffeine);

  worrying;

  sleeping more or less than is needed;

  throwing, kicking, or breaking things;

  falling behind in school;

  drinking alcohol or using drugs;

  engaging in early sexual behavior;

  withdrawing from favorite friends and activities; and

  taking out frustration by mistreating friends, parents, siblings, teachers, or school-age staff.

- **Healthy** ways to handle stress include:

  exercising—taking a walk, going for a bike ride, dancing, doing aerobics, jumping on a trampoline;

  taking a shower or bath;

  meditation or yoga;

  listening to music;

  talking to someone about one's feelings;

  making a homework "to do" list and a schedule for completing work; and

  asking parents, teachers, staff, or other professionals for help.

The school-age program can reduce sources of stress.

The school-age program can play a significant role in reducing sources of stress and helping children handle stress in healthy ways. Some examples follow.

When offering a competitive activity, always offer an alternative. Some children find the stress of competition difficult to handle. They prefer to participate without worrying about winning or losing, or having their work judged.

Mr. Wolfe tells the children about an upcoming photography contest. He also talks about a photography display the school-age program will set up in the lobby of their building.

Anticipate situations children may find stressful and take steps to minimize the stress. Many children find it easier to handle changes and new situations when they know about them in advance.

Ms. Shere tells the children about next week's field trip to the state park. She places brochures describing the park in the quiet area. Tomorrow she will review the rules and procedures for field trips.

Listen to children when they express their feelings, and let them know you understand what they are saying. Very often children can overcome feelings of stress by talking about them. The talking releases their tension and allows them to move on.

> Ms. Marianno listens and responds to 9-year-old Zara. "You think Dana and Renée don't want to be your friends any more. Tell me more about what happened."

Conduct frequent observations of children in different settings to learn more about their behavior, interactions with others, favorite activities, sources of pain or frustration, and strategies for coping with frustration or stress. (Module 12, Program Management, discusses observation in depth.) Observation records are an excellent information source when a child's behavior seems unusual.

> Mr. Penn thinks Lionel is spending a lot of time by himself. He reviews the observation records for Lionel. The records confirm Lionel usually spends more time in group activities. He decides to spend some one-on-one time with Lionel. He thinks Lionel might feel like talking about what's bothering him.

Accept and respect each child as an individual. Avoid expecting all children to respond to a situation or behave in the same way. Remember, what is easy for one child may be a source of stress for another.

> Gina likes to jump into new games. She learns the rules while she is playing. Whit likes to watch for a while, then join in. He learns the rules by watching and listening to the other children.

Encourage children to recognize when they feel stress and to use their own techniques for stress management. Some children know themselves very well and are able to handle their stress without adult intervention.

> Charnelle knows she gets in more fights with her friends when she's feeling bad about her mom being away. When she begins to feel tense, she removes herself from the group and looks at magazines or listens to music.

Provide a variety of activities that help children release tension such as sand and water play, playdough and clay, open-ended art materials, books about children handling difficult situations, and active games and sports.

> Terrence wants to roller-skate, but all the skates are being used. Ms. Ross asks him if he would like to jog around the field with her until a pair of skates are free.

Arrange the environment so there are places where children can be alone when they need to take a break from the group—a single beanbag chair in a corner, a large open box set on its side and lined with pillows, a tape player and earphones, and a one-sided easel.

Jasmine is having a hard time playing with the other children. She picks out a few books to read and curls up in the beanbag chair.

Applying Your Knowledge

In this learning activity you select a child to observe for three days in various situations. Next, you review your observation notes to summarize what seems to cause the child to experience stress and how the child copes. Finally, you develop and implement a strategy to help reduce the stress and help the child cope more effectively. Review the example that follows, then begin the activity.

Helping Children Cope With Stress

(Example)

Child: _Dylan_   **Age:** _8 years_   **Dates:** _February 6-8_

Situation	Observation Summary
Departure for school	The first day Dylan was flustered because he couldn't find his homework assignment. It had fallen on the floor, and someone had put it in Marcy's cubby. He yelled at Marcy and accused her of taking his paper on purpose. The second day went smoothly, no problems. The third day, Dylan wasn't ready when the bus came. He was finishing breakfast. (Breakfast was served late that day.)
Arrival after school	Dylan arrives each day with a smile on his face, full of energy and ideas about what he wants to do. He almost always helps with snack.
Outdoor play	The first day Dylan joined a game of kickball organized by Ms. Ross. He got on base a few times and scored a run. He stayed fully involved in the game. The next day was rainy, so Dylan went to the gym. He played basketball with some friends, but got into a fight when one of them "fouled" him. The friends said they weren't playing a real game, so it didn't count. He left the game before resolving the problem. The third day Dylan played volleyball, again led by Ms. Ross. She gave him some pointers for serving. He got the ball over the net.

What situations might this child find stressful?

Dylan seems to feel stress when he makes the transition from the program to school.

He does well in adult-led games but may have trouble when he has to negotiate with other children.

What can you and your colleagues do to reduce stress for this child and help him/her cope with stress?

We can anticipate when Dylan might be feeling stress. For example, if breakfast is late, we can make sure Dylan has his stuff ready for school before he sits down to eat.

We can intervene to help Dylan solve disagreements with friends so they can continue their game. Also, we can teach him to use conflict resolution techniques.

Helping Children Cope With Stress

Child: _____ **Age:** _____ **Dates:** _____

Complete the sections of this chart that are relevant to your program.

Situation	Observation Summary
Departure for school	
Arrival after school	
Outdoor play	
Group meeting	
Cleanup	

What situations might this child find stressful?

_____

_____

_____

_____

What can you and your colleagues do to reduce stress for this child and help him/her cope with stress?

_____

_____

_____

_____

Discuss this activity with your trainer and with your colleagues.

Learning Activity IV.
Recognizing Child Abuse and Neglect

In this activity you will learn to:

- identify the four types of child abuse and neglect; and

- recognize the signs of child abuse and neglect.

Definitions of Child Abuse and Neglect

Child abuse that occurs in a child's own home is called familial child abuse. Child abuse that occurs outside a child's home, for example in a child care program, is called institutional abuse. Child abuse and neglect cases are often first identified in a school-age program. Staff members who are in daily contact with children, often detect and report suspected child maltreatment that otherwise might go unnoticed. You are responsible for knowing how to identify signs of child abuse or neglect and to report your suspicions to the appropriate authorities. The first step is to know the definitions of child abuse and neglect in federal and state laws and how they apply to your program.

Child abuse and neglect is defined in Public Law 104-235.

The Child Abuse Prevention and Treatment Act (CAPTA), Section 111; 42 U.S.C. 5106g, Public Law 104-235, as amended and reauthorized in October 1996, provides the following definitions:

(1) the term "child" means a person who has not attained the lesser of

(A) the age of 18; or

(B) except in the case of sexual abuse, the age specified by the child protection law of the State in which the child resides;

(2) the term "child abuse and neglect" means, at a minimum, any recent act or failure to act on the part of a parent or caretaker, which results in death, serious physical or emotional harm, sexual abuse or exploitation, or an act or failure to act which presents an imminent risk of serious harm;

(4) the term "sexual abuse" includes

(A) the employment, use, persuasion, inducement, entice-ment, or coercion of any child to engage in, or assist any other person to engage in, any sexually explicit conduct or simulation of such conduct for the purpose of producing a visual depiction of such conduct; or

(B) the rape, and in cases of caretaker or inter-familial relationships, statutory rape, molestation, prostitution, or other form of sexual exploitation of children, or incest with children…

Each state and many communities also have specific definitions of child maltreatment. Most definitions cover the following types of abuse:

- **physical abuse** which includes burning, kicking, biting, punching, or hitting a child;

- **sexual abuse** which includes using a child (can be by a child or adult) in any sexual context which includes fondling, rape, sodomy, and using a child in pornographic pictures or films;

- **emotional abuse or maltreatment** which includes blaming, belittling, ridiculing, badgering, and constantly ignoring a child's needs;

- **neglect** which includes failing to provide a child with food, clothing, medical attention, or supervision.

Child abuse and neglect could result from **acts** (doing something to injure a child) or **omissions** (not doing or taking actions necessary to protect a child) on the part of a responsible person.

There are four types of child abuse and neglect.

Children who are being abused or neglected may exhibit physical and/or behavioral signs of their maltreatment. Physical signs are those you can actually see. Whether mild or severe, they involve the child's physical condition. Frequently, physical signs are skin or bone injuries, or evidence of lack of care and attention manifested in conditions such as malnutrition.

Behavioral clues may exist alone or may accompany physical indicators. They range from subtle changes in a child's behavior to graphic statements by children describing their abuse.

School-age staff play an important role in preventing or stopping child maltreatment by identifying and reporting signs of possible abuse or neglect. (Reporting is addressed in more detail in the next learning activity.) To fulfill this duty, you must be able to recognize the relevant signs.

Signs of Abuse and Neglect

Clues to abuse and neglect may be found in how a child looks and acts, what the parent says, how the parent relates to the child, and how the parent and child behave when they are together. No single sign or clue proves abuse or neglect, but repeated signs or several signs together should alert you and others to the **possibility** that a child is being abused or neglected.

Signs of possible physical abuse can be physical or behavioral.

Physical abuse of children includes any nonaccidental physical injury caused by the child's caretaker in single or repeated episodes. Although the injury is not accidental, the adult may not intend to hurt the child. The injury might be the result of overdiscipline or inappropriate physical punishment. This usually happens when an adult is angry or frustrated and strikes, shakes, or throws a child. Occasionally, physical abuse is intentional, such as when an adult burns, bites, pokes, cuts, twists limbs, or otherwise harms a child.

Active school-age children sometimes fall down and bump into things. This may result in injuries to their elbows, knees, chins, noses, foreheads, and other bony areas. Bruises and marks on the soft tissue of the face, back, neck, buttocks, upper arms, thighs, ankles, backs of legs, or genitals, however, are more likely to be caused by physical abuse as are bruises in patterns from a belt or rope. Other physical signs are repeated injuries or cigarette burns. Also consider the possibility of abuse if the explanation given for the injury doesn't make sense to you.

When a child changes clothes to go swimming, or rolls up the sleeves of a shirt on a hot day, you might see bruises or burns that are covered by clothing. Often abusive parents are consciously or unconsciously aware that the signs of their abuse should be concealed, so they dress their children in long sleeves or long pants. Another sign to look for is bruises that are at various stages of healing, as if they are the result of more than one incident.

Injuries to the abdomen or head, which are particularly vulnerable spots, often go undetected until there are internal injuries. Injuries to the abdomen can cause swelling, tenderness, and vomiting. Injuries to the head may cause swelling, dizziness, blackouts, retinal detachment, and even death.

In addition to the physical signs that a child has been physically abused, the child **might** also exhibit behavioral signs. Here are some examples:

• When a staff member notices another big bruise on his leg, Troy tells her, "I fell down the stairs again."

- When Daniel is picked up by his mother, he often takes a long time to finish what he's doing before gathering his belongings. When he sees his father come to get him, he quickly stops what he's doing, saying, "Uh oh, I've got to get my stuff ready. My dad doesn't like to wait." Earlier that day a staff member asked him about a drawing. Daniel told her, "This is a bad boy. He got a whipping because he acted like a baby."

Sexual abuse includes a wide range of behaviors: fondling a child's genitals, intercourse, rape, sodomy, exhibitionism, and commercial exploitation through prostitution or pornography. These behaviors are contacts or interactions between a child or adult(s) in which the child is used for the sexual stimulation of the adult or another perpetrator (in this scenario, both are considered perpetrators of sexual abuse). Sexual abuse may be committed by a person under the age of 18 when that person is either significantly older than the victim or in a position of power or control over another child. For example, if a 14-year-old babysitter forces an 8-year-old child to look at his or her genitals, this would be considered exploitation, a form of sexual abuse. Although only 14 years old, this offender would be considered in a position of power over the child, and therefore his or her actions could be defined as sexual abuse.

The physical signs of sexual abuse include some that might be noticed by caregivers of younger children but are not generally noticed by school-age staff. Signs such as torn, stained, or bloody underclothing, or bruises or bleeding in the child's external genitalia, vaginal, or anal areas are likely to go unnoticed because school-age children go to the bathroom without adult assistance. However, if a child says that it hurts to walk or sit, or if he or she complains of pain or itching in the genital area, you should take note and watch to see if this is a recurring condition.

Children who have been sexually abused may also exhibit behavioral signs. They might act out their abuse with other children, or you might overhear them talking about sexual acts. Their premature sexual knowledge can be a sign that they have been exposed to sexual activity. They might show excessive curiosity about sexual activities or touch adults in the breast or genitals. Some children who have been sexually abused are very afraid of specific places, such as the bathroom. Older children who have been sexually abused may be very uncomfortable in situations where they have to undress. For example, such a child might avoid having to put on a swimsuit.

Signs of possible child sexual abuse can be physical or behavioral.

135

Some examples of signs that **might** indicate a child is being sexually maltreated include the following:

- The children and staff are outside on the playground. Simone needs to go inside to the bathroom. Jonathon says, "I have to go, too." Neil, says, "But you just went." Jonathon insists he has to go, too. Simone says, "I don't have to go any more." Ten minutes later Simone comes up to Ms. Ellis and says, "Could you please come inside with me when I go to the bathroom? I don't want to go alone."

- The children are sitting at the table eating breakfast. Nancy is wiggling around in her seat a lot. A staff member asks her if she needs to go to the bathroom. Nancy says, "No, I'm just having trouble getting comfortable." For several days, Nancy continues to exhibit signs of discomfort when sitting.

Signs of possible emotional maltreatment are usually behavioral.

Emotional maltreatment includes blaming, belittling, or rejecting a child; constantly treating siblings unequally; or exhibiting a persistent lack of concern for the child's welfare. This type of maltreatment is the most difficult to identify, as the signs are rarely physical. The effects of mental injury, such as lags in physical development or speech disorders, are not as obvious as bruises and lacerations. Some effects might not show up for many years. Also, the behaviors of emotionally maltreated and emotionally disturbed children are often similar.

Although emotional maltreatment does occur alone, it often accompanies physical and sexual abuse. Emotionally abused children are not always physically abused, but physically abused children are almost always emotionally maltreated.

The following are examples of signs that **might** indicate a child is being emotionally maltreated:

- Each time he picks up nine-year-old Nathan, Mr. Wheeler makes fun of his son's efforts. Typical comments include: "Can't you button that coat right? You never get the buttons lined up with the holes. You look like an idiot." "What's that a picture of? It looks like a five-legged horse." "Can't you climb to the top of the ropes yet? All those other kids climbed to the top. What's the matter with you, are your legs too weak?" Mr. Wheeler told a staff member, "I like to give him a hard time. I don't want him to think he's better than anyone else. He needs to remember that he's got a lot to learn."

- The Jackson family has two children enrolled in the school-age program. Seven-year-old Neesie is a child who excels at everything—she's a great athlete, a talented artist and musician, and an excellent student. Nine-year-old Tiffany is a quiet child who tends to spend most of her time playing with a small group of friends. Her strength is her flexible and adaptable nature. She is able to get along with almost everyone. Usually, when Mrs. Jackson picks up the girls she ignores Tiffany and lavishes praise and attention on Neesie. Today she says, "Neesie, let me see what you made today. Did you get another 'A'?" "Where's Tiffany? Sitting in the corner again? Tell her we have to go." Mrs. Jackson tells a staff member, " I know Neesie's going to do well in life. And Tiffany—I hope she stays as cute and quiet as she is so she can catch a rich husband."

Child neglect is characterized by a failure to provide for a child's basic needs. Neglect can be physical (for example, refusal to seek health care when a child clearly needs medical attention), educational (for example, failure to enroll a child of mandatory school age), or emotional (for example, chronic or extreme spouse abuse in the child's presence). Neglect results in death as frequently as abuse. Neglectful families often appear to have many problems they are not able to handle.

Signs of possible neglect can be physical, educational, or emotional.

When considering the possibility of neglect, it is important to look for consistencies. Do the signs of neglect occur rarely or frequently? Are they chronic (present almost every day), periodic (happening after weekends, vacations, or absences), or episodic (for example, seen twice during a period when the child's mother was in the hospital)?

Some examples of signs that **might** indicate a child is being neglected include the following:

- Sara falls down outside and badly scrapes her knee. A staff member cleans the knee with soap, puts on a bandage, and prepares an injury report for Sara's parents. Four days later, Sara complains her knee hurts. The staff member looks at her knee and notices the bandage has not been changed and the wound is becoming infected.

- Ten-year-old Andrea tells a staff member she missed school again yesterday because she was tired in the morning. She says, "My baby brother Max woke me up in the night. My mom wasn't home yet, so I made Max a bottle and gave it to him. Then he finally went back to sleep. This morning I slept so late I missed the bus." Andrea stays home from school at least once a week.

Recognizing Signs of Possible Child Abuse and Neglect Through Conversations and Interviews

School-age programs are generally family oriented, encouraging a great deal of formal and informal communication between staff and parents. You may gather important information about families from routine conversations with parents and children. During daily drop-off and pick-up times and at scheduled conferences, parents provide details of family life, discuss discipline methods, or ask for help with problems. Some children enjoy talking about their families, so they too may provide information about the family's interactions and home life.

Conversations with parents can provide clues to how the parent feels about the child. The presence of child abuse and neglect may be indicated if the parent constantly:

- blames or belittles the child ("I told you not to drop that. Why weren't you paying attention?")

- sees the child as very different from his or her siblings ("His older sister Terry never caused me these problems. She always did exactly what she was told to do.")

- sees the child as "bad," "evil," or a "monster" ("She really seems to be out to get me. She's just like her father, and he was really an evil man.")

- finds nothing good or attractive in the child ("Oh well, some kids are just a pain in the neck. You can see this one doesn't have much going for her.")

- seems unconcerned about the child ("She was probably just having a bad day. I really don't have time to talk today.")

- fails to keep appointments or refuses to discuss problems the child is having in the program ("That's what I pay you for—if she's getting into trouble, it's your job to make her behave.")

- misuses alcohol or other drugs.

Isolation and extreme stress can lead to child abuse and neglect.

When you know a family well, you are in a better position to gauge whether a problem may be a sign of possible child abuse and neglect or something else; a chronic condition or a temporary situation; a typical childhood problem that the program can readily handle or a problem that requires outside intervention. Family circumstances may also provide clues regarding the possible presence of abuse or neglect. The risk of abuse or neglect increases when families are isolated from friends, neighbors, and other family members, or if there is no apparent "lifeline" to which a family can turn in times of crisis. Marital, economic, emotional, or social crises are among the causes of family stress that can lead to child abuse or neglect.

You may find it hard to imagine that child abuse and neglect could take place at a school-age program, but it happens. Thinking of this possibility may make you feel as though you are "spying" on your colleagues or that your supervisors will be "spying" on staff. It may help to remember that your primary responsibility is to keep children safe. One important way to do this is to be alert to the possibility of child abuse and neglect taking place right at the program site.

Much of the information provided already applies to both familial and institutional child abuse and neglect. There are, however, some specific signs that may indicate child abuse or neglect in a school-age setting. Here are some examples:

- A child refuses to participate in activities supervised by a particular staff member.

- A child shows extreme fear of a staff member.

- A staff member notices that a colleague spends long periods of time out of sight with one child.

- A staff member takes unscheduled breaks without telling his or her colleagues.

- A staff member talks about children very negatively, saying a child is "bad," "spoiled," or "needs to be taught some respect."

- A staff member hears screams or cries coming from a room used by the program.

- A child states that he or she has been hurt by a staff member.

- A staff member shows favoritism to one child and gives that child special attention and treats. The staff member holds the child excessively, although the child appears uncomfortable and tries to get away.

If you see any of these signs, or others that cause you to suspect the possibility of child abuse or neglect, discuss your observations with your supervisor.

Indicators of Abuse and Neglect in School-Age Programs

There are some specific signs of possible child abuse or neglect in a school-age setting.

Applying Your Knowledge

In this activity you answer several questions about defining and recognizing child abuse and neglect. If you can't answer a question, review the information provided in this learning activity, then try again. An answer sheet is provided at the end of the module.

Defining and Recognizing Child Abuse and Neglect

1. A parent refuses to get medical care for a child who will die without treatment. Is this considered abuse?

_____

_____

_____

_____

2. What are the four types of child abuse and neglect?

_____

_____

_____

_____

3. What are "acts and omissions"? Give an example of child abuse or neglect that is the result of an act and an example that is the result of an omission.

_____

_____

_____

_____

4. Does sexual maltreatment always include physical contact between an offender and child?

_____

_____

_____

_____

5. Why is it difficult to identify emotional maltreatment?

_____

_____

_____

_____

6. **Why are school-age staff in an excellent position to identify signs of possible child abuse and neglect?**

_____

_____

_____

_____

Review the answer sheet at the end of this module. Discuss this learning activity with your trainer.

Learning Activity V.
Reporting Suspected Cases of Child Abuse and Neglect

IN THIS ACTIVITY YOU WILL LEARN TO:

- identify state and local requirements for reporting suspected cases of child abuse and neglect; and

- overcome emotional and other barriers to reporting.

School-age staff must follow established reporting requirements.

In every state and the District of Columbia, school-age staff are mandated reporters of suspected child abuse and neglect. This means you have a legal obligation to report your suspicions. In addition, you have an ethical and professional responsibility to know, understand, and follow the reporting requirements and procedures of your state, community, and program.

State laws specify where to report suspected child abuse and neglect.

Each state law specifies one (or more) agencies to receive reports of suspected child abuse and neglect. Usually reports are made to the Department of Social Services, the Department of Human Resources, the Division of Family and Children's Services, or Child Protective Services of the local city, county, or state government. In some states the police department may also receive reports of child maltreatment. It is important to know who receives reports of suspected child abuse and neglect in your jurisdiction. The state reporting statute includes this information.

Some states require that either a written or an oral report be made to the responsible agency. In other states an oral report is required immediately, and a written report must follow in 24 to 48 hours. You will need to check your state law for the specific requirements. The National Clearinghouse on Child Abuse and Neglect Information (www.calib.com/nccanch) maintains current on-line reports on state statutes.

Most states require reporters to provide the following information:

- the child's name, age, and address;

- the child's present location (for example, at the school-age program);

- the parent's name and address;

- the nature and extent of the injury or condition observed; and

- the reporter's name and location (sometimes not required but very useful for the agency conducting the investigation).

Many programs have established policies defining the duties and responsibilities of all staff in reporting child abuse and neglect. If you don't have a copy of your program's child abuse and neglect reporting procedures, ask your director for one. Use it to complete the following chart.

State and Local Policy on Child Abuse and Neglect

I report suspected child abuse and neglect to:

_____

At the following phone number: _____

I must give the following information:

_____

_____

_____

I also must follow these state and local reporting requirements:

_____

_____

_____

_____

My report must be: ☐ Oral

☐ Written

☐ Both

Overcoming Barriers to Reporting

When you suspect a child is being abused or neglected, you may feel very reluctant to report your suspicions. It helps to remember that a report of child maltreatment is not an accusation; rather, it is a request to begin the helping process. But the reporting process does not always go smoothly. You may encounter difficulties that will discourage you from making future reports. If you are aware of these difficulties beforehand and plan ways to overcome them, you will be better able to fulfill your legal and ethical responsibilities.

You do not have to prove your suspicions.

Some staff find their personal feelings are a barrier to reporting child abuse or neglect. They simply prefer not to get involved. They are afraid they have made a mistake and convince themselves that there is a perfectly good explanation for the child's injuries or behavior. They may fear other staff or parents will think them incompetent or alarmist. It is important to remember that while adults wait for positive proof of a child's maltreatment, the child is vulnerable to continued maltreatment.

Your primary responsibility is to protect children.

Another potential barrier to reporting is the special relationship parents and a staff member (or two staff members) might develop over months or years, which may hinder a person from reporting suspected cases of child maltreatment. At times, when staff observe signs of abuse or neglect, they may give parents or colleagues the benefit of the doubt. Even when they do suspect child maltreatment, they may fear that confronting the parent or colleague will result in a hostile, indignant, or distressed reaction or retaliation. It may help to remember that as a professional, your primary responsibilities are to protect children and to support their families. By reporting your suspicions to the appropriate authorities, you are actively protecting children. In addition, you are helping their families (or your colleague) get the assistance they need to change their behavior.

Getting Ready to Report

Once you suspect a child is being maltreated, **you must not waste time in reporting**. Taking this action will probably make you feel at risk, confused, and generally uncomfortable. It is not a pleasant task. To alleviate some of your discomfort, you can use the following checklist to prepare for the report. (Note: some items may not be applicable to your situation.)

Checklist for Child Abuse and Neglect

	Done
1. Document your suspicions and review your observation notes and anecdotal records.	☐
2. Analyze your information to identify the things that cause you to suspect abuse or neglect. Make a list of the physical and behavioral signs you have observed.	☐
3. Describe the parent (or staff member) and child interactions you observed. Note instances when the parent indicated he or she finds the child difficult, worthless, or impossible to handle. Include examples of the parent's lack of interest in the child.	☐
4. Discuss with your colleagues the physical and behavioral signs you have documented. If they have reason to suspect abuse or neglect, discuss their reasons.	☐
5. Ask your supervisor what support he or she will provide once you file the report and what the program will do if the parent tries to remove the child.	☐
6. Set up a support system for yourself. (After making the report, you may feel vulnerable and need to talk with others about your feelings and concerns, without breaching confidentiality.)	☐
7. Review the program's reporting policy.	☐
8. Collect the information needed to file the initial report.	☐
9. Obtain the exact telephone number and address of the agency to which you should report.	☐
10. If a written report is required, obtain the reporting forms or use a piece of paper.	☐
11. File your report.	☐
12. Notify the parents that you have filed a report.	☐

This checklist can help you organize your thoughts and secure the support you will need once the report is filed. You might not be able to wait until you have completed all the items on this checklist. In some cases, you may have to report your suspicions immediately.

Offer support to the child and family.

You will note that the last step on this checklist is to notify the child's parents that you have filed a report. In most cases this will be a difficult conversation. You want to be supportive, while carrying out your primary responsibility—to keep the child safe. Try to maintain a professional tone. Let the parents know **what** you reported ("repeated incidences of cigarette burns on Carl's arm"), **when** the report was filed ("this morning"), and **to whom** ("Child Protective Services"). Explain that you have carried out your legal, professional, and ethical responsibilities to file a report of suspected child abuse and neglect and are not involved in "proving" that abuse or neglect took place. In addition, let parents know that you want to offer the family support as they deal with this difficult situation. They may not respond to your offer immediately; however, it is important to let them know that you are not passing judgment on anyone's behavior. Instead, you have reported signs of possible abuse so their child and the family can get the help they need.

After Filing the Report

In some states and local jurisdictions, CPS is so overwhelmed by reports of child abuse and neglect that staff cannot respond to every case. There may be internal policies that require the agency to respond first to cases that are life-threatening or extremely clear-cut. You may see no response to a report you have filed. If this happens, remember it is extremely important for the school-age program to continue supporting the child and family and advocating for them to receive needed services. In addition, you should continue to be alert to physical and behavioral signs of abuse or neglect. If necessary, file a second, or even third report. Some states have hotline numbers set up for filing reports. Find out if there is one in your state, and use it if necessary.

Applying Your Knowledge

This learning activity will help you understand your responsibilities for reporting child abuse and neglect. Answer the questions, then respond to the case study that follows. Answers are provided at the end of the module. There can be more than one good answer to each question.

School-Age Staff Responsibilities for Reporting Child Abuse and Neglect

1. Why do child maltreatment laws exist?

_____

_____

_____

_____

2. How do maltreated children get assistance?

_____

_____

_____

_____

3. What happens to children if nobody reports child maltreatment?

_____

_____

_____

_____

4. Under what circumstances do I have to file a report?

_____

_____

_____

_____

5. What will happen to me if I don't report?

_____

_____

_____

_____

6. What if I'm wrong and the parents sue me?

_____

_____

_____

Case Study

Ms. Benson and Ms. Altman have worked together in the school-age program for several months. They get along well and have become friends outside work. Today Ms. Benson is assigned to supervise the children playing outside. Ms. Altman is supervising children who have chosen to stay inside. Ms. Altman looks outside and sees nine-year-old Teresa come running towards the building. Then Ms. Benson comes running after Teresa. When Ms. Benson catches up with Teresa she grabs her by both arms and turns the child around. Still holding Teresa by both arms, Ms. Benson shakes Teresa and appears to be shouting at her. Teresa struggles to get free, then runs into the building. When she reaches Ms. Altman, she shouts through her tears, "I hate her. I'm going to tell my mother she squeezed my arms." Ms. Altman sees Teresa's arms are very red. She says, "I'm sure there must be a misunderstanding. Ms. Benson probably didn't realize she was hurting you." Teresa responds, "How can you take her side? I saw you watching. I know you saw what she was doing."

What should Ms. Altman do, and why?

_____

_____

_____

_____

_____

_____

_____

_____

Compare your response to the one at the end of the module, and discuss it with your trainer.

SUMMARIZING YOUR PROGRESS

You have now completed all the learning activities for this module. Whether you are an experienced school-age staff member or a new one, this module has probably helped you develop new skills for helping children stay healthy. Before you go on, take a few minutes to review your responses to the pre-training assessment for this module. Write a summary of what you learned, and list the skills you developed or improved.

_____

_____

_____

_____

_____

_____

_____

_____

_____

_____

_____

_____

If there are topics you would like to know more about, you will find recommended readings listed in the Orientation.

Your final step in this module is to complete the knowledge and competency assessments. Let your trainer know when you are ready to schedule the assessments. After you have successfully completed them, you will be ready to start a new module. Congratulations on your progress so far, and good luck with your next module.

ANSWER SHEETS

Promoting Good Health and Nutrition

Maintaining Indoor and Outdoor Environments That Promote Wellness and Reduce the Spread of Disease

1. **What are three things Ms. Nunes did to maintain a healthy environment?**

   a. She opened the windows a few inches to let in fresh air. Because it was a cool day, she didn't open them all the way.

   b. She checked the paper towel and soap supply and made a note to ask one of the children to put out more paper towels.

   c. She conducted a health check on the children.

2. **What did Ms. Nunes do to keep germs from spreading?**

   a. She reminded a child to use a tissue and then wash his hands.

   b. She washed her hands and made sure Lacey washed hers after vomiting.

Encouraging Children to Develop Habits That Promote Good Hygiene and Nutrition

1. **How did Mr. Berry help the children develop healthy habits?**

   a. He reminded them to wash their hands.

   b. He washed his own hands.

   c. He shared the recipe for one of his favorite snacks.

2. **How did Mr. Berry teach the children about good nutrition?**

   a. He helped them see how much fat was in a hamburger.

   b. He suggested they look for recipes that are low in fat, salt, and sugar.

   c. He planned a healthy snack for their first cooking project.

1. **What are the clues to possible child abuse in this situation?**

   a. Carolyn has been spending more time alone than usual.

   b. Carolyn has been short-tempered with the younger children.

   c. Carolyn says she hates her brother and that he made her do something bad.

   d. Carolyn tells Ms. Charles her brother made her touch him.

2. **How did Ms. Lee support Ms. Charles?**

   a. Ms. Lee tells Ms. Charles she's glad she came to her.

   b. She encourages Ms. Charles to discuss her concerns and to maintain confidentiality.

   c. She supports Ms. Charles' decision to file a report to Child Protective Services.

Recognizing and Reporting Child Abuse and Neglect

Defining and Recognizing Child Abuse and Neglect

1. A parent refuses to get medical care for a child who will die without treatment. Is this considered child abuse or neglect?

Yes. This is failing to provide health care, a form of neglect.

2. What are the four types of child abuse and neglect?

Physical abuse, sexual abuse, emotional abuse or maltreatment, and neglect.

3. What are "acts and omissions"? Give an example of child abuse or neglect that is the result of an act and an example that is the result of an omission.

Acts refers to what a parent or other caretaker actively does to a child; for example, burning a child's arm. Omissions refers to what the person does not do; for example, failing to provide appropriate supervision.

4. Does sexual maltreatment always include physical contact between an offender and child?

No. The definition of sexual maltreatment includes exploitation, which might include forcing a child to look at pornography or the offender's genitals, or could include photographing a child for use in pornographic publications.

5. Why is it difficult to identify emotional maltreatment?

The signs are rarely physical and some effects do not show up for years. Also, the behaviors of emotionally maltreated and emotionally disturbed children are often similar.

6. Why are school-age staff in an excellent position to identify signs of possible child abuse and neglect?

School-age staff see children every day. They might detect signs of possible child maltreatment that would otherwise go unnoticed.

School-Age Staff Responsibilities for Reporting Child Abuse and Neglect

1. Why do child maltreatment laws exist?

To provide protection for children who cannot protect themselves.

2. How do maltreated children get assistance?

If a child is a victim of maltreatment, the only way the child and family will receive help is if a report is filed.

3. What happens to children if nobody reports maltreatment?

If the maltreatment goes unnoticed and unreported, it is likely it will continue and perhaps escalate.

4. Under what circumstances do I have to file a report?

If your knowledge of the child and his or her family and your professional training and experience lead you to suspect child maltreatment, then you must file a report.

5. What will happen to me if I don't report?

If you fail to report, under your state's laws you might be subject to fines or even a jail sentence.

6. What if I'm wrong and the parents sue me?

When you make a report in good faith, the law protects you. You cannot be sued for reporting child maltreatment because as a school-age staff member, you are mandated to do so.

Case Study

What should Ms. Altman do, and why?

Ms. Altman needs to remember it is her job to protect children such as Teresa from harm. Some signs of physical abuse are evident. She witnessed a colleague using physical force to restrain a child, and she saw the results of the physical actions—red marks on Teresa's arms. It is not Ms. Altman's job to investigate or determine if her colleague's actions are poor practice or child abuse or neglect. Based on what she saw, it is her job to file a report of **suspected** abuse.

GLOSSARY

Body fluids   Liquids and semi-liquids eliminated by or present in the body, such as feces, urine, mucus, blood, vomit, and saliva.

Diet   The kind and amount of food and drink regularly consumed.

Disinfectant   A cleaning solution that destroys the causes of infection.

Hygiene   Practices that preserve good health and eliminate disease-producing germs.

Infection   Invasion of the body by tiny organisms that cause disease.

Nutrient   A component of food that offers nourishment to the body.

Nutritious   Having large amounts of vitamins, minerals, complex carbohydrates, or protein, and being low in fats, salt, and sugar.

Sodium   A mineral normally found in seafood, poultry, and some vegetables; one of the components of table salt.

Starch   A carbohydrate food such as cereal, potatoes, pasta, and bread.

Module 3:
PROGRAM ENVIRONMENT

OVERVIEW

CREATING AND USING THE SCHOOL-AGE PROGRAM ENVIRONMENT INVOLVES:

- organizing indoor and outdoor areas to support a variety of activities;

- selecting and arranging developmentally appropriate materials and equipment; and

- planning and implementing a schedule and routines to meet children's developmental and individual needs.

The school-age program environment includes the indoor and outdoor space you regularly use. Some, or all, of the environment may be used solely by your program, or it might be shared with other groups. For example, a program located in a school might have its own room, supplemented by regular access to the gymnasium, cafeteria, and playground.

The quality of the physical environment affects how children and staff feel. Features such as the size of the space, wall colors, the type of flooring, the amount of light, the acoustics, and the number of windows all influence the quality of the environment.

The quality of the environment affects how children and staff feel.

A good outdoor environment for school-age children has soft and hard surfaces and shady and sunny areas. There is an area for ball games, challenging equipment for large muscle development, space set aside for construction and digging, a storage area, and a place to read or play quiet games. Ideally, the outdoor play area is adjacent to a field for large group games and sports.

In school, children spend a large part of their day following directions, completing assignments, and developing skills in a relatively structured classroom setting. They are in a very real sense "on the job" during the school day. The most appropriate environments for school-age programs complement rather than duplicate the school day. They allow children to unwind, relax, be themselves, and socialize with peers and adults. They also support children's special projects and encourage involvement in the community beyond home and school. Activities and materials allow children to develop special talents and master new skills. A good program environment would support Renaldo's interest in building a geodesic dome, allow Tiffany to learn more about her community's recycling efforts, and give Amy a chance to master her woodworking skills.

Effective environments complement the school day.

157

School-age children can help plan and organize the environment.

It's important to allow children to feel a sense of ownership of their environment. Include them as you plan, organize, set up, or rearrange your space. Their suggestions may surprise you. Although some materials and equipment are already in place, the children will have ideas about additional items they would like to have at the program. If the environment is planned and organized in cooperation with the children, they are likely to take more responsibility for taking care of it, and your job will be easier.

Your program's schedule and routines also contribute to creating a comfortable atmosphere. Each day will probably go more smoothly if the schedule and routines meet the diverse needs of the children enrolled in the program.

Listed below are examples of how school-age staff demonstrate their competence in creating and using program environments.

Organizing Indoor and Outdoor Areas to Support a Variety of Activities

Establish a variety of well-defined and equipped indoor and outdoor interest areas that reflect children's skills and interests.

Rotate interest areas or create sub-areas to respond to children's changing skills and interests.

Create soft, cozy areas where children can play alone, read books and magazines, do homework, listen to music, daydream, or talk with a friend.

Provide sufficient space and appropriate equipment for group games and sports, indoors and outdoors.

Define separate spaces indoors and outdoors for active and quiet play so children don't get in the way of each other.

Provide sufficient storage for children's personal belongings—for example, labeled lockers, cubbies, and shelving units.

Arrange the outdoor area to support a variety of activities such as group games, painting at easels, eating snack, and reading under a shady tree.

Help older children create special places that are reserved for their use only.

Involve children when arranging and rearranging the space used by the program.

Locate interest areas near the resources, such as light and water, that are used in the area.

Designate storage space for long-term projects and works-in-progress.

Adapt the environment, if necessary, to accommodate children with special needs.

Select materials such as board games, puzzles, and manipulatives of varying degrees of difficulty to accommodate a wide range of skill levels.

Follow up on field trips, school, and community activities by providing related materials at the program. (For example, after a field trip to a nature center, display nature books, magazines, posters, and collections in the science and nature area.)

Offer open-ended materials (for example, collage supplies) and equipment (such as playground balls) children can use in different ways.

Use low, open shelves and storage units so children can easily select and replace materials.

Store special projects and items to be used with supervision on tall shelves and lockable storage units.

Provide materials such as puppets, dramatic play props, posters, books, and magazines that present or reflect different ethnic backgrounds, diverse roles for men and women, and people with disabilities.

Store materials and supplies that are used together, near each other.

Provide a variety of materials and equipment that can be used by children with a wide range of abilities.

Selecting and Arranging Developmentally Appropriate Materials and Equipment

Find out what children would like to have at the program through observations, conversations, surveys, and listening to their interactions with each other.

Planning and Implementing a Schedule and Routines to Meet Children's Developmental and Individual Needs

Allow children to meet their personal needs (using the bathroom, eating snack, resting/relaxing) on individual schedules.

Provide things to do during transitions (for example, leaving for school) so children do not have to stand in line or wait with nothing to do.

Plan a schedule that includes large blocks of time when children choose what they want to do.

Provide sufficient time in the schedule for children to carry out their plans and engage in long-term projects.

Offer a balance of activity choices including active and quiet; indoors and outdoors; and individual, small group, and large group.

Schedule time for rests or naps for children who come to the program after morning kindergarten.

Include sufficient time for clean-up at the end of the morning, afternoon, and full-day sessions.

Creating and Using a Program Environment

In the following situations school-age staff are creating and using program environments. As you read them, think about what the staff are doing and why. Then answer the questions that follow.

Mr. Johnson watches the children on the playground. Several older girls are sitting under a tree randomly drawing lines in the dirt with sticks. Jason, Bobby, and Derrick are running around in circles teasing each other. They nearly knock down several roller skaters, disrupt a ball game, and get in the way of two children painting at easels. Some younger children are trying to play volleyball, but they can't get the ball over the net and it keeps rolling down the hill. The rest of the children are at the storage shed looking for something to do. They pull out some jump ropes tangled up with skates and sandbox toys. "This place needs some organizing," Mr. Johnson thinks.

Over the next week, Mr. Johnson and the children reorganize the storage shed. They hang up the jump ropes where they can be reached easily, and put the skates and sandbox toys in separate boxes. Next they make three activity boxes: one with colored chalk for sidewalk drawing, another with trowels and magnifying glasses to examine insects and plants, and a third with small games such as jacks and cards. Mr. Johnson and the children also discuss how to use the areas of the playground and how to help each other. Several older children offer to hold a "sports clinic" to help the younger ones learn to play volleyball. Jason, Bobby, and Derrick ask to set aside an area for running relay races.

Organizing Indoor and Outdoor Areas to Support a Variety of Activities

1. **How did Mr. Johnson know the outdoor environment was not working?**

   _____

   _____

   _____

2. **How did Mr. Johnson and the children work together to improve the outdoor area?**

   _____

   _____

   _____

Selecting and Arranging Developmentally Appropriate Materials and Equipment

Ms. Rodriguez and Mr. Sullivan are discussing special projects the children could explore over the next month. They have noticed that even though it's January, many children have been talking about summer vacations and how they wish they could go to the beach—right now! At the next group meeting they present some ideas for learning more about ocean life; painting large murals of underwater life—to create an underwater atmosphere; adding paper maché materials to the arts and crafts area to make large underwater creatures—such as an octopus or a starfish; turning the drama area into a sunken ship, complete with a broken mast, a crow's nest, and a treasure chest. The children respond enthusiastically and offer some of their own ideas. Nancy suggests they learn some sailing songs. Daniel says he will ask his mother, who is a marine biologist, to visit the program and talk about life under the sea. Terrence asks, "What happened to the aquarium we had last year?" Mr. Sullivan replies, "It's in the closet. We could use some of our supply budget to set it up again. Would you like to be in charge?" "Sure," says Terrence. "I'll help him," joins in Jack.

To involve families, Ms. Rodriguez puts a notice in the newsletter asking for donations of old jewelry and coins for the treasure chest. She arranges for Daniel's mother to speak to the group and gathers books and magazines on sea life for the quiet area. Mr. Sullivan is a scuba diver so he brings in his gear and explains how it works. For the science and nature area, children bring in items they've collected on beach trips—shells, shark's teeth, driftwood. Over the next two weeks the children and staff become totally immersed in their study of ocean life.

1. **What did Ms. Rodriguez and Mr. Sullivan know about the children?**

   _____

   _____

   _____

2. **How will the planned activities and new materials help children learn?**

   _____

   _____

   _____

As she sees the first bus pull up, Ms. Chan thinks about how lately roll call and snack are taking longer than ever. The children can't seem to quiet down, and she has to shout over the noise to be heard. Some of the children have wrestling matches while waiting for snack, and others complain they're not hungry and just want to go outside.

At the next planning meeting Ms. Chan shares her observations with her colleagues. They decide to adjust the schedule to create a more comfortable, relaxed atmosphere that will be in tune with children's needs. First they decide it really isn't necessary to call the roll aloud. Instead, Mr. Trent will stand near the door, greeting and checking off the children as they arrive. Three activities will be available to the children during the first 30 minutes of the program: (1) going outside with Ms. Chan to unwind after the school day; (2) going to a self-service area where snacks will be set out in advance; and (3) gathering in the quiet area to relax and talk with friends, play a short game, read a magazine, or listen to music on headphones. Staff will remind children who don't eat snack right away to serve themselves 15 minutes before the area closes. After children have settled in during the first 30 minutes, Ms. Chan and the other staff will gather everyone for brief announcements about activity options for the rest of the afternoon.

Planning and Implementing a Schedule and Routines to Meet the Developmental and Individual Needs of Children

1. **How do the changes planned by Ms. Chan and her colleagues reflect the needs of children after school?**

   _____

   _____

   _____

2. **In what ways might the new approach reduce the amount of noise and tension in the program?**

   _____

   _____

   _____

Compare your answers with those on the answer sheet at the end of this module. If your answers are different, discuss them with your trainer. There can be more than one good answer.

How Your Environment Affects You

All people are affected by their environments.

We are all affected by our environments. Whether sitting in the living room, shopping in a store, climbing a mountain, or lying on the beach, we react to where we are. Our surroundings affect:

- how we feel;

- how comfortable we are;

- how we behave; and

- how effectively we can accomplish what we need to do.

Think for a moment about how you feel and behave in the following situations:

- Standing in a hot, crowded bus or subway where you are sandwiched among strangers. (Perhaps you pull in your shoulders, try to avoid any contact with others, and count the minutes until you get off.)

- Eating in a special restaurant with a favorite friend. The lights are low, and the noise level is muffled. The food smells delicious, and attractive pictures hang on the walls. (You are probably relaxed, enjoying a delightful dinner, feeling special and unhurried.)

- Preparing a meal in a strange kitchen when the owner is not there to help you. (You can't figure out how the kitchen is organized and you spend lots of time looking for the things you need. It's inefficient, and you may not cook as well as you usually do.)

Sometimes we don't know how the environment affects us.

It's easy to see in these examples how environments can affect our actions and our feelings. But the influence of our surroundings isn't always so clear. Sometimes we aren't aware of how the environment is making us feel and act.

To identify some less obvious factors in the environment that can support you or work against you, take time to answer the following questions. Think about a store where you enjoy shopping. It can be a grocery store, clothing store, hardware store, or any other store. As you imagine yourself there, think of what makes it a good experience. What makes it easy to find and purchase the things you need?

Then think about a store you dislike. When you are there, you feel frustrated and angry. You may decide never to return again. What's different about this store?

Type of store: _____

Why do you *enjoy* shopping there?

_____
_____
_____
_____

Type of store: _____

Why do you *dislike* shopping there?

_____
_____
_____
_____

Look over your answers to these two questions. Many of the factors you identified that make shopping enjoyable or difficult apply to your work environment as well. Your work environment should be organized and planned to support your goals for children and to make your job easier and more enjoyable.

Now think of your favorite place to be; it can be indoors or outdoors. Close your eyes for a moment and imagine yourself in that space. How does it feel? smell? look? What do you hear? What are you doing? Are you alone, or are other people with you? Describe your favorite place below.

Favorite Place:

_____
_____
_____
_____

Often when people describe their favorite place, they identify features such as the following:

- a quiet place to be alone;
- a place where only the sounds of nature can be heard;
- a soft and comfortable place to stretch out;
- a place where music is playing;
- a place where the air smells fresh and clean;
- a bright and sunny place; or
- a colorful and attractive place.

Keep the features of your favorite space in mind as you examine your work environment. An environment that is comfortable for both you and the school-age children will make your job more satisfying.

When you have finished this overview section, you should complete the pre-training assessment. Refer to the glossary at the end of this module if you need definitions of the terms used.

PRE-TRAINING ASSESSMENT

Listed below are the skills school-age staff use to create and use program environments. Think about whether you do these things regularly, sometimes, or not enough. Place a check in one of the boxes on the right for each skill listed. Then discuss your answers with your trainer.

Organizing Indoor and Outdoor Areas to Support a Variety of Activities	**I Do This**		
	Regularly	Sometimes	Not Enough
1. Establishing a variety of well-equipped indoor and outdoor interest areas that reflect children's skills and interests.	☐	☐	☐
2. Rotating interest areas or creating sub-areas to respond to children's changing skills and interests.	☐	☐	☐
3. Creating soft, cozy areas where children can play alone, read, listen to music, daydream, or talk with a friend.	☐	☐	☐
4. Providing sufficient space and appropriate equipment for group games and sports, indoors and outdoors.	☐	☐	☐
5. Defining separate spaces, indoors and outdoors, for active and quiet play so children do not get in the way of each other.	☐	☐	☐
6. Providing sufficient space for children to safely store their belongings.	☐	☐	☐
7. Arranging the outdoor area to support a variety of activities.	☐	☐	☐
8. Helping older children create special places that are reserved for their use only.	☐	☐	☐
9. Involving children when arranging and rearranging space used by the program.	☐	☐	☐

Organizing Indoor and Outdoor Areas to Support a Variety of Activities (continued)	**I Do This**		
	Regularly	Sometimes	Not Enough
10. Locating interest areas near resources, such as light and water, that are used in the area.	☐	☐	☐
11. Designating storage space for long-term projects and works-in-progress.	☐	☐	☐
12. Adapting the environment, if necessary, to accommodate children with special needs.	☐	☐	☐

Selecting and Arranging Developmentally Appropriate Materials and Equipment

	Regularly	Sometimes	Not Enough
13. Selecting materials such as board games, puzzles, and manipulatives of varying degrees of difficulty to accommodate a wide range of skill levels.	☐	☐	☐
14. Following up on field trips, school, and community activities by providing related materials at the program.	☐	☐	☐
15. Offering open-ended materials and equipment children can use in different ways.	☐	☐	☐
16. Using low, open shelves and storage units so children can easily select and replace materials.	☐	☐	☐
17. Storing special projects and items to be used with supervision on tall shelves or in lockable storage units.	☐	☐	☐
18. Providing materials such as puppets, drama props, posters, books, and magazines that present or reflect different ethnic backgrounds, diverse roles for men and women, and people with disabilities.	☐	☐	☐
19. Observing, talking with, listening to, and surveying children to find out what materials and equipment they would like to have in the program.	☐	☐	☐

Planning and Implementing a Schedule and Routines to Meet Children's Developmental and Individual Needs

	I Do This		
	Regularly	Sometimes	Not Enough

20. Allowing children to meet their personal needs (for example, toileting, eating, and resting or relaxing) on individual schedules.

☐ ☐ ☐

21. Providing things to do during transitions (for example, leaving for school) so children do not have to stand in line or wait with nothing to do.

☐ ☐ ☐

22. Planning a schedule that includes large blocks of time when children can choose what they want to do.

☐ ☐ ☐

23. Providing sufficient time in the schedule for children to carry out their plans and engage in long-term projects.

☐ ☐ ☐

24. Offering a balance of activity choices including active and quiet; indoor and outdoor; and individual, small group, and large group.

☐ ☐ ☐

25. Scheduling time for children to rest or nap after their morning kindergarten session.

☐ ☐ ☐

26. Including sufficient time for clean-up at the end of morning, afternoon, and full-day sessions.

☐ ☐ ☐

Review your responses, then list three to five skills you would like to improve or topics you would like to learn more about. When you finish this module, you can list examples of your new or improved knowledge and skills.

_____

_____

_____

_____

_____

_____

_____

_____

Begin the learning activities for Module 3, Program Environment.

LEARNING ACTIVITIES

Learning Activity I.
Understanding How Children Use the Environment

IN THIS ACTIVITY YOU WILL LEARN TO:

- recognize some typical behaviors of school-age children; and

- apply what you know about children to creating and using a program environment.

What 5- to 7-Year-Old Children Are Like

No longer preschoolers, 5- to 7-year-old children begin to develop a sense of themselves as "big kids." They want to make friends and play with others. Their emerging sense of themselves includes an awareness of what it means to be a "boy" or a "girl."

Children in this age group generally prefer cooperative rather than competitive games and sports. They like teamwork and following rules. They enjoy making up new games—complete with rules— and inventing new rules for familiar games.

Climbing, running, skipping, and hopping are favorite physical activities, along with tumbling and simple ball games. Children may tire easily during physical activities, so it is a good idea to have a place for them to rest or cool down.

Younger school-age children enjoy "hands-on" activities, but may not have the fine motor coordination needed to hold and manipulate small tools and materials. They enjoy the process of making things, but also are interested in the tangible products of their efforts. Simple arts and crafts projects and a wide variety of open-ended materials help them develop their fine motor skills and feel good about their accomplishments.

With rapidly expanding vocabularies, 5- to 7-year-olds are learning to express their interests, thoughts, and feelings. They enjoy reading and being read to (by staff or older children), and use their thinking skills to solve puzzles and problems. They use their active imaginations in dramatic play, music, dancing, and art.

The youngest children in this age group are just beginning to shift their interests from a world centered around the family to one that includes school, friends, and community. Playing with familiar household materials in the dramatic play area may be very appealing. This age group also enjoys more complex dramatic play that helps them explore and make sense of the larger world.

Most 5- to 7-year-olds can take care of their personal needs independently. They use the bathroom, eat meals, wash hands, and make a wide range of decisions without adult assistance.

How do 5- to 7-year-old children use the environment?

Below are some examples of 5- to 7-year-old children using a program environment.

- Brenda and Tran are using the wok and chopsticks in the house corner to cook and serve dinner.

- Janet and Cindy are outside under a tree with a box of puppets. Janet's puppet says to Cindy's, "It feels terrible when someone makes fun of you."

- Carla and Betty stand in the back row during aerobics so they can copy what the bigger kids are doing.

- Tommy and Bobby jump from the bus and run inside to put away their backpacks. Tommy hurries outside to play on the climber. Bobby stops first to get a snack from the self-service counter.

- Maria, a kindergartner, is pleased to see her older friend Monica arrive at 3 p.m. The two girls choose a beginning reader from the quiet area and curl up in the beanbag chair. Monica reads Maria a story.

- Patty is working on her favorite jigsaw puzzle—which she can do very quickly. Ms. Jacobs says, "You are so good at doing that puzzle. Would you like to try one with more pieces?"

- Galen and Marshall are building a large block structure. Some older children run by, making the blocks fall down. They complain to Ms. Dobson, who suggests they bring up their problem at the group meeting. "Yeah," says Marshall, "maybe we can move the block corner to a safer place."

Observe how the 5- to 7-year-olds in your program use the environment, and list some examples below.

_____

_____

_____

_____

_____

Based on your observations, what changes would you like to make in the environment to address the needs of 5- to 7-year-olds?

_____

_____

_____

_____

_____

_____

_____

What 8- to 10-Year-Old Children Are Like

During the middle elementary years, most children are cooperative and enjoy group activities that focus on a common interest—for example, sports, clubs, drama, music, or gymnastics. They may be interested in contests and other competitive activities that allow them to be "good at something." Younger children in this age group tend to prefer being with their own gender. The older ones begin to show interest in the opposite sex, although they are probably too embarrassed to admit it.

As cognitive abilities increase, children stretch their creativity—writing stories and plays, acting, inventing and designing things, and making up jokes and riddles. They can use their math and thinking skills in fresh, entertaining ways. Their thinking skills also help them negotiate with others, solve problems, and exercise good judgment. They use words to express their anger and other feelings. Children begin to set standards for their own behavior and learn greater self-control.

The increased body strength and coordination of most 8- to 10-year old children is used in organized sports and games and individual physical activities. They are developing a sense of rhythm and balance and like to move and dance to music. Sometimes they create their own dance steps and routines.

Fine motor control also is increasing, so children enjoy activities and projects that require manual dexterity and control. Crocheting, playing musical instruments, doing macramé, performing magic tricks, using hand looms, and playing computer games are among the many activities these children find appealing.

Children in this age group tend to feel grown up and like to experiment and try out new ideas and activities. Their growing confidence may lead them to take risks and try things they are not ready for. Increased physical and mental skills allow them to do complex tasks, follow detailed directions, and play complicated games of strategy without adult assistance. They may enjoy the challenge of playing games such as chess and backgammon, following directions to build models, and using a special recipe to make a new snack.

With their growing attention spans, 8- to 10-year-olds like long-term projects and activities: organizing, categorizing, and displaying a shell collection; weaving a wall hanging; or mastering a physical skill such as turning a cartwheel. They may pursue special interests for days, weeks, or even months.

How do 8- to 10-year-old children use the environment?

Below are some examples of 8- to 10-year-old children using a program environment.

- Ronald and Dirk are members of a community soccer league. They run up and down the field, practicing their dribbling and passing skills.

- Sam and Laura find a garden snake on the playground. They come inside to see if they can find its picture in one of the nature books.

- Jodie, Mark, and Eddie are telling each other jokes and rolling on the floor laughing. Ms. Donahue shows them some joke and riddle books. The three "comedians" decide to put on a comedy show in the large-group activity area.

- Judy and Eli are arguing about whose turn it is to use the computer. Judy says, "I know what we can do. Let's ask Ms. Kelly to think of a number from 1 to 5. Whoever guesses closest to her number can have the first turn." Eli agrees, and they both go to ask for Ms. Kelly's help.

- Dani is at the homework table studying for her spelling test. She asks Molly, an 11-year-old, to give her a "practice test."

- Doreen, Eric, and Damian are playing a new board game. When they get to a point where nobody knows what to do, Eric reads the instructions out loud.

Observe how the 8- to 10-year-olds in your program use the environment, and list some examples below.

_____

_____

_____

_____

_____

Based on your observations, what changes would you like to make in the environment to address the needs of 8- to 10-year-olds?

_____

_____

_____

_____

_____

_____

In general, older school-age children can focus on challenging tasks for long periods of time. Hobbies and interests begun during these years may develop into lifelong pursuits. Children's increased attention spans are accompanied by the development of abstract thinking skills. They can think about the future, make plans, reflect on the past, and grapple with events happening outside their immediate community. They are thirsty for information as they try to see how they relate to the rest of the world. As their awareness and thinking capacities grow, they may worry about situations reported in the news and need opportunities to express their concerns and feelings. They can empathize with others and may want to get involved in community projects such as helping the homeless, establishing a recycling center, or visiting the elderly. Older children also enjoy creative activities that help them shape and express their feelings and ideas.

Many 11- and 12-year-olds are entering or already in early adolescence—the period of most rapid physical growth since infancy. As a result, they need lots of opportunities to exercise. Sports such as basketball, tennis, and gymnastics allow children to develop complex coordination skills, for example, running and dribbling at the same time. Older children may take risks as they test the limits of their physical skills. They may feel they are invincible—accidents happen to other people, not to them. They need equipment that is sturdy enough for larger bodies and more vigorous play. Outdoors, the climbing equipment, swings, and slides designed for younger children may not be strong enough for use by older children. Indoors, programs should provide tables, chairs, and other furniture large enough to accommodate older children.

What 11- to 12-Year-Old Children Are Like

Peer groups provide the arena for this age group to test their opinions and practice social skills. This process allows them to develop relationships with the opposite sex and with others in the community. There is a strong desire to be accepted by peers, who may be a positive or negative influence. It's common for these children to imitate teenagers and the adult world as they "try on" what it's like to be grown up. Fads in dress, music, and language are common. Although 11- and 12-year-olds are struggling to gain autonomy, they seek out adults who can provide guidance, encouragement, and support without making them feel like "little kids."

How do 11- to 12-year-old children use the environment?

Below are some examples of 11- to 12-year-old children using a program environment.

- Lisa is sitting at the homework table writing a letter to a friend she met at overnight camp.

- Natalie is making a display for her poetry. First she uses a calligraphy pen to copy her poems. Then she uses an X-acto knife to mat the copies on heavy board.

- George and Aseem set up the volleyball net on the far end of the field. They are teaching some younger children how to serve.

- Melinda and JoWanda are leading a "Double Dutch" jump rope contest outside on the blacktop.

- Ben, Kelly, and Marcia are sorting clothes and toys the program collected for a homeless shelter. Later in the week several children will help to deliver the items.

- Nicky and Meredith are using poster board, fabric scraps, and other collage materials to design a new line of kids' fashions.

- Wayne and Haki are signing out to go to a mime class offered by a local acting company. The school-age staff coordinated with the children's families so the boys could take advantage of this community resource.

Observe how the 11- to 12-year-olds in your program use the environment, and list some examples below.

_____

_____

_____

_____

_____

_____

Based on your observations, what changes would you like to make in the environment to address the needs of 11- to 12-year-olds?

_____

_____

_____

_____

_____

_____

_____

_____

Discuss with your trainer and your colleagues what changes you should make in your environment to make sure it addresses the needs of children of different ages.

Learning Activity II.
Creating an Indoor Environment

IN THIS ACTIVITY YOU WILL LEARN TO:

- plan and set up interest areas in the indoor environment; and

- create an environment in shared space.

Establishing Interest Areas

Many school-age programs divide their environments into interest areas—clearly defined spaces with materials and equipment focused on a theme or type of activity. This is done for several reasons. It structures the environment so children can choose their own activities. It also gives them the freedom to work and play alone or with a small group of friends. Well-organized and inviting interest areas allow children to engage in activities with little help or assistance. This frees staff to support and encourage children who do need attention and assistance.

Popular interest areas are available every day.

Regardless of the size or shape of your program's environment, you can set up interest areas. In a large room the areas can be relatively permanent, defined by architectural features and furniture. In smaller rooms, some areas may remain in place throughout the year, while others are created by using rolling carts, baskets, or boxes to store and display materials. Even programs that share space and must set up and take down each day can create interest areas. Suggestions for creating an environment in shared space are discussed later in this learning activity.

In deciding which interest areas to create in your program, consider the number, ages, and interests of the children enrolled; size and characteristics of your space; and requirements related to sharing space. Some interest areas, such as the arts and crafts area, are so popular they should be available every day. Others, such as a collections area, can be established in response to children's interests and left up until children have moved on to other endeavors. Sub-areas can also address special interests. For example, a basket of materials and books on tie-dying could be a sub-area within the arts and crafts area.

Some popular interest areas are described below. Discuss with your colleagues which ones are priorities for your program.

The **Board and Table Games Area** includes board and card games, puzzles, word games, crossword puzzles, and other small games. There are tables and chairs and protected space on the floor for playing games. Materials for inventing and making new games and puzzles are stored on a shelf or in a box or basket. Board and table games allow children to develop the skills needed to work and play cooperatively with others. Most younger children enjoy simple games that are played for 20 to 30 minutes. These games can be rotated every few weeks to give children new options. Older children prefer more complex games that take a long time to play. They may play challenging games such as chess and backgammon daily, over a long period of time, gradually mastering the skills involved.

The **Quiet Area** is located near a good source of light for doing homework and reading. It is an inviting, comfortable, restful place where children can read, relax, do homework, play paper-and-pencil and blackboard games, use a computer, listen quietly to music or recorded stories, or talk with a friend. This area is stocked with materials such as paper, pens, pencils, erasers, index cards, rulers, computer programs, and a wide variety of books and magazines.

The **Large-Group Activity Area** is located away from quiet activities with lots of space for children to move freely. This flexible area is used for gross motor activities, meetings, play rehearsals, dancing, and performances. (Clubs may meet here or in other areas, such as science and nature, math, or arts and crafts). Some programs have access to a gymnasium or separate room for these activities. Because a variety of activities take place here, there is ample storage for props and costumes, club supplies, musical instruments, and CD and tape players.

The **Blocks and Construction Area** is located in a well-protected space, out of the line of traffic. Shelves define the area and a flat carpet provides a smooth surface for building. Ideally, structures can be saved from one day to the next. Blocks of different sizes and types (e.g., unit blocks and Legos), construction materials (e.g., Lincoln logs), and props (e.g., small cars and trucks) are stored on open shelves. Block building encourages children to think, play, and solve problems. They learn about sizes and shapes and how to cooperate as they plan and carry out their ideas. Unit blocks help children grasp basic mathematical concepts. Some children build complex structures and play with them for several days. A sub-area can provide materials for creating huts, hideaways, caves, and tents children can use in dramatic play.

The **House Corner** is defined by shelves and furniture. It is equipped with props and materials that encourage imaginative play. Because the family is so important to them, younger children especially enjoy a house corner filled with familiar objects. If your program doesn't have many younger children, or if the children begin to outgrow or tire of this kind of play, you can dismantle the area or create a dramatic play area with a broader range of props and costumes.

The **Long-Term Project and Hobby Area** is located in a protected place with shelves and tables for storing and displaying children's ongoing projects. This area is a must if older children are enrolled in your program. They have the skills and attention spans to carry out projects over a long period of time.

The **Dramatic Play Area** is stocked with prop boxes that encourage play around a specific theme such as a travel agency, veterinarian's office, or a television station. (See Module 9, Social, for a discussion on prop boxes.) This area might focus on a specific theme for several weeks. Older children especially enjoy developing a total environment around a theme of their choice. For example, they might create a mini-mall with different shops "selling" things made by the children. Other children could purchase items with pretend money.

The **Arts and Crafts Area** is located near the sink and has a washable (rather than carpeted) floor. It includes easels and a table and chairs. Basic art supplies such as paper, glue, scissors, paint, and markers are within easy reach on a nearby shelf. Children use art materials to express ideas and feelings and to explore their creativity. Craft projects help develop small muscle coordination. Sub-areas (rotated if space is limited) encourage children to explore modeling and carving, sculpting, collage making, weaving and stitchery, printing, and batik and tie-dye.

The **Sand and Water Area** adds softness and sensory experiences to the environment. Younger children especially enjoy this area; sand and water are very calming materials. Located near the sink and away from carpeting, it includes a sand and water table and a variety of props children use to explore the properties of these natural materials. You don't need more than two inches of sand or water to make this a great activity. If space is limited or shared, or if only a few younger children are enrolled, you can use a small, light table on wheels.

The **Science and Nature Area** is located near windows and the sink. It is a place to set up experiments, observe and learn about animals, and display collections and special items, such as a snake's molted skin or an abandoned hornet's nest. If space allows, this area can include basic materials and supplies for exploring science (for example, tools and items for measuring, weighing, magnifying, examining, and taking apart). Every few weeks, new materials, equipment, and experiments can be introduced to keep interests alive. The area allows children to investigate and think about nature and the environment and encourages them to become involved in community projects. Older children may become engrossed in long-term projects for many weeks. Sub-areas might include: natural science, physical science, and club projects such as inventions, pet care, or how things work.

If space is limited, you can establish interest areas such as the following on a rotating basis.

The **Woodworking Area** includes a workbench set up outdoors or indoors, with a variety of simple tools, safety equipment, wood scraps, and books of suggested projects. It is located near other noisy activity areas and is constantly supervised when in use. This area provides hands-on, practical learning opportunities.

The **Music Area** includes instruments, music books, CD and tape players, and CDs and tapes representing a wide range of musical styles, including music from different cultures. When space is limited, equipment and supplies can be stored in a closet or wheeled shelving unit and used in the large-group activity area. This area encourages children to use their imaginations as they explore and express their feelings through singing, dancing, listening to, and creating music. Music activities also help children develop small and large muscle coordination.

The **Math Area** includes graph and plain paper, pencils, measuring tools, calculators, small blocks, and Cuisenaire rods for children to use in problem solving. It provides many opportunities to test thinking capacities. To minimize distractions and interruptions, it is helpful to locate this area near other quiet activities. The math area can be a useful resource for children in the blocks and construction and science and nature areas.

The **Collection Area** provides a safe space where children can categorize, store, and display items related to their special interests. As children become more independent, collections are an excellent way for them to work on their own projects. A Collections Club can accommodate a wide range of interests. The club might have rotating monthly exhibits—Tony's rocks this month and Regan's toys from foreign lands next month. If you don't have room for a separate collection area, you can have sub-areas in other interest areas (for example, arts and crafts or science and nature).

The next step is deciding where to set up your interest areas. Careful placement of your interest areas will make it possible for children to work and play without disturbing each other.

Some interest areas can be rotated.

Try these suggestions for arranging interest areas.

- Separate quiet areas (such as arts and crafts and board and table games) from noisier ones (such as blocks and construction and dramatic play).

- Store materials that are used together near each other—collage materials near glue and paper, reference books and writing supplies in the quiet area, small vehicles with the blocks.

- Define the boundaries of each area using shelves, furniture, different floor coverings, and room dividers. In shared space, children can help to define interest areas each day by laying out carpet squares, using masking tape to mark boundaries, or setting up large blocks or cardboard building materials.

- Locate areas near the resources children need to carry out their plans. For example, place the science and nature area near light and water so children can conduct experiments such as growing plants or hanging prisms that make rainbows.

- Set up the quiet area where there is a good source of light for writing, using the computer, and reading.

Suggested materials for each interest area are provided in the next learning activity.

Creating an Environment in Shared Space

Your program may be housed in shared space such as a multipurpose room, gymnasium, cafeteria, or recreation center, or you may share your space with another part-day child development program. Even if the space is used for other purposes before and after program hours, your environment should make children feel as if it's designed for them while they're using it.

As discussed earlier, programs held in shared space can include a variety of interest areas. Begin by viewing interest areas as well-organized, portable modules or kits that can be set up quickly and stored easily. It will not be feasible to set up every interest area each day; however, you can develop a number of modules or kits to combine in different ways to keep the program varied and stimulating. Try to also put out materials that give the program a homelike, relaxed feeling (for example, beanbag chairs or cushions, small rugs, or carpet squares).

Sharing space will influence your choice of supplies, equipment, and room arrangement. Before you make these choices take time to gather information about your space and other parts of the facility used by the program. Answering the following questions will help you learn more about your shared space.[1]

- What is the size and shape of the space? Where in the building is it located? Do you have access to other areas? If so, where are they located?

- What other groups use the space? When?

- How can the different groups using the space have **regular** and **direct** communication with each other?

- Can some program equipment remain permanently set up, or must everything be dismantled daily?

- What storage area is available? How large is it? How close is it to the space where most program activities take place?

- What furniture and supplies are already in the space? Are any of these "off limits" to the school-age program?

Most programs that share space need to create and dismantle the environment each day. Include ample time in your schedule for staff and children to complete this process. Certain types of furniture and equipment can be set up, taken down, moved around, and stored with relative ease in a short amount of time. The following list of equipment, furniture, and supplies will help you plan an appropriate environment in shared space. For each item listed, there is a description of why it is suitable for shared space and how it might be used. All of the items are available commercially; however, a volunteer with carpentry skills could make low-cost versions of some of them.

Take time to identify the best equipment, furniture, and supplies for shared space.

Before making final decisions about what furniture and equipment best suit your program's needs, review your answers to the planning questions listed earlier. Keep in mind your goal is to select items that will help you create a rich and varied program for the children.

[1] Adapted with permission from Roberta Newman, *Presto Environments in Shared Space, Keys to Quality in School-Age Child Care Viewer's Guide for School-Age Professionals* (Rockville, MD: Montgomery County Public Schools Television Foundation, Inc., 1993), pp. 98–107.

Equipment, Furniture, and Supplies for Shared Space

Basic Equipment and Furniture

Item	Description	Suggested Uses
Tables	Sturdy and light: -rectangular (3' x 6' or 3' x 8') -round -fold-out type -wooden with wheels	Play games, do homework, work on crafts Eat meals and snack Display projects Use audiovisual and other equipment Store materials underneath (camouflage with cloth) Create a staff administrative area
Chairs	Stack on a wheeled base Folding	Define areas for relaxation and work Store coats, books, and personal belongings Sit down
Shelves	No more than two to four shelves per unit (higher units limit visibility and may be unsafe): -wooden with pegboard, on wheels -open-up cabinet type	Create borders to define and contain supplies for interest areas Divide the room (cover backs with attractive, sturdy material) Store staff supplies (face open shelves to wall or cover with a curtain)
Cabinets	With built-in or attached locks: -wooden on wheels -metal on rolling base	Store supplies Divide the room Create displays (front or back)
Cubbies	Wooden units on wheels with sections (most have 10 to 30 sections) large enough for coats and books	Screen, hide, or protect storage areas Divide the room Create displays (on the back) Hang coats and store belongings
Roll carts	Metal on wheels with two to three shelves	Transport equipment and supplies from storage to rooms Set up moveable interest areas Store heavy equipment such as stereos
Storage bins	Cardboard, plastic, or wooden crates with tops for easy storage/stacking Labeled to store related items together	Store materials for interest areas Store supplies Transport supplies

Equipment and Supplies to Make the Space Attractive and Comfortable

Item	Description	Suggested Uses
Bean bag chair, large pillows, or mattress	Light versions that hold one to two children, are sturdy, comfortable, durable, and washable Single-size mattress with attractive, sturdy, washable cover	Create a home-like, comfortable environment Add softness to the room Encourage children to socialize, listen to music, and play quiet games
Area Rugs*	Low pile with pads underneath Large enough for a few children to sit on, but small enough to carry to and from storage areas if necessary	Create softness and warmth Encourage children to use the space Create an area for relaxing Cut down noise levels
Curtains*	Shower curtains or fabric hung from a dowel rod attached to the ceiling or window, or hung between large pieces of portable furniture	Create a soft feeling Define boundaries in the room
Styrofoam sheets	Light insulation sheeting in 2' x 3', 3' x 5', or 4' x 6' sizes	Create bulletin boards (use push pins to hang items) Screen storage areas Create more private areas
Tri-Wall cardboard	Sheets of thick, sturdy, corrugated cardboard	Create room dividers (designed, built, and decorated by the children) Make clubhouses or private nooks (again, created by the children) Build constructions Create bulletin boards (use push pins to hang items)
Blocks	Large, hollow cardboard or wooden blocks	Create private areas Define interest areas

*Check your local fire regulations to make sure these items are permitted in your space.

Applying Your Knowledge

In this learning activity you will review two different room arrangements for school-age programs and identify the strengths and weaknesses of each. Then draw a plan of your own indoor space and decide on what changes you want to make to improve the environment.

Room Arrangements

Using the guidelines for arranging indoor space, identify the strengths and weaknesses of Floor Plan A.

Floor Plan A

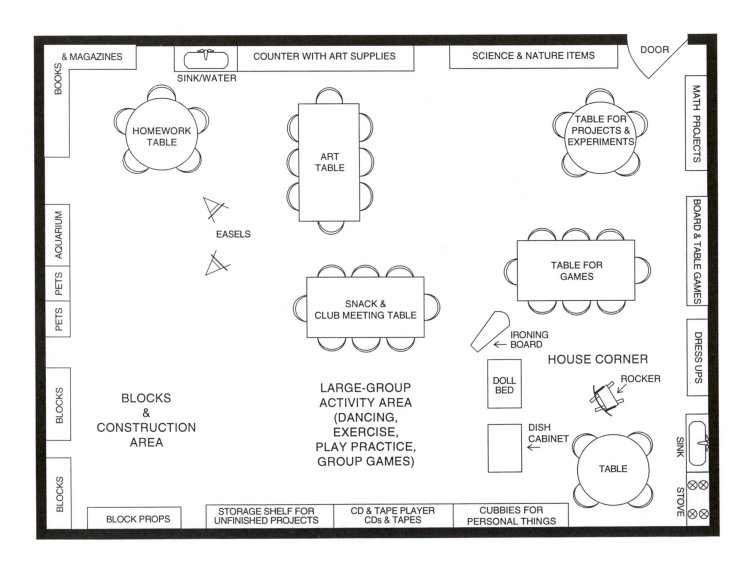

Strengths:

_____

_____

_____

_____

_____

_____

_____

_____

_____

_____

_____

Weaknesses:

_____

_____

_____

_____

_____

_____

_____

_____

_____

_____

_____

Now look at Floor Plan B, which shows the same room rearranged. What is different? In what ways is this arrangement better?

Floor Plan B

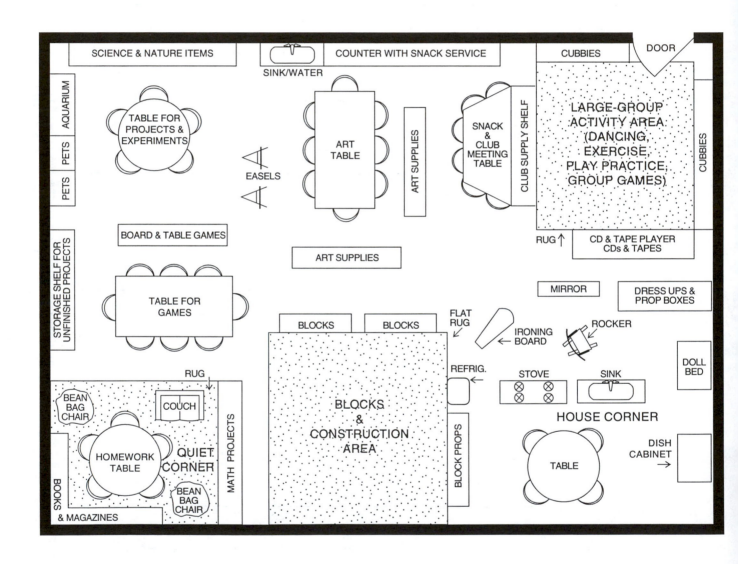

Differences in Floor Plan B:

_____

_____

_____

_____

_____

_____

_____

_____

_____

_____

_____

How is Plan B better?

_____

_____

_____

_____

_____

_____

_____

_____

_____

_____

_____

Compare your answers to those on the answer sheet at the end of this module.

Use the space below to draw a plan of your indoor space as it is now. Include all areas that are available to you, even if you cannot use them every day. Also include fixed items, especially if you share space and cannot rearrange these items. Use additional paper if necessary.

Current Floor Plan

On the basis of what you've learned, what changes do you want to make?

_____

_____

_____

_____

_____

What special challenges would you face in making these changes?

_____

_____

_____

_____

_____

Now, redo your plan, showing how you want to rearrange your space. Even in shared space, the basic principles of arranging interest areas apply. Whatever special challenges your space offers, try to think of ways to set up and arrange the space to accommodate children's interests and needs.

Before your final version, you may want to experiment with different arrangements. An easy way to do this is to use graph paper marked with the dimensions of your space (for example, one square = one square foot) and its special features (for example, windows, electrical outlets, sink, and closets). Then, using the same scale, cut out small pieces for furniture and equipment. This allows you to move the pieces around on the paper to find the best possible arrangement for your space. This will save a lot of time in the long run, because you won't have to actually move large pieces of equipment to find out whether they will fit in the space you intended. Working with scale models will also help you decide where to place equipment such as CD players or aquariums that need electrical outlets.

Revised Floor Plan

Discuss your revised floor plan with your trainer and colleagues who use the same space. Decide what changes you will make.

Learning Activity III.
Using the Outdoor Environment

IN THIS ACTIVITY YOU WILL LEARN TO:

- organize the outdoor environment by interest areas; and

- determine what materials and equipment are needed to improve your program's outdoor environment.

Whether your program operates in a school immediately adjacent to playgrounds and ball fields, a recreation center located next to a neighborhood park, or an apartment complex surrounded by parking lots, children should be allowed to play outdoors. For some children, it may be their only chance to get fresh air, stretch their muscles, and explore the outdoor world. Some schools have a very short recess or none at all. By the time children get home from the program, it may be too late and too dark to play outdoors. Weekends may be filled with family activities. And, in some neighborhoods, violence, drug and alcohol abuse, and criminal activities are so prevalent, there are no outdoor areas where children can play safely.

The school-age program may provide children with their only opportunities to be outdoors.

The most effective outdoor environments for school-age children support a wide range of activities. There is a large area for ball games, equipment for climbing and other large muscle activities, and space for construction and digging activities. There is also room to set up activities typically done indoors. For example, children can play board games, eat snack, model with clay or playdough, or listen to music outdoors.

If at all possible, the outdoor environment should include the following:

Does your outdoor environment include these features?

- easy access to and from the indoor space used by the program;

- a drinking fountain and water spigot for attaching a hose;

- nearby bathrooms;

- a storage shed outdoors or indoors, near the door to the outdoor area;

- soft materials such as sawdust, sand, or bark under swings, slides, and climbers;

- a paved or hard-surfaced area for riding, skating, chalk drawings, and games;

- a covered area for use in wet weather;

- sunny areas;

- shady areas;

- places to be alone or with one or two friends (boxes, tents, logs, bushes);

- open, grassy spaces for tumbling, running, and sitting; and

- ball fields for active or group play.

Outdoor interest areas allow for many different kinds of play.

Like the indoor environment, the outdoor space used by school-age programs can be organized by interest areas that provide a variety of materials and activities. Active play areas are located near each other and separated from the quiet ones. There are clear pathways and enough space between areas to avoid crowding and accidents. Equipment and materials used in the interest areas are kept in a storage shed or brought outdoors from the indoor space. Examples of outdoor interest areas include the following:

- Large Muscle (the playground equipment includes swings, slides, and climbers)

- Science and Nature (activity kits are kept in the storage shed and used to explore the plant and animal life present in the outdoor space)

- Woodworking (a bench is set up in an area away from active games and sports, tools are kept in the storage shed)

- Gardening (a vegetable garden is in a sunny spot near the building, tools and a hose are kept in the storage shed, an outside spigot provides water)

- Sports and Active Games (there is a large field and an outdoor basketball court; balls, equipment, and rule books are kept in the storage shed)

- Construction (saw horses, boxes, planks, tires, and boards are located on the grassy area next to the playground equipment)

- Sand Play (a covered sandbox is next to the playground equipment, digging tools and a variety of props are kept in the storage shed)

- Reading and Quiet Games (a picnic table with two benches sits under a shady tree, away from the noise and hubbub, books come from indoors, cards and small games are kept in the storage shed)

- Riding and Skating (a section of the paved surface is marked with safety cones, bikes, skates, and safety gear are kept in the storage shed)

- Jumping Rope (a section of the paved surface is marked with safety cones; ropes and books of jump rope jingles are kept in the storage shed)

- Arts and Crafts (easels, paper, paints, and brushes are carried from indoors to a designated area of the blacktop; tote boxes filled with craft supplies are kept in the storage shed; there is a picnic table with benches)

- Water Play (the water table and props are carried from indoors to an area of the blacktop near the water spigot; on hot days a sprinkler is set up on the grass)

- Club Meetings (several sizes of cable spools from the telephone company are set up on the grass under a tree; materials are kept in the storage shed brought from indoors)

An ideal school-age program environment allows children to move between the indoor and outdoor areas, participating in activities of their own choosing. The schedule doesn't include a set time to go outdoors, because the outdoor area is always staffed and available for children's use. If your outdoor area is not immediately adjacent to the building, your program schedule may have a set time, when interested children, accompanied by assigned staff, go outdoors and choose from a variety of activities or plan and carry out their own. You will want to encourage all children to spend some time outdoors; however, they should be allowed to stay indoors if that is their choice for the day.

Some children (and staff) don't like to go outdoors because they think it is too cold or too hot. They prefer to stay indoors where the temperature is at a constant level. Children and staff will feel more comfortable outdoors if they are dressed appropriately for the weather. On cold days this includes dressing in layers (long sleeve shirt, sweater, and coat), and wearing a hat and gloves or mittens. On warm days, dress in loose clothing, made from light fabrics, and perhaps wear a hat with a visor. You can keep on hand a box of extra clothes—loose t-shirts, shorts, and baseball caps in the summer; and scarves, hats, gloves, and sweaters in the winter. Remember, you are a model for the children in the program. If you dress appropriately and enjoy spending time outdoors, children are more likely to follow your lead.

Children and staff need to dress for the weather.

Applying Your Knowledge

In this learning activity you and a small group of children (2 to 3) use a checklist to take an inventory of the materials and equipment your program provides for the outdoor environment. When you come to items on the checklist that your program doesn't have, ask the children if they think you should add them to your inventory. There is also space to suggest additional items you and the children think would enhance everyone's enjoyment of the outdoor environment.

When you have completed the checklist, invite the children to meet with you, your colleagues, and the director to pass on your recommendations for improving the outdoor environment.

Materials and Equipment Checklist for the Outdoor Environment*

Date: _____

Children: _____

Physical Activities

- ☐ Bats
- ☐ Balance beam
- ☐ Hoops
- ☐ Swings
- ☐ Roller skates
- ☐ Ice and/or roller skates
- ☐ Yo-yos
- ☐ Street hockey sticks and pucks
- ☐ Wagons and carts
- ☐ Tumbling mats
- ☐ Balls (playground and specific sports)
- ☐ Tunnels
- ☐ Knotted rope
- ☐ Seesaws
- ☐ Safety helmets and pads (for skating, bike riding, and street hockey)
- ☐ Safety cones to designate areas for riding, skating, or playing hockey
- ☐ _____
- ☐ _____
- ☐ _____

- ☐ Ring toss sets
- ☐ Jump ropes
- ☐ Slides
- ☐ Punching bag
- ☐ Badminton and volleyball equipment
- ☐ Pogo sticks
- ☐ Batons
- ☐ Portable goal net
- ☐ Horse shoes
- ☐ Chalk (for hopscotch)
- ☐ Air pumps for balls
- ☐ Tennis rackets and balls
- ☐ Barrels
- ☐ Platforms
- ☐ Long ropes for "Double Dutch"
- ☐ Pump (to reinflate balls)
- ☐ _____
- ☐ _____
- ☐ _____

Construction

- ☐ Large cartons and crates
- ☐ Large blocks
- ☐ Fabric, wood, or cardboard for "roofing"
- ☐ _____
- ☐ _____
- ☐ _____

- ☐ Large spools
- ☐ Saw horses
- ☐ Boards to extend structures and build ramps
- ☐ _____
- ☐ _____

This list does not include items brought from the indoor interest areas.

Water play

- ☐ Hoses
- ☐ Pails
- ☐ Shallow pans
- ☐ Squeeze bottles
- ☐ Cups
- ☐ Sponges and brushes
- ☐ Soap
- ☐ Dolls and doll clothes
- ☐ _____
- ☐ _____

- ☐ Short lengths of rubber hose
- ☐ Measuring cups
- ☐ Corks
- ☐ Plastic bottles
- ☐ Funnels
- ☐ Egg beaters
- ☐ Tea kettle
- ☐ Sprinkler tops
- ☐ _____
- ☐ _____

Sand play

- ☐ Milk cartons
- ☐ Plastic bottles
- ☐ Gelatin molds
- ☐ Cookie cutters
- ☐ Spoons
- ☐ Dishes
- ☐ Small blocks
- ☐ Ladles
- ☐ Screens
- ☐ Coffee pots
- ☐ Human figures
- ☐ _____
- ☐ _____

- ☐ Plastic food containers
- ☐ Nest of painted cans
- ☐ Muffin tins
- ☐ Pans
- ☐ Cups
- ☐ Watering cans
- ☐ Sieves
- ☐ Pitchers
- ☐ Sifters
- ☐ Sugar scoops
- ☐ Animal figures
- ☐ _____
- ☐ _____

Hot-weather

- ☐ Hoses
- ☐ Buckets
- ☐ _____

- ☐ Pools (must meet safety requirements)
- ☐ Sprinklers
- ☐ _____

Snow

- ☐ Shovels
- ☐ Mallets for breaking ice
- ☐ Forms for making snow bricks
- ☐ _____

- ☐ Snow saucers
- ☐ Sleds
- ☐ _____
- ☐ _____

Discuss the completed checklist with the children who helped you. Schedule a meeting with your colleagues and director so you and the children can pass on your recommendations for improving the outdoor environment.

Learning Activity IV.
Selecting Materials

IN THIS ACTIVITY YOU WILL LEARN TO:

- select materials that are developmentally and culturally appropriate; and

- determine what materials to add to your program's interest areas.

Selecting the right materials for each interest area depends partly on what items are available in your program. Established programs may already have a supply of developmentally appropriate materials and equipment. However, as children's skills and interests are constantly changing, the materials in each area must be regularly updated to provide new challenges and build on current "passions."

Many good materials for school-age children can be recycled from home and community businesses. For example, recycled items might include dress-up clothes; dramatic play props; fabric scraps, yarn, buttons, and wallpaper and paint samples for the arts and crafts area; collections for the science table; and back issues of sports, hobby, and other magazines for the quiet area. Also, excellent materials and games can be made—by staff, by volunteer parents, and by the children.

In selecting materials for your program, consider the following questions:

Consider the following when selecting materials.

Will it interest the children? Your daily observations of the children will help you identify special interests. Ask them what they like to do and pick up cues from their conversations with each other. You might also invite children to take turns helping to plan the activities for the next week or month or include a weekly evaluation and planning discussion in a group meeting. Children who can write might use a suggestion box to let you know their ideas for new materials and activities.

Do the children have the skills to handle the material? For example, does 7-year-old Sara have the coordination needed to use a crochet hook or serve a volleyball? Does 9-year-old Derek have the thinking skills to do crossword puzzles or play chess and other complex games of strategy?

Will it challenge children to think and explore? For example, weaving with natural items—grasses, feathers, twigs and other items found in nature—may be more interesting than using yarn and other commercial supplies. While working with these materials, children may also explore how people in different countries and cultures use natural materials for both practical and decorative purposes.

Does the material reflect the children's ethnicity, show people with disabilities engaged in meaningful tasks, or allow both boys and girls to see themselves in nonstereotyped roles? For example, books and magazines, puppets, and posters should reflect the diversity of our society and help children value and respect these differences. The arts and crafts area should have varied colors of paints, papers, crayons, and markers so children can easily paint and draw people with different skin tones.

Is the item durable and in good condition? This means it has no broken parts or missing pieces and will stand up to heavy use by many children. Materials should be clean and free of splinters or any jagged edges.

Does it help achieve your goals for children? For example, will it help children develop creativity? Practice independence? Learn to solve problems? Use language skills? Explore a special interest? Express humor? Develop small and large muscle control? Connect children with the community?

Although you can answer the last question now, you may want to review and expand your answer after you have completed Modules 4 through 10. These modules include many ideas for selecting materials that promote children's creativity and physical, cognitive, social, and language development.

Applying Your Knowledge

In this learning activity you use a checklist to identify the materials and equipment in your program's interest areas. There is space to suggest additional items you think would enhance the areas.

Materials Checklist for Indoor Interest Areas

House Corner

Equipment and Furniture

☐ Stove
☐ Dish cabinet
☐ Highchair
☐ Ironing board
☐ Small table and three to four chairs
☐ Place to hang dress-up clothes

☐ _____
☐ _____

☐ Sink
☐ Refrigerator
☐ Rocking chair
☐ Mirror—full-length
☐ Bed for small doll
☐ _____

☐ _____
☐ _____

Props and Materials

☐ Dishes
☐ Standard pots and pans
☐ Silverware
☐ Cooking utensils
☐ Apron (for man or woman)
☐ Pot holders
☐ Plastic flowers
☐ Tablecloth or mats
☐ Items that reflect diverse cultures

☐ _____
☐ _____

☐ Telephones (at least two)
☐ Jewelry
☐ Suitcases and purses
☐ Hats
☐ Shoes
☐ Dress-up clothes (male and female)
☐ Plastic fruits, vegetables, and foods
☐ Empty food containers
☐ Dolls (reflecting children's ethnic backgrounds) and doll clothes

☐ _____
☐ _____

Dramatic Play Area

☐ Costumes
☐ Books of simple plays
☐ Miscellaneous props for plays
☐ Prop boxes related to specific themes (e.g., travel agent, magic show, auto mechanic, fitness club)

☐ _____
☐ _____

☐ Puppets
☐ Materials for making more puppets
☐ Clothes, shoes, scarves, hats, gloves
☐ Props related to history and geography (e.g., Alaska, The Roaring Twenties, The Year 2010)

☐ _____
☐ _____

Board and Table Games Area

- [ ] Shelf for displaying games and puzzles
- [ ] Table with five to eight mid-sized chairs
- [ ] Table to save puzzles or games that take more than a day to complete
- [ ] Cardboard, tape, scissors, markers, and other items for making games and puzzles
- [ ] Puzzles of varying levels of complexity
- [ ] _____
- [ ] _____
- [ ] _____

- [ ] Jacks and pick-up sticks
- [ ] Crossword puzzles and word games
- [ ] Playing cards (standard deck and specialized games for different ages)
- [ ] Board games of varying levels of difficulty, such as Candyland, Chutes and Ladders, Sorry, Connect Four, Monopoly, Scrabble, trivia games, chess, checkers, and backgammon
- [ ] _____
- [ ] _____

Math Area

- [ ] Table or shelf for displays and games
- [ ] Pegs and pegboards
- [ ] Beads and laces
- [ ] Colored inch cube blocks
- [ ] Legos
- [ ] Geo set
- [ ] Calculators
- [ ] _____
- [ ] _____
- [ ] _____

- [ ] Rulers, yardsticks, measuring tapes, and meter sticks
- [ ] Abacus
- [ ] Parquetry blocks
- [ ] Attribute blocks
- [ ] Cuisenaire rods
- [ ] Magnetic board and numbers
- [ ] Paper and pencils
- [ ] _____
- [ ] _____

Blocks and Construction Area

- [ ] Storage shelves (preferably two)
- [ ] Complete set of unit blocks
- [ ] Lincoln logs
- [ ] Wood or rubber people and animals
- [ ] Large hollow blocks
- [ ] Sheets of cardboard or Tri-Wall board
- [ ] Crates, large boxes, or appliance cartons
- [ ] Sheets or large pieces of fabric for tents, caves, or clubhouses, and "roofing."
- [ ] _____
- [ ] _____

- [ ] Small cars and trucks
- [ ] Small blocks (Legos, Bristle Blocks)
- [ ] Traffic signs
- [ ] Giant paper fasteners
- [ ] Tarps
- [ ] Boards
- [ ] Colored inch cube blocks
- [ ] _____
- [ ] _____
- [ ] _____

Arts and Crafts Area

General

- ☐ Table with five to eight mid-sized chairs
- ☐ Storage shelves or cabinets
- ☐ Easel (two-sided)
- ☐ Paint holders
- ☐ Water-based paint in a range of colors
- ☐ Finger paint
- ☐ Water color sets
- ☐ Water-based markers
- ☐ Colored chalks
- ☐ Crayons in a wide variety of colors
- ☐ Long and short handled easel paintbrushes
- ☐ Scissors
- ☐ Rubber cement
- ☐ Stapler
- ☐ Playdough and utensils
- ☐ Collage items
- ☐ _____
- ☐ _____

- ☐ Paper cutter
- ☐ Easel paper
- ☐ Finger paint paper
- ☐ Drawing paper
- ☐ Butcher paper for murals
- ☐ Tissue paper
- ☐ Construction paper
- ☐ Crepe paper
- ☐ Felt scraps
- ☐ Poster board
- ☐ Burlap
- ☐ Needles with large eyes and thick yarn
- ☐ Glue
- ☐ Glitter
- ☐ Sponges for cleanup
- ☐ Oilcloth to protect table
- ☐ _____
- ☐ _____

Drawing and Painting

- ☐ Acrylics
- ☐ Pastels
- ☐ Felt pens
- ☐ Calligraphy pens
- ☐ _____

- ☐ Chalks
- ☐ Charcoal
- ☐ Drawing pencils
- ☐ Colored inks
- ☐ _____

Modeling and Carving

- ☐ Oil-based clays
- ☐ Aluminum foil
- ☐ Soap stone
- ☐ Newspaper
- ☐ _____
- ☐ _____

- ☐ Moist clays
- ☐ Soap flakes
- ☐ Plaster of Paris
- ☐ Wheat paste
- ☐ _____
- ☐ _____

Sculpting

- ☐ Wire
- ☐ Glue
- ☐ Pipe cleaners
- ☐ _____
- ☐ _____

- ☐ Wood scraps
- ☐ Metal scraps
- ☐ Styrofoam pieces
- ☐ _____
- ☐ _____

Collages, Weaving, and Stitchery

- ☐ Yarns (knitting, rug, and weaving)
- ☐ Mesh backings
- ☐ Frames and hand looms
- ☐ Hooks (crocheting and rug making)
- ☐ Fabric scraps
- ☐ Stuffing (scraps or white polyester)
- ☐ Buttons
- ☐ Toothpicks
- ☐ Cotton balls
- ☐ Pods
- ☐ Weeds and grasses
- ☐ Mosses
- ☐ Shells
- ☐ Pine cones
- ☐ _____

- ☐ Papers
- ☐ Needles (knitting and sewing)
- ☐ Beads and beading needles
- ☐ Ribbons
- ☐ Felt
- ☐ Rickrack
- ☐ Leather and fur scraps
- ☐ Thread (sewing and embroidery)
- ☐ Hooks and eyes, snaps
- ☐ Seeds
- ☐ Twigs and branches
- ☐ Leaves and bark
- ☐ Feathers
- ☐ Acorns
- ☐ _____

Batik and Tie-Dye

- ☐ Dyes
- ☐ Basins
- ☐ String
- ☐ Drying rack
- ☐ _____

- ☐ Paraffin
- ☐ Dyeable fabric pieces (not polyester)
- ☐ Rubber bands
- ☐ Books with suggested designs
- ☐ _____

Quiet Area

- ☐ Soft carpeting
- ☐ Small table with three to five chairs
- ☐ Tape or CD player with headphones
- ☐ Tapes and CDs
- ☐ Writing supplies (paper, pens, pencils, erasers)
- ☐ Books (a variety of fiction and non-fiction that reflect children's abilities and interests and depict characters without using stereotypes)
- ☐ Current events board (maintained by children) for community, sports, and music news and scheduled events
- ☐ Several large pillows, beanbag chairs, or an easy chair
- ☐ Decorations (a plant, pictures, or posters)
- ☐ _____

- ☐ Dictionaries
- ☐ *Guinness Book of World Records*
- ☐ *World Almanac*
- ☐ Local newspaper
- ☐ Local, U. S., and world maps
- ☐ Globe or national and international atlases
- ☐ Computer and a variety of software (may also be in math, science, or large-group activity area, depending on how it's used)
- ☐ Magazine on topics of interest to children (e.g., sports, cars, music, pets, hiking, fitness, animals)
- ☐ Flannel board, puppets, and props for storytelling, role playing, and problem solving
- ☐ Display shelves for books and magazines (at least one that shows front covers)
- ☐ _____

Large-Group Activity Area

- ☐ Table with six to eight mid-sized chairs for holding club meetings
- ☐ Balance beam
- ☐ Loft with a ladder
- ☐ Song books
- ☐ Fancy dress-up clothes
- ☐ Hats
- ☐ Cardboard cartons or Tri-wall for building simple stage sets
- ☐ Storage space for supplies used on a rotating basis
- ☐ Tapes and CDs (popular, ethnic, classical, jazz, folk, and traditional children's songs and dancing games)
- ☐ _____

- ☐ Large flat rug to make dancing and other exercises more comfortable
- ☐ Large indoor climber
- ☐ Tumbling mats
- ☐ Books on cooperative indoor games
- ☐ Capes
- ☐ Dance costumes
- ☐ Beanbags, foam balls, and other items for indoor games
- ☐ Tape or CD player for dancing, singing, exercise, and drama
- ☐ Scarves, streamers, hula hoops, jump ropes, pom-poms, and other items for dancing and exercise
- ☐ _____

Sand and Water Area

- ☐ Sand/water table (small or large)
- ☐ Shelf or box for equipment
- ☐ Plastic squeeze bottles
- ☐ Plastic pitchers
- ☐ Plastic hoses
- ☐ Plastic tubing
- ☐ Plastic sifters and beach toys
- ☐ _____

- ☐ Basins to hold sand and water
- ☐ Waterproof aprons
- ☐ Funnels
- ☐ Plastic basters or eye droppers
- ☐ Plastic boats
- ☐ Plastic measuring cups
- ☐ Sponges and mops for cleanup
- ☐ _____

Science and Nature Area

General

- ☐ Table
- ☐ Hand lenses
- ☐ Containers (basins, jars, cans, cartons, trays)
- ☐ Rulers and yardsticks
- ☐ Balance scales
- ☐ Access to water
- ☐ Old clocks, radios, and machines
- ☐ Reference materials (books, magazines, charts, and posters) related to current projects and displays
- ☐ Mallets and tools for taking things apart and/or exploring their insides
- ☐ _____
- ☐ _____

- ☐ Shelves
- ☐ Microscope and slides
- ☐ Notebooks and pencils
- ☐ Tape measures
- ☐ Egg and clock timers
- ☐ Hotplate or electric skillet
- ☐ Rocks, seeds, and nuts to take apart
- ☐ Tools (trowels, beaters, sieves, measuring cups, scissors, mixing utensils, pitchers, clippers, pumps)
- ☐ _____
- ☐ _____
- ☐ _____

Natural Science

- ☐ Ant farm
- ☐ Terrarium with glass cover
- ☐ Insect nets and boxes
- ☐ Cages with removable bottoms for pets or visiting animals (if allowed)
- ☐ Pets and supplies for their care
- ☐ _____

- ☐ Aquarium
- ☐ Bird feeders
- ☐ Collection containers
- ☐ Plastic bags for viewing insects, sand, earth, and water
- ☐ Gardening containers, weeds, soil, and tools
- ☐ _____

Physical Science

- ☐ Pendulums
- ☐ Prisms and crystals
- ☐ Mirrors
- ☐ Thermometers (indoor and outdoor)
- ☐ Electric bells with wires and dry cells
- ☐ Basins
- ☐ Bubble pipes
- ☐ Gelatin
- ☐ Hose pieces
- ☐ Magnetic compass
- ☐ Bicycle pump
- ☐ Oil, colorings, and powders for water experiments
- ☐ _____

- ☐ Batteries
- ☐ Magnets and related objects
- ☐ Balloons
- ☐ Barometer
- ☐ Photography kit
- ☐ Basters
- ☐ Straws
- ☐ Salt
- ☐ Astronomy kit
- ☐ Weather vane
- ☐ Tuning fork
- ☐ _____
- ☐ _____

Woodworking Area

- ☐ Sturdy workbench
- ☐ Pegboard or shelf for storing tools
- ☐ T-square
- ☐ Saws
- ☐ Hand drill and bits
- ☐ Assorted screws and screw eyes
- ☐ Tri-wall sheets
- ☐ Sandpaper
- ☐ Screwdriver and screws
- ☐ Tongue depressors
- ☐ Books and/or kits with instructions for easy projects—bird houses or feeders, small boxes, musical instruments
- ☐ _____
- ☐ _____

- ☐ Ruler
- ☐ Hammers
- ☐ Assorted nails
- ☐ Vise
- ☐ C-clamps
- ☐ Soft wood (pine and balsa)
- ☐ Dowel rods
- ☐ Wood glue
- ☐ Protective eye goggles
- ☐ Popsicle sticks
- ☐ Bottle caps, wooden wheels, leather scraps, fishing line (for making simple instruments)
- ☐ _____
- ☐ _____

Music Area

- ☐ CD or tape player
- ☐ Scarves and streamers
- ☐ Musical instruments (e.g., tambourines, claves, sticks, castanets, drums, autoharp, ukulele, guitar, electric keyboard), homemade or purchased
- ☐ _____

- ☐ CDs or tapes
- ☐ Storage cabinet or shelves for resources
- ☐ _____
- ☐ _____
- ☐ _____

Collections Area

This area may begin with displays prepared by the staff to get children interested in collecting. From then on, children can collect, research, and display items such as the following:[2]

- ☐ Autographs
- ☐ Bottle caps
- ☐ Coins
- ☐ Decals
- ☐ Flags
- ☐ Jokes
- ☐ License plates
- ☐ Magic tricks
- ☐ Matchbox cars
- ☐ Model cars, trains, planes, ships
- ☐ Patches
- ☐ Postcards
- ☐ Rocks
- ☐ Stamps
- ☐ Trading cards
- ☐ _____
- ☐ _____

- ☐ Bird nests
- ☐ Buttons
- ☐ Comics
- ☐ Dolls
- ☐ Insects
- ☐ Kites
- ☐ Marbles
- ☐ Maps
- ☐ Miniatures
- ☐ Music boxes
- ☐ Puppets
- ☐ Recordings
- ☐ Shells
- ☐ Stickers
- ☐ Travel souvenirs
- ☐ _____
- ☐ _____

Discuss your ideas with your colleagues and trainer. Decide what items you can add to your program's interest areas.

---

[2]Adapted with permission from Judith Bender, Barbara Schuyler-Haas Elder, and Charles H. Flatter, _Half a Childhood: Time for School-Age Child Care_ (Nashville, TN: School-Age NOTES, 1984).

Learning Activity V.
Managing the Day

IN THIS ACTIVITY YOU WILL LEARN TO:

- plan routines and a daily schedule that meet children's needs;

- provide time and space for homework; and

- use a variety of strategies to handle transitions smoothly.

Your program schedule should reflect the children's needs and interests.

The daily schedule defines the events that happen each day at your program. It shows what events take place, in what order, and for how long. What is a good schedule for school-age children? No one schedule will work for all groups and all staff. Each program needs a schedule that reflects its unique circumstances. For example, if a program offers breakfast before school, it must be served early enough for children to eat, clean up, and get ready to go to school. It's also important to allow for flexibility—for example, a planned crafts activity could be postponed if children are eager to go sledding before the snow melts. In addition, the schedule should provide a balance between structure and free choice. Children gain a sense of security from knowing that on most days, events at the program take place in the same order and at the same time. However, because most children have spent the day in a structured school setting, it is also important to plan a schedule that provides many opportunities for children to make choices. The program schedule should allow children to decide what to do, where to do it, with whom to spend time, and what materials to use.

Should homework be included in the program schedule?

Most school-age children receive homework assignments—every day or several times a week. In the early primary grades, homework may be minimal; however, by the time children reach the upper elementary grades, homework assignments can be quite lengthy and, for some children, difficult and frustrating. The decision to offer time and space to do homework at the program raises several issues related to the needs of children and families.

Some school-age professionals believe that homework should not be a part of the daily schedule. They think that it is more important for the program to give children opportunities to engage in different kinds of activities than those they experience in school. Homework should be done at home, they feel, where parents can give children structure and support, keep track of their progress, and congratulate them for their accomplishments.

Other professionals have a different view. They believe that providing time and space for doing homework at the program is a way to support children and families. They believe in offering children a variety of choices—with homework being one of them.

In discussing this issue in your program, it is important to consider the needs of the children and families you serve. Some children do not have a quiet space at home for doing homework and there may be nobody in the family who can provide encouragement and assistance if needed. In addition, some parents come home from work exhausted. By the time they pick up their children from the program, cook dinner, put younger siblings to bed, and do other household chores, there is little time left to answer children's questions about an assignment. The school-age program can provide the structure and support children need to do their homework and succeed in school.

You may encounter some parents who want their children to work on their homework as soon as they arrive at the program and do nothing else until it is finished. They want their children to do well in school and think homework should always come first. In such cases, it is important to explain that most children need a break from academic work after school and benefit from participating in a variety of activities. Some children actually do a better job on their homework after expending energy and engaging in active play. It is best if you can work with the parents and the child to reach a compromise. Perhaps the child can play for an agreed upon length of time before beginning homework, work for a set period of time, or do the assignments for some subjects at the program and for other subjects at home.

If your program does provide an opportunity to do homework, you might find the following suggestions helpful:

Try these suggestions.

- Establish a place in the environment for doing homework. In many programs, the quiet area includes the space and materials children need to work on their assignments. Like any workplace, the area should be well-lit and well-stocked.

- Keep in mind that children have different learning styles. Some learn best through reading, some by listening, some need to be shown how to do something, some need hands-on experiences, and most need a combination of approaches.

- Encourage children to take a break every 15 or 30 minutes. Taking a break relieves stress and helps them do their best work.

- Respect children's individual approaches to doing homework. In her book *Mega Skills,* Dorothy Rich says, "I am more and more convinced that what works for one person does not necessarily work for another. There are those who have to do it standing up, those who do it sitting down, those who need complete quiet, and those who do well studying with lots of background noise."[3]

- Maintain a positive attitude. This lets children know that you think it is important for them to do their homework, and do it well. Try to emphasize quality over speed. Encourage children to take as much time as they need to do their best.

- Remember that homework is a child's responsibility. It is an opportunity for the child to practice and reinforce lessons learned in school and it gives teachers information about the child's skill level. Teachers need to know if an assignment is too simple, too difficult, or just right.

- Resist the temptation to give the correct answer when a child asks for help. First, ask lots of questions and encourage the child to try again: "Can you show me how to set up the problem?" "I think the answer is in the first paragraph. Try reading it again." "Let's do a similar problem together. Then you can try that one again." If the child continues to struggle with the assignment, suggest putting it aside for a while and going on to another one.

- Tell children if you don't know the answer or have no idea how to help. Suggest asking another child for help or asking the teacher at school. Share your observations with the child's parents so they can go over the assignment later and perhaps notify the teacher that their child is having difficulty.

- Offer support that reinforces children's learning. You might quiz a child studying for a test, listen to an oral presentation, read an essay, or discuss a book the child is reading.

- Suggest study tips that help children do their best. For example, introduce the "COPS" method for checking a paper. The child checks the paper four separate times: for Capitalization, Organization, Punctuation, and Spelling. Focusing on a separate item each time helps children catch their own mistakes. You can also show children how to make flash cards to study math facts or vocabulary words.

- Encourage children to apply their thinking and arithmetic skills as they play board games; writing skills when they make up plays and stories; and reading skills when they read a magazine to catch up on the activities of a favorite sports star.

Routines and transitions are also part of the schedule.

In addition to the adult- and child-initiated activities that take place each day, the daily schedule includes routines and transitions. Routines are the daily events that must take place:

---

[3]Dorothy Rich, *MegaSkills* (Boston, MA: Houghton Mifflin Company, 1988), p. 56.

- arriving and leaving;
- eating;
- resting (after kindergarten);
- toileting;
- dressing and undressing to go outdoors (in cool weather); and
- cleaning up.

Some routines involve groups of children—everyone cleans up before school. Others are performed on an individual basis—eating, resting or relaxing, using the bathroom, washing hands. The program should be structured so children can take care of these personal routines according to their own schedules and with little or no adult assistance.

The period of time between one activity and the next is called a transition. Transitions take place when a busload of children arrives from school, a group gets ready to go bowling, or children clean up activities and interest areas at the end of the day. In these situations it is important to plan how to make the transitions go smoothly.

Children can become restless if they have nothing to do while waiting. They sometimes act in ways staff don't like—wrestling with one another or running around the room. This may be because they are bored or excited about the next event.

Here are some suggestions for handling transitions:

Try these suggestions.

- Ask children to walk quietly from one area to another (for example from your room to the gym), on their own or in small groups. Asking children to stand in line usually creates problems because they find it very difficult to stand close together without touching or bumping into each other.

- Lead songs, guessing games, and other activities that need no props with children who are ready before the others. It's helpful to make a list of "back-pocket" ideas you are comfortable leading on the spur of the moment. Put the list on a 3" x 5" index card, laminate it, and keep it with you as a resource for planned transition times and for unexpected emergencies (for example, the bus breaks down on the way to the museum and you have to wait 30 minutes for a replacement).

- Involve children in transition activities such as setting up for meals, collecting the trash, or washing the paint brushes.

- Be flexible whenever possible. Allow children extra time to complete projects or activities when they are very interested and involved. "We're going to let the Drama Club finish their rehearsal while the rest of us start clean up. Then we can all hear their plans for performing at Parent Night next week."

- Allow time for children to share their work before asking them to clean up. This can be especially important if you think other children might like to join the activity or club the next day. You can call a brief meeting or encourage children to look at projects and activities before they are dismantled.

- Establish a signal (for example, blinking lights, a special hand sign, a bell) to let children know you need quiet or that it will be time to clean up in five minutes.

- Play a clapping game when you want to quiet children down so they can listen to you. For example, ask children to follow as you clap out different beats and rhythms.

- Ask older children to make up special songs and chants to sing with the younger ones.

Consider the following criteria in planning your schedule.

An appropriate schedule for school-age programs meets the following criteria:

Before school, children can:

- choose from a number of quiet, short-term activities;
- rest if they are tired;
- have breakfast if they have not eaten at home;
- clean up quickly;
- gather homework and belongings without feeling rushed; and
- participate in transition activities while waiting for the bus.

After kindergarten, children can:

- take care of personal routines—storing belongings, using the bathroom, handwashing;

- eat a relaxed, family-style lunch;

- rest or do quiet activities;

- choose what they want to do; and

- help prepare for the arrival of older children.

After school, children can:

- take care of personal routines—storing belongings, using the bathroom, handwashing;

- select a snack if they wish;

- meet as a group—daily, weekly, or as often as needed;

- choose what they want to do—use interest areas, participate in planned activities, hold club meetings, go outdoors, use other areas (such as the gymnasium) available to the program, attend community activities (such as scouts), work on long-term projects and so on;

- join planned activities "in progress" as long as they don't cause disruptions;

- leave planned activities as they finish or lose interest;

- clean up without feeling rushed;

- gather their projects and belongings, then participate in a quiet activity or interest area until their parents arrive; and

- reconnect with their parents.

The sample daily schedule on the next page shows how a school-age program might be organized to meet the needs of children.

Sample Daily Schedule

Before School

6:30–7:00 AM
Arrival

As children arrive, they participate in quiet activities (card games, puzzles, reading, listening to music with headphones, coloring, reviewing homework, or resting if still tired) and prepare for breakfast.

7:00–7:30
Breakfast

Children who eat before coming to the program continue quiet activities. As they finish breakfast, children move back to activities.

7:30–8:10
Interest areas and staff-led activity

Children participate in short term, quiet activities that do not require significant setup or cleanup or projects that can be saved if not completed (for example, an ongoing macramé project, cutting out pictures for a scrapbook collection).

A staff member leads or oversees a low-key group game or activity (for example, charades, cooperative games, storytelling, mixing a batch of cookies for baking later in the day, morning stretching exercises).

8:10–8:25
Cleanup

Children help clean up the interest areas and gather belongings for school.

8:25–8:30
Leave for school (walk and/or ride school buses)

Children are released to go to school—either as walkers or bus riders. One staff member and/or older child plays short guessing games, asks riddles, or leads songs while children wait for the buses.

After Kindergarten—Early Afternoon

12:00–12:30 PM
Arrival and lunch

Kindergarten children arrive from morning session, wash hands, and eat lunch with staff, family style.

12:30–1:00
Story time

Group gathers for story time.

1:00–2:00
Quiet activity time

Children participate in quiet activities or use a separate area to rest or nap.

2:00–2:10
Transition time

Children pick up or get up from resting.

2:10–2:40
Interest areas and staff-led activity

Interest areas are open. A staff member oversees a short-term art activity.

2:40–3:00
Group time

Children and staff sing songs and share; prepare for the arrival of older children; and discuss activities planned for the rest of the day.

After School

3:00–3:30 PM Arrival	Children arrive on school buses. One staff member takes attendance by doing a visual check as children arrive (rather than trying to maintain quiet for calling the roll).
	Children put away their belongings and play outside, eat a self-service snack, use the bathroom, or participate in quiet activities. Staff circulate and remind children to eat, use the bathroom, wash hands.
3:30–3:50 Group meeting time (daily, weekly, or as needed)	Children meet with their primary staff member. In small programs, all ages may meet together "family-style." In larger programs the different age groups may meet separately. The meeting might consist of one or more of the following:

- Describing plans for the day (activity options and special projects);
- Making announcements;
- Discussing directions/rules;
- Discussing or role-playing problems and solutions;
- Sharing exciting news;
- Inviting ideas for new projects and activities; and
- Making up a group song, game, or mascot.

3:50–4:00 Transition	Children move to activities or interest areas.
4:00–5:30 Activity choices	Children select from the following:

- Indoor interest areas;
- Planned activities (such as a craft project or science experiment);
- Club meetings (indoors or outdoors);
- Community activities (such as scouts);
- Outdoor games and/or interest areas;
- Homework; and
- Games and activities in gym or multipurpose room (after dark or in poor weather).

Duration of activities depends on children's interests and attention spans. Children can choose when to join and leave ongoing activities as long as they don't cause disruptions.

5:30–5:45 Transition and clean up	Indoor and outdoor activities are closed. Children clean up long-term and messy projects in progress in interest areas. Children gather belongings and projects they want to take home.

5:45–6:30
Indoor activity
choices and
parent pick-up

The following areas are open:

- Science and nature area;
  (playing with pets or projects that need little or no clean-up);

- Quiet area;

- Board and table games area (short-term games and puzzles or those that can be stopped in progress and saved); and

- Large-group activity area (listening to music, conversations, charades, dramatic play activities requiring no props, and guessing games).

A staff member greets parents and helps them find their children.

Why is this schedule appropriate for school-age children?

_____

_____

_____

_____

_____

_____

Daily Schedule

In the space below, write down your program's schedule. Complete the sections that apply to your program. Use the checklist that follows to assess your schedule.

Time   **Before School**

_____   _____

_____   _____

_____   _____

_____   _____

_____   _____

Time   **After Kindergarten**

_____   _____

_____   _____

_____   _____

_____   _____

_____   _____

Time   **After School**

_____   _____

_____   _____

_____   _____

_____   _____

_____   _____

Daily Schedule Checklist

☐ 1. Children always can choose between active and quiet things to do.

☐ 2. There is sufficient time for routines and transitions.

☐ 3. There are times for outdoor and indoor play.

☐ 4. Most of the time children can choose what they want to do.

☐ 5. The schedule offers structure and flexibility.

☐ 6. Children can be in small groups doing independent activities for most of the time.

☐ 7. There are opportunities for children to be part of the whole group.

☐ 8. There are opportunities for children to be alone.

☐ 9. Sufficient time is allowed for cleanup and other chores.

On the basis of your responses to the checklist, are there any changes you need to make to enhance your daily schedule? If so, note them on this revised daily schedule.

Revised Daily Schedule

Time	Before School
_____	_____
_____	_____
_____	_____
_____	_____
_____	_____

Time	After Kindergarten
_____	_____
_____	_____
_____	_____
_____	_____
_____	_____

Time	After School
_____	_____
_____	_____
_____	_____
_____	_____
_____	_____

Discuss your ideas with your trainer and your colleagues before changing your daily schedule.

SUMMARIZING YOUR PROGRESS

You have now completed all the learning activities for this module. Whether you are an experienced school-age staff member or a new one, this module has probably helped you develop new skills for creating an appropriate program environment. Before you go on, take a few minutes to review your responses to the pre-training assessment for this module. Write a summary of what you learned, and list the skills you developed or improved.

_____
_____
_____
_____
_____
_____
_____
_____
_____
_____
_____
_____

If there are areas you would like to know more about, you will find recommended readings listed in the Orientation.

Your final step in this module is to complete the knowledge and competency assessments. Let your trainer know when you are ready to schedule the assessments. After you have successfully completed them, you will be ready to start a new module. Congratulations on your progress so far, and good luck with your next module.

ANSWER SHEETS

Creating and Using a Program Environment

Organizing Indoor and Outdoor Areas to Support a Variety of Activities

1. **How did Mr. Johnson know the outdoor environment was not working?**

   a. Some children's work and play was being interrupted by other children running around.

   b. The older children in particular seemed to need more interesting and challenging materials and equipment.

   c. The younger children did not have the skills used to play volleyball and needed a more appropriate place to play.

2. **How did Mr. Johnson and the children work together to improve the outdoor area?**

   a. They cleaned and reorganized the storage shed so equipment and toys are easy to see and within reach.

   b. They set up activity boxes with materials to reflect children's interests.

   c. They discussed how to use the different areas of the playground and thought of ways to help each other.

Selecting and Arranging Developmentally Appropriate Materials and Equipment

1. **What did Ms. Rodriguez and Mr. Sullivan know about the children?**

   a. The children enjoy summer vacations at the beach with their families and wished they had a way to go there even though it was winter.

   b. The children have lots of imagination and enjoy creative projects such as turning the program into an underwater world.

   c. The children like to learn about "real-life" activities such as scuba diving.

   d. The children enjoy dramatic play.

   e. The children enjoy bringing things from home to share with friends.

   f. The children have lots of ideas and suggestions.

2. How will the planned activities and new materials help children learn?

a. All the planned activities and materials will encourage children's creativity.

b. The books and magazines and the visit from a parent who is a marine biologist will stimulate children's interests and independent learning about sea life.

c. Setting up the aquarium will give children a chance to learn new skills and have increased responsibility.

d. The "sunken ship" will provide fresh opportunities for dramatic play.

e. The children will have an opportunity to learn more about scuba diving, a sport they might like to try some day.

Planning and Implementing Schedules and Routines to Meet Children's Developmental and Individual Needs

1. How do the changes planned by Ms. Chan and her colleagues reflect the needs of children after school?

a. They respect that different children have different needs at the end of the school day.

b. They provide for a smooth transition from the structured school day to a more informal tone appropriate for the school-age program.

c. They reduce the need for structure and control.

d. They allow children to choose what they want to do until it's time for group meeting.

2. In what ways might the new approach reduce the amount of noise and tension in the program?

a. Children who need to be physically active will not get impatient or fidgety while they try to sit still quietly and wait for roll call and snack.

b. Children who want to talk with friends will be free to do so.

c. Children who are hungry won't complain while they wait for others to be quiet so roll can be called before snack is served.

d. Children who need some time alone will have a chance to relax at the program before they begin activities.

Classroom Arrangements

Strengths of Floor Plan A:

- The homework table is in a quiet corner near books and magazines.
- The shelves holding science and nature materials are near the table for science and nature projects and experiments.
- Board and table games are near a table where children can sit to play games.
- Blocks and block props are in the blocks and construction area.
- The house corner equipment and furniture are together.
- The large-group activity area includes a CD and tape player along with CDs and tapes.

Weaknesses of Floor Plan A:

- All the shelves are against the walls.
- There are almost no enclosed areas.
- The easels are not near the storage area for art supplies.
- The blocks and construction area is open to the rest of the room, not protected from the large-group activity area, and too close to the pets and aquarium.
- The shelves holding math projects are too far from other areas where they could be used (for example, homework table, blocks and construction area).
- The table used for snack and club meetings is too far from the sink. It is in the center of the room where traffic will disturb children.
- The house corner furniture is not logically arranged.
- The large-group activity area is too open.
- The traffic pattern for entering the room is likely to result in children disturbing others working at the science and nature tables or playing games.
- Cubby space for personal belongings is too small and too far from the door.
- The shelves holding unfinished projects are in the large-group activity area where projects might easily be disturbed or broken.

Differences in Floor Plan B:

- Shelves are used to define different areas.

- Easels are close to the art supplies and in a protected area.

- The blocks and construction area is protected and near other active areas.

- The quiet corner is far from noisy areas; soft items (such as a rug, couch, and beanbag chairs) make this area homelike.

- The table used for snack and club meetings is closer to the water supply, and a counter is available for self service. The table is positioned to one side of the room and is near the meeting area where larger club activities could take place (for example, Drama Club practice). A shelf is available for projects and supplies.

- Pets and the aquarium have been moved to the science and nature area.

- The science and nature table is closer to the sink so it will be easier to do experiments that need water.

- Shelves holding unfinished projects are on one side of the room away from active areas where they might be disturbed.

- Rugs provide comfort and definition for the quiet area, large-group activity area, and the blocks and construction area.

- House corner furniture is more logically arranged.

- Shelves for math projects are closer to the quiet corner and the blocks and construction area.

- The meeting and large-group activity area is near the entrance and is a convenient place for children to gather at arrival and dismissal times and during transitions. There is more space for cubbies, and they are close to the entrance.

How Is Plan B Better?

- Children can work in small interest areas and feel more protected.

- The blocks and construction area is protected so block buildings are not as likely to be knocked down.

- Quiet interest areas (arts and crafts, science and nature, and board and table games) are grouped together.

- The pets and aquarium are more logically located—in the science and nature area, near the water supply.

- Materials are stored on shelves in the areas where they are to be used.

- The house corner can spill over into the blocks and construction area for related dramatic play activities.

GLOSSARY

Daily schedule

How you anticipate and plan for the day's activities. The plan includes the times of day and the order in which activities will occur.

Environment

The complete makeup of the indoor and outdoor areas used by the children. The environment includes the space and how it is arranged and furnished, routines, materials and equipment, planned and unplanned activities, and the people who are present.

Interest Area

A clearly-defined space with materials and equipment focused on a theme or type of activity.

Routines

Scheduled activities that occur every day, including meals, rest times, toileting, washing hands, and going outdoors, which can all offer opportunities for children to learn.

Sub-area

Materials and equipment related to children's specific interests, housed in a related interest area.

Transitions

The in-between times in a daily schedule when children have completed an activity or routine and are moving to the next one.

Module 4:
PHYSICAL

OVERVIEW

PROMOTING SCHOOL-AGE CHILDREN'S PHYSICAL DEVELOPMENT INVOLVES:

- reinforcing and encouraging physical development through an appropriate environment, activities, and interactions;

- providing equipment and opportunities for gross motor development; and

- providing equipment and opportunities for fine motor development.

Adults use a wide range of physical skills every day. We walk and run, often several miles a day, in our homes and at work. We open car doors, carry boxes, and climb stairs. We grasp pencils, cups, and other small items and use tools such as scissors and computer keyboards. Because we regularly use our large and small muscles, we rarely think about the skills involved. In fact, however, we have developed these physical skills through many years of practice.

Physical development refers to the gradual gaining of control over large and small muscles. It includes acquiring gross motor skills such as walking, running, and throwing, and fine motor skills such as holding, pinching, and flexing fingers and toes. Coordinating movement is also an important part of physical development. For example, eye-hand coordination (the ability to direct finger, hand, and wrist movements) is used by school-age children to accomplish fine motor tasks such as fitting a piece in a puzzle or threading a needle. In addition, children use all their senses—sight, sound, touch, taste, and smell—to coordinate the movement of their large and small muscles.

Physical development involves fine and gross motor skills and coordination.

A tremendous amount of physical development takes place before and during the school-age years. Children learn to control their body muscles and to refine the physical skills they will use for the rest of their lives. Although these skills are retained during adolescence and adulthood, new skills are not usually acquired. Therefore, it is crucial for children to have many opportunities to learn and practice basic physical skills.

School-age children practice the physical skills they will use all their lives.

229

Children develop physical skills in a similar pattern of progression. Most children control their head movements first. Next, they develop control of their torsos and arms, and finally their legs. Generally, moving hands and feet in highly skilled ways comes last. Gross motor skills usually appear before those involving small muscles. Movement normally begins with muscles close to the body center and progresses outward as the child matures.

Each child learns and uses physical skills according to his or her own "body clock." For example, some children can ride a two-wheeler at age 5; others are 9 years old before they master this skill. Although the age when children accomplish a skill varies from child to child, the pattern rarely does.

Physical development is often tied to self-esteem.

For most school-age children, acquiring physical skills is closely tied to feeling accepted by peers, having strong self-concepts, and developing positive attitudes toward their own bodies. Some children have well-developed physical skills; others may seem awkward because of their uneven physical growth. For example, Stacy is not a strong swimmer yet, but she is already an accomplished ice skater. Children who have had many successful experiences using their fine and gross motor skills tend to believe they are competent. They are likely to continue to accept new challenges without worrying about failure.

Adults play an important role in promoting children's physical development. They provide ample, safe spaces indoors and outdoors for children to engage in physical activities that are fun and will keep them fit. Programs need to schedule time for active play each day, offer a range of interesting sports, games, and fitness activities, and encourage all children to participate. Staff can promote physical development by encouraging children's efforts as they practice new skills and eventually master them.

Listed on the next page are examples of how school-age staff demonstrate their competence in promoting children's physical development.

Schedule time for active outdoor play every day. "The snow is still deep enough for sledding. You can use the snow saucers to go down the hill by the playground."

Provide opportunities for indoor active play during bad weather. "It's raining hard today, so the gym will be open all afternoon."

Help and encourage children as they learn new skills. "Yannick, I think the birds will all want to build a nest in your birdhouse. I'm impressed by how you used the jigsaw to cut out scalloped edges for the roof."

Encourage children to use their large and small muscles in coordinated ways. "The clay may need some water, Mickey. You can add a little at a time and work it into the clay until it is easier to use."

Help children develop an awareness of rhythm so they can coordinate their movements. "Reggae music has its own beat. Can you hear the way the beat repeats itself over and over?"

Provide a variety of materials that challenge a wide range of skill levels. "While you're learning to crochet, try using the thick yarn and fat crochet hooks. When you get more experienced, it will be easier to use the thin yarn and hooks."

Introduce children to games and activities that build physical skills and encourage cooperation. "If you think it's a good idea, we're going to try playing softball in a way that allows everyone to keep trying until they get a hit. It should be fun and will help everyone improve their hitting skills."

Encourage children to make up and organize their own games. "We don't have soccer on today's schedule, Wendy, but you and your friends can get out the equipment and organize your own game."

Encourage children to use their large muscles during daily routines. For example, ask children to help you move equipment safely.

Plan and implement increasingly difficult activities involving the use of large muscles that children use in sports and games. "Margo and Janice, now that you've mastered the obstacle course, can you rearrange the tires and boards to make it more challenging?"

Reinforcing and Encouraging Physical Development Through an Appropriate Environment, Activities, and Interactions

Providing Equipment and Opportunities for Gross Motor Development

Plan and implement activities that help all children develop and maintain physical fitness. "Next month we're going to have weekly guest instructors from the health center who will introduce us to different ways to stay fit—aerobics, jogging, yoga, and old-fashioned exercises such as jumping jacks."

Make sure children take breaks and have plenty of drinking water available during active play periods. "Everyone needs to drink a little water before we start jogging."

Introduce new games and activities regularly so children are exposed to different ways to use their muscles. "Serena suggested we set up an interest area for children who like to work out. We have aerobics tapes, jump ropes, and hula hoops. What else could we include for a work-out area?"

Suggest children use stopwatches and graph paper to measure and keep track of their own progress in activities such as running, bike riding, or jump roping. "Carla, your chart shows that since you started running you've improved your time by more than a minute. At this rate you're going to end up in the Olympics!"

Providing Equipment and Opportunities for Fine Motor Development

Provide a variety of materials that require children to use their small muscles. "Lloyd and Maddie, would you like to use the tools to take apart the broken radio?"

Plan and implement increasingly difficult activities in which small muscles are used. "The Stitchery Club has been meeting for about a month now. At first we sewed pictures using thick yarn, needles with large eyes, and burlap. Now we are sewing cross-stitch pictures using embroidery floss."

Provide materials that fit together, such as puzzles and Legos, so children can use their fine motor skills. "Raoul and Emma are building a skyscraper. They used boxes of different sizes for the bottom floors, and now they've switched to small plastic bricks for the top ones. So far it's four feet tall."

Provide activities, materials, and equipment that accommodate different skill levels. "You can use the wood scraps for your project, or you can learn to measure and cut wood to fit your own design."

Offer children the chance to learn real skills as well as to explore materials on their own. "Aaron is an accomplished baker. He experiments with different combinations of ingredients, then he braids the dough and shapes the loaves like different animals."

Follow up on adult-led projects with opportunities for children to explore the same materials on their own. "Today we're going to learn how to make shadow puppets. We'll leave the supplies in the arts and crafts area so you can make more puppets on your own."

Promoting Children's Physical Development

In the following situations, school-age staff are promoting children's physical development. As you read them, think about what the staff are doing and why. Then answer the questions that follow.

Reinforcing and Encouraging Physical Development Through an Appropriate Environment, Activities, and Interactions

Diana and Bradley are eating snack and talking. "My sister is in seventh grade and she's going to a dance at school," says Diana. "My brother is going to that dance, too," says Bradley. "I saw him practicing in front of the mirror. He thought nobody was watching." "I like to dance," says Diana. "My sister has been teaching me how." "Maybe we could have our own dance here," says Bradley. "Let's ask Bob." They find Mr. Brody in the arts and crafts area helping Sandra get her knitting back on the needles. "Can we have our own dance at the program?" asks Diana. Sandra joins in: "Yeah, that would be so much fun! Can we?" Mr. Brody asks the children what kind of dance they would like to have. "Well," says Bradley, "when my mom heard about the dance my brother is going to, she asked him if it was a sock hop. He laughed, but she told me sock hops are really fun. Maybe we can have a sock hop." "I've heard of sock hops, too," says Diana. "You listen to old rock and roll songs, and wear white socks and twirly skirts with poodles on them." Mr. Brody suggests the children bring up their idea at the next group meeting. If other children are interested, they can learn dances from the fifties, make costumes, and plan when and where to have the dance. "I already know how to do some rock 'n roll dances," says Sandra. "My mom's a great dancer." Mr. Brody responds, "I'm not a great dancer, but I could learn. Do you think your mom would come in to teach us?" "I'll ask her tonight," says Sandra. "This will be so much fun," says Bradley. "I can hardly wait for tomorrow."

1. **What did Mr. Brody do to encourage the children's physical development?**

_____

_____

_____

2. **Why did Mr. Brody suggest the children bring up their idea at the next group meeting?**

_____

_____

_____

Whether he's playing basketball or learning a new dance step, Renaldo likes to be active. Today during free play time, he goes to the gym to use the movement stations. Ms. Tunis has posted eight skill cards on the walls at one end of the gym. Each card describes a different activity. Renaldo wants to improve his jump shot in basketball, so he starts at the first station, which lists ten different ways to jump. Renaldo jumps high, claps his hands over his head, then lands on his feet with knees bent. He jumps high and claps his hands behind his back. After several more jumps, he finishes the station by jumping as high as he can, as far as he can, and as quietly as he can. He asks Ms. Tunis which other station would be good for a basketball player. She suggests the throwing and catching station. Renaldo proceeds to the new station where he performs a variety of movements that involve throwing a ball up in the air, clapping hands, letting the ball bounce, and dribbling with his right and left hands. For the last movement Renaldo dribbles the ball down a line and back, sits down with his legs spread apart and dribbles the ball between his legs, and lies down on his back and throws the ball up in the air and catches it. Ms. Tunis watches him finish the last movement and says, "You're really getting to be a good ball handler." "Thanks," says Renaldo. "These movement stations are really fun. I think I'll try the hopping one next." "Okay," says Ms. Tunis, "But first go have a drink of water. It's easy to get overheated when you're exercising."

Providing Equipment and Opportunities for Gross Motor Development

1. **Why did Ms. Tunis set up the movement stations?**

   _____

   _____

   _____

2. **How did Ms. Tunis support Renaldo's development of gross motor skills?**

   _____

   _____

   _____

Providing Equipment and Opportunities for Fine Motor Development

Playing jacks is the latest fad among the older children at the program. Three children, Penny, Kate, and Ruthie are playing a game. Dana and Charles, both seven, watch intently. "Will you teach us to play?" asks Dana. "You're too little," says Kate. "When I was your age I couldn't play jacks." You'll have to wait until you're older." Ruthie joins in, "Besides, Charles can't play jacks, he's a boy." Mr. Shepard overhears and strolls over. "Charles," he says, "Did I hear you want to learn to play jacks?" "Yeah," responds Charles. "Do you know how?" Mr. Shepard bends down to Charles' level and replies, "Yes, I know how to play jacks. I also know another game like jacks that you might enjoy. Would you like to learn to play?" "Yes," says Charles. "Me, too," says Dana. Mr. Shepard retrieves a box labeled Chopstick Jacks from the supply cabinet and hands it to Dana and Charles. Inside are ten chopsticks, two small balls like the ones used for jacks, and an instruction card. The instructions say to lay the chopsticks in a straight line. Dana and Charles lay them end to end. Mr. Shepard demonstrates throwing the ball up in the air, then immediately picking up a stick and catching the ball in the same hand after letting it bounce once. "Can you do that?" he asks. Charles and Dana nod. Each child takes a ball and tries to pick up a chopstick. It takes a few tries to get the hang of it. Mr. Shepard explains, "Now, take turns until all the chopsticks have been picked up. Then you start again." Charles and Dana begin their game. Penny, Kate, and Ruthie come over to watch. Mr. Shepard thinks, "Maybe this is the start of a new fad!"

1. **How did Mr. Shepard accommodate the different skill levels of the children?**

_____

_____

_____

2. **How did Mr. Shepard encourage the fine motor development of Charles and Dana?**

_____

_____

_____

Compare your answers with those on the answer sheet at the end of this module. If your answers are different, discuss them with your trainer. There can be more than one good answer.

Taking Care of Your Own Body[1]

As a school-age staff member, you are concerned about children's physical development. Yet to work well, it is essential that you take care of yourself, too. How many times a day do you:

You need to take care of yourself.

- bend from the waist to pick up an item on the floor?

- participate in active games without first warming up?

- carry heavy boxes or equipment?

- sit on the floor and bend forward to play with a child?

- sit on a child-sized chair?

These are normal activities for staff in school-age programs. They are also activities that can produce sore backs and limbs. There are ways to maintain good posture and flexibility and to avoid physical pain as you work with active children. Here are some suggested practices:

Try these suggestions.

- Keep your lower back as straight as possible and avoid slouching when sitting or standing.

- Put one foot up on a stool or step when standing for a long time.

- Bend your knees, not your back, when you are leaning forward.

- Wear low-heeled, soft-soled, comfortable shoes to maintain proper posture.

- Bend your knees, tuck in your buttocks, and pull in your abdominal muscles when lifting a heavy object.

- Avoid twisting when lifting or lowering a heavy object. Hold the object close to you.

- Stretch your muscles before playing an active game with children. (It's a good idea for children to stretch their muscles, too.)

- Use adult-sized tables and chairs, whenever possible.

- Talk with your supervisor and colleagues about staff coverage for short breaks. Relax during these breaks! (Doing some stretching exercises is also a good way to spend breaks.)

[1] Based on Susan S. Aronson, M.D., "Coping With the Physical Requirements of Caregiving," *Child Care Information Exchange* (Redmond, WA: Exchange Press, May 1987), pp. 39-40.

Working with children is physically demanding.

Working with children is a physically demanding job. To be fully involved with school-age children, you need to be in good physical shape. Think about your daily movements and your environment, and answer the questions below.

How can you improve your posture and movements throughout the day?

_____

_____

_____

_____

What changes to the environment or the schedule can you suggest so you and your colleagues can avoid sore backs and limbs?

_____

_____

_____

_____

The suggestions you have just read and the ones you noted above, along with regular exercise and good health and nutrition practices, can help you promote your own physical development along with that of school-age children.

When you have finished this overview section, you should complete the pre-training assessment. Refer to the glossary at the end of this module if you need definitions of the terms used.

Pre-Training Assessment

Listed below are the skills school-age staff use to promote children's physical development. Think about whether you do these things regularly, sometimes, or not enough. Place a check in one of the boxes on the right for each skill listed. Then discuss your answers with your trainer.

Reinforcing and Encouraging Physical Development Through an Appropriate Environment, Activities, and Interactions

	I Do This		
	Regularly	Sometimes	Not Enough
1. Providing space and time so children can engage in active play every day.	☐	☐	☐
2. Encouraging children when they are learning new skills and providing assistance upon request.	☐	☐	☐
3. Suggesting ways children can coordinate movement of their large and small muscles.	☐	☐	☐
4. Helping children develop an awareness of rhythm so they can coordinate their movements.	☐	☐	☐
5. Observing and recording information about each child's physical strengths, interests, and needs.	☐	☐	☐
6. Providing a variety of materials and activities to challenge a wide range of physical capabilities.	☐	☐	☐
7. Introducing children to games and activities that encourage physical development and cooperation.	☐	☐	☐
8. Encouraging children to make up and organize their own games.	☐	☐	☐

Providing Equipment and Opportunities for Gross Motor Development

	Regularly	Sometimes	Not Enough
9. Encouraging children to use their large muscles during daily routines.	☐	☐	☐
10. Planning and implementing increasingly difficult activities involving the use of large muscles that children use in sports and games.	☐	☐	☐

239

	I Do This		
Providing Equipment and Opportunities for Gross Motor Development (continued)	Regularly	Sometimes	Not Enough
11. Providing activities, materials, and equipment that allow all children to develop and maintain physical fitness.	☐	☐	☐
12. Making sure children take breaks from vigorous activity and drink plenty of water to prevent dehydration.	☐	☐	☐
13. Introducing new games and activities regularly so children learn different ways to use their muscles.	☐	☐	☐
14. Encouraging children to keep track of their own progress, rather than comparing themselves to each other.	☐	☐	☐

Providing Equipment and Opportunities for Fine Motor Development

	Regularly	Sometimes	Not Enough
15. Providing a variety of materials that require children to use their small muscles.	☐	☐	☐
16. Providing activities, materials, and equipment that accommodate different fine motor skill levels.	☐	☐	☐
17. Planning and implementing increasingly difficult activities in which small muscles are used.	☐	☐	☐
18. Offering children opportunities to learn real skills as well as to explore materials on their own.	☐	☐	☐
19. Following up on adult-led projects by providing materials children can explore on their own.	☐	☐	☐
20. Providing materials that fit together such as puzzles and Legos, so children can use their fine motor skills.	☐	☐	☐
21. Follow up on adult-led projects with opportunities for children to explore the same materials on their own.	☐	☐	☐

Review your responses, then list three to five skills you would like to improve or topics you would like to learn more about. When you finish this module, you can list examples of your new or improved knowledge and skills.

_____

_____

_____

_____

_____

_____

_____

_____

Begin the learning activities for Module 4, Physical.

LEARNING ACTIVITIES

Learning Activity I.
Using Your Knowledge of Child Development to Encourage Physical Fitness[2]

IN THIS ACTIVITY YOU WILL LEARN TO:

- recognize some typical behaviors of school-age children; and

- use what you know about children to encourage physical fitness.

Most children are naturally drawn to physical activity. In school playgrounds, back yards, and on city streets, children organize their own activities—running races, climbing trees, or playing hopscotch. After a day at school, children are usually eager to participate in active physical play.

It's important to encourage all children to be physically active.

Some children do not have enough opportunities to exercise, play sports, or otherwise play actively. Although physical education is offered in most schools, only one state, Illinois, provides daily physical education for all children from kindergarten through grade 12. A 1987 study conducted by the Harvard School of Public Health found from age 6 on, today's children weigh more and have more body fat than did children 20 years ago. Since the 1960s, obesity (defined as being 20 percent above the ideal weight for age, sex, and height) has increased by more than 50 percent among children aged 6 to 11.

Your school-age program can play an important role by providing a wide variety of physical activities that appeal to as many children as possible—not just the athletically talented. Children are likely to make physical exercise a lifelong habit if they are given the time and space to stretch and use their muscles, along with sincere encouragement for their efforts and accomplishments.

Physical skills develop according to individual time clocks. Within a given age group there can be great variation in physical skills. A few of the children who learn skills earlier than their age mates have natural ability. Others who develop earlier are on a "faster" time clock, which does not necessarily lead to becoming a star athlete. School-age children tend to be very aware of their

Children's physical skills can vary greatly from those of their peers.

---

[2] Parts of this learning activity are based on Kenneth H. Cooper, M.D., M.P.H., *Fit Kids* (Nashville, TN: Broadman and Holman, 1999).

own physical skills and those of their peers. Those who have "slower" time clocks may get discouraged and give up favorite sports and activities because they feel they are "no good" and never will be. With continued encouragement, however, they can eventually develop physical skills and enjoy a wide variety of sports and exercise activities.

Descriptions of the physical development of school-age children of different ages appear below.

5- to 7-Year-Old Children

In the early school-age years (approximately ages 5 to 7), physical growth slows, weight gain is moderate and even, and boys and girls are relatively equal in physical skills. Children want to do things well but are not always as coordinated as they would like to be.

Typically, after a day in school, these younger children have lots of energy to burn but can become easily tired. They need a schedule that alternates periods of activity and rest. Physical activities such as swimming, skating, riding bikes, doing gymnastics, playing hopscotch, jumping rope, climbing, running, and playing tag are most appropriate for this age group.

In the early school-age years, children are beginning to enjoy organized group play and team sports; however, they are not really ready for competition. Organized sports, played without the pressure of winning or losing, can help them stay fit and develop physical skills they will continue to use as they get older.

Children in this age group are perfecting coordination of large and small muscles and perceptual motor coordination. They are developing a sense of rhythm and enjoy dancing and activities that involve moving their bodies to music.

The following examples depict the physical development of children ages 5 to 7. At the end, add an example of the physical development of a 5- to 7-year-old child enrolled in your program.

- Nathan loves to play T-ball. He's a strong runner—when he catches the ball he is as likely to run with it as he is to throw it to first base. During games he often daydreams and may forget important rules. He has to stop to think before following instructions such as "Throw the ball to Daniel." After he hits the ball he stops to think before running. Once, he hit the ball, then ran around the bases the wrong way.

- Peter is not interested in team sports, but he enjoys other kinds of physical activity. He can hop on one foot for a long distance and likes to skip across the playground. He can walk the full length of a balance beam without stepping off. He likes to climb to the top of the jungle gym and "walk" across the monkey bars with his arms.

- Marisa has been playing soccer for two years. She recently developed the ability to react spontaneously—she can kick the soccer ball and automatically run up the field after it. She used to stop after she kicked the ball while thinking about what to do next. She's becoming more aware of her physical skills and limits. When other children make fun of her or tell her she can't kick the ball far enough, she gets very discouraged.

Example of the physical development of a 5- to 7-year-old child in your program:

_____
_____
_____
_____

Describe something you do to encourage the physical fitness of children in this age group:

_____
_____
_____
_____

8- to 10-Year-Old Children

In the middle school-age years (approximately ages 8 to 10), body strength increases and coordination and reaction times improve. Children learn to coordinate their physical skills; for example, they are able to run and dribble a basketball at the same time. Some children become interested in competitive sports—either team sports such as soccer or individual sports such as swimming. A National Children and Youth Fitness Study conducted in 1987 reported 84 percent of children in this age group participated in physical activity through at least one community group.

At this age many children compare their abilities to their peers. If they believe their skills are not as good as another's, they may become discouraged and stop participating in physical activities. This is unfortunate because most children in this age group have not yet begun their growth spurt and have not developed their muscle power. They may also lack the nerve connections necessary to activate the full force of the muscles they do have.

There is wide variation in the muscle strength and physical power in any given group of children aged 8 to 10. Adults may consider some children to be unathletic when in fact they are "late bloomers" who will eventually be able to develop many physical skills. You can encourage children to exercise to release tension, to make their muscles strong, and to practice and develop skills. This encouragement will help children make exercise part of their lifelong routines.

The following examples depict the physical development of children ages 8 to 10. At the end, add an example of the physical development of an 8- to 10-year-old child enrolled in your program.

- Paul, Nick, and Terrence are good friends. They spend a lot of time discussing each other's physical abilities, often in very critical terms. "We would have won if you hadn't dropped the ball." "I can throw much further than you can." "I'm younger than you are, but I can skate backwards and you can't skate forward without falling down." Ms. Cikovsky overhears their conversation and writes herself a note to be sure to plan some cooperative games that accommodate a wide range of skill levels.

- Teresa really enjoys basketball. She is tall for her age and is a high scorer in games. She's not very good at passing the ball to her teammates, however. She knows she needs to practice passing, so she asks a friend to run up and down the gym with her, passing the ball back and forth. After 30 minutes of this vigorous activity, both girls are exhausted. (Sweat glands of children who have not entered puberty produce only about 40 percent as much sweat as do adult glands. They get overheated easily and need to drink plenty of water when exercising vigorously.)

- Lisa has stopped playing in the daily after-school soccer games. When asked by Ms. Jones why she isn't playing any more, Lisa explains, "The boys think they are bigger and stronger, so they never pass the ball to girls. It's just not fun any more." Ms. Jones agrees it can be frustrating when the boys don't recognize her skills—she's very fast and an expert dribbler. She encourages Lisa to continue playing soccer. She also plans to observe the children's soccer game and work with her colleagues to encourage the players to include everyone in the game.

Example of the physical development of an 8- to 10-year old child in your program:

_____

_____

_____

_____

Describe something you do to encourage the physical fitness of children in this age group:

_____

_____

_____

_____

11- to 12-Year-Old Children

Most 11- to 12-year-old children like to move their bodies and may work hard to polish their physical skills. Some may test the limits of their physical skills; therefore, they continue to need close supervision. It's important to supervise without being overprotective, as these children have a great need to be independent and to control their own activities.

Up to about age 10, boys and girls are generally equal in physical development. Typically girls go through a growth spurt at age $11\frac{1}{2}$ to 12, while boys go through a similar stage about two years later. After age 10, as girls enter puberty, they may develop increased body fat, and decreased size, endurance, and muscle power in comparison to boys. These changes may cause girls to feel sports are for boys and less rigorous activities are for girls. You and your colleagues can counteract this trend by encouraging girls to stay involved in sports. When girls maintain their interest in sports they are likely to develop physical skills later in their teens.

The height increases and weight gains triggered by entering puberty generally are an advantage for boys. The boys in this age group who are slower to develop, however, tend to be less skilled athletically and may drop out of organized sports because they feel they can't keep up with their age mates. This does not mean they will remain less skilled. When encouraged to continue physical fitness programs, many boys who mature later in their teens become outstanding athletes.

The following examples depict the physical development of children ages 11 to 12. At the end, add an example depicting the physical development of an 11- or 12-year-old child in your program.

- Brenda is the program's Double Dutch Champion. Until this year she didn't participate in many sports or games; however, she did spend a lot of her free time dancing and doing aerobics with her friends. When Ms. Reynolds congratulated her for winning the jump rope contest, Brenda said she couldn't have done it without the support of her two friends who turned the ropes. Ms. Reynolds said, "Well, yes, that's true—they did help you a lot. And I remember seeing you practicing every afternoon for the last few months. You worked hard to develop those skills." Brenda needs to be reminded her physical accomplishments are the result of her athletic ability and hard work.

- Jonathan is small for his age and has a hard time keeping up with some of the more developed boys in games and sports. He loves to run, however, and participates in the school-age program's Jogging Club. Three times a week this group goes on a 20-minute jog around the field. This activity is increasing Jonathan's strength and building his endurance. It's also keeping him interested in physical activities and giving him the opportunity to develop a lifelong fitness habit.

- Marisa is going through puberty. She used to be one of the best basketball players at the school-age program. Even though she is still a skilled athlete, she sometimes has trouble keeping up with the athletic boys her age who are taller and stronger and never seem to get tired. Mr. Knight has noticed Marisa tends to spend less and less time enjoying physical activities. Instead, she listens to music or makes up plays with her friends. He asks Marisa to help him plan some new physical activities for the program. Together they come up with several ideas for games and activities she and the others will enjoy. Mr. Knight will run a basketball clinic for the younger children, with Marisa's help. This will allow her to stay active and to feel good about her physical abilities.

Example of the physical development of an 11- to 12-year-old child in your program:

_____

_____

_____

_____

Describe something you do to encourage the physical fitness of children in this age group:

_____

_____

_____

_____

Discuss this activity with your trainer.

Learning Activity II.
Observing and Planning for Children's Physical Development

> **IN THIS ACTIVITY YOU WILL LEARN TO:**
>
> • identify children's developing fine and gross motor skills; and
>
> • offer activities that help children practice fine and gross motor skills.

School-age children use their fine motor skills in many activities.

Fine motor skills such as holding, pinching, and flexing fingers and toes involve use of small muscles. School-age children use their small muscles in many different ways. Coordinating hands, fingers, and wrists is necessary for writing, drawing, and lacing shoes. Strength in small muscles is needed for typing on a computer keyboard and using woodworking tools. Control is required for holding cooking utensils, playing musical instruments, and tying macramé knots. Fine motor skills are refined, adapted, and used throughout life for activities such as sewing, baking bread, and repairing car engines.

Children use their senses to coordinate movements.

Sensory awareness—using sight, sound, touch, taste, and smell to get information—is a large part of fine motor development. Activities in which children use their senses as they manipulate objects help them coordinate movements. For example, an activity such as making carrot muffins and lemonade for snack can provide experiences such as these:

• sight: peeling, slicing, and grating carrots;

• sound: cracking eggs on the side of a bowl;

• touch: rolling the lemons to make them juicier;

• taste: sipping the lemonade to see if it needs more sugar; and

• smell: breathing the fragrance of the spices in the hot muffins.

While a variety of cognitive concepts are learned during this type of activity, fine motor skills are also developed as children get information from their senses.

On the next page are some examples of school-age children using their fine motor skills. For each one, note the ways in which the child used fine motor skills.

When Antwan arrived at the program this morning, he undid his coat zipper, took off the coat, and hung it in his cubby. He tightened the buckles on his overalls and retied his sneaker laces. Next, he played a board game with two friends, drew a picture, and turned the pages in the dinosaur book looking for the picture of the Stegosaurus. At breakfast he ate cereal with a spoon, poured juice from a pitcher, and buttered a muffin with a knife. While waiting for the school bus, he used a pencil to write his name over and over on a piece of paper until the page was filled.

How did Antwan use his fine motor skills?

_____

_____

_____

_____

When Stacy arrived at the program after school, she unbuckled her backpack, took out her social studies homework, and stuffed the backpack in her cubby. She unbuttoned her sweater, took it off, and hung it up by looping the tag over a hook. She put her homework down on the table and went to get her snack. She chose some fresh fruit (grapes and orange slices) and returned to the homework table. As she read her assignment, she plucked each grape and popped it in her mouth. Next, she picked the seeds out of each orange slice and then held the slices with two fingers as she sucked the juice out. She popped one slice between her teeth and lips and turned to Kyle. "That's gross," said Kyle. Her homework finished, Stacy decided to listen to music. She selected a tape, placed it in the player, and closed the lid. She hooked up the head phones, put them on her head, and pushed the play button. While she was listening, she moved her fingers in time with the music.

How did Stacy use her fine motor skills?

_____

_____

_____

_____

Gross motor skills are used in sports, games, routines, and activities.

Gross motor skills such as walking, running, and throwing involve large muscles. These are the skills used for many of the physical fitness activities discussed in Learning Activity I. Professor Vern Seefeldt of Michigan State University has identified 21 basic gross motor skills children and adults use in sports and games.[2] He suggests teaching these skills to children who are developmentally ready to learn them as early as possible so they can enjoy a wide variety of physical activities. These skills are listed below. For each one, give an example of how it is used by children in a routine, game, sport, or other activity. One example is provided for each skill area.

Object control skills

kicking, as when *playing kickball* _____

throwing overhand, as when _____

throwing underhand, as when _____

catching, as when _____

punting, as when _____

dribbling or bouncing a ball several times in a row, as when _____

striking a ball with a bat or racket, as when, _____

trapping a ball with the feet, as when _____

Locomotor skills

running, as when *doing laps around the gym* _____

jumping over an obstacle, as when _____

hopping, skipping, as when _____

balancing on one foot, as when _____

galloping, as when _____

leaping forward, as when _____

rolling forward (somersault), as when _____

rolling backward, as when _____

sliding while standing, as when _____

---

[2] Based on Kenneth H. Cooper, M.D., M.P.H., *Fit Kids* (Nashville, TN: Broadman and Holman, 1999).

Non locomotor skills

lifting, as when _carrying a heavy box_ _____

pulling, as when _____

pushing, as when _____

These skills can serve as the basis for more complex movements and abilities. For example, if Kerry can use a plastic bat to hit a ball placed on the ground, she might be ready to try hitting the ball as it is rolled to her. If Jared can slide while standing, then he can probably try roller skating.

Applying Your Knowledge

In this learning activity you observe one of the children in your group over two three-day periods. During the first three days, identify the gross motor skills you see the child using; during the second three days, identify the fine motor skills you see the child using. Then plan activities that give the child opportunities to practice and refine his or her gross and fine motor skills. Begin by reviewing the example that follows.

Gross Motor Skills
(Example)

Child: _Alex_   **Age:** _8 years_   **Date:** _May 5-7_

Gross motor skills this child has mastered:

>*Riding a two-wheeler*
>*Dribbling soccer ball the full length of field*
>*Bouncing on a pogo stick*
>*Pitching a ball underhand*

Gross motor skills this child is learning:

>*Passing the ball to another player*
>*Dancing to music*
>*Doing a pull-up*

Activities that are appropriate for this child:

>*A sports clinic to practice passing*
>*Movement activities to focus on rhythm and moving to music*
>*A variety of strength development activities, such as arm curls with small cans or more time playing on the monkey bars*

Fine Motor Skills
(Example)

Child: _Alex_   **Age:** _8 years_   **Date:** _May 10-12_

Fine motor skills this child has mastered:

>*Cursive writing*
>*Hammering a nail straight*
>*Using eating utensils*
>*Playing the recorder*

Fine motor skills this child is learning:

>*Cutting with an X-acto knife*
>*Using a whisk to beat eggs*
>*Threading small beads to make jewelry*

Activities that are appropriate for this child:

>*Using a greater variety of woodworking tools*
>*Making clay beads*
>*Soap carving*

Gross Motor Skills

Child: _____   Age: _____   Date: _____

Gross motor skills this child has mastered:

_____

_____

_____

_____

_____

_____

Gross motor skills this child is learning:

_____

_____

_____

_____

_____

_____

Activities that are appropriate for this child:

_____

_____

_____

_____

_____

Fine Motor Skills

Child: _____   **Age:** _____   **Date:** _____

Fine motor skills this child has mastered:

_____

_____

_____

_____

_____

_____

Fine motor skills this child is learning:

_____

_____

_____

_____

_____

_____

Activities that are appropriate for this child:

_____

_____

_____

_____

_____

_____

Discuss your observations and plans with your trainer.

Learning Activity III.
Providing a Variety of Physical Activities

IN THIS ACTIVITY YOU WILL LEARN TO:

- plan and implement a wide range of physical activities to accommodate the needs and interests of all children in the program; and

- encourage all children to use and practice their physical skills.

Physical fitness is an important goal for children and adults. Therefore, it is important to encourage **all** children to participate in physical activities—those with highly developed skills and those who are slower to develop skills. Some children enjoy playing sports that require specific skills such as throwing, hitting, or dribbling a ball. Others like activities such as aerobic dancing that promote overall fitness.

Some children may resist physical activity. They might have "dropped out" of a once-favorite sport or they might think of themselves as unathletic. You can encourage their participation by pointing out the benefits of physical fitness—"you'll be able to hike all the way around the lake without getting tired"—rather than telling them they need to spend less time enjoying their favorite sedentary activities.

Another excellent strategy for encouraging chidren's participation in physical activities is to get involved yourself. When you jog around the track, take a turn jumping rope, or play volleyball with the children you are sending the message that staying fit is important throughout our lives. (See Module 13, Professionalism, for more information on taking care of your physical well-being.)

Listed below are physical fitness activities the children in your program may enjoy. Add your own suggestions in the space provided.

Create an obstacle course. Children can build a challenging obstacle course using barrels, tires, inner tubes, tumbling mats, hula hoops, orange safety cones, and anything else they can think of. When the group has mastered the course, the builders can redesign it to create new challenges.

Physical Fitness Activities

Try these suggestions.

Establish an exercise activity area. Include jump ropes, instructions for floor and other exercises, a tape player and music tapes for aerobic dancing, soft balls and beanbags, and other popular exercise paraphernalia.

Make an "Around the World" dance prop box. Include pictures of dancers in traditional dress, instructions for different dances, props to wear or dance with, and tapes with music from different lands. Staff can introduce the dances; children can then use the prop box on their own.

Hold sports clinics. Some days, instead of playing sports, you can hold clinics to build the skills children use in these games. For example, during a kickball clinic, staff and older children could review the rules of the game, lead the children in drills to practice kicking, pitching, and fielding the ball as if in a game, and play games that help improve their running and throwing.

Provide a variety of equipment to be used alone or with a friend. This is particularly important for children who are not drawn to sports or organized games. Examples include hula hoops, stilts, pogo sticks, soft balls and paddles, yo-yos, chalk for hopscotch, roller skates (and safety equipment), jump ropes, bean bags, and ring tosses.

Offer exercise clubs such as Aerobics, Jogging, or Tumbling Clubs. Children of all ages and abilities can participate in clubs such as these. Staff, community volunteers, or children can serve as leaders/instructors.

_____

_____

_____

Activities for Building Skills

Some children are reluctant to join in organized games and sports because they think they don't have the skills to be a successful player. School-age children are very sensitive to their physical abilities and frequently compare themselves with their peers. Rather than trying to explain that some children's physical development "time clocks" work at a slower pace than others, you can offer activities that will help children build skills such as catching, kicking, jumping, balancing, dribbling, and hitting. Children will enjoy these activities because they are challenging, there are no winners or losers, and, most importantly, they are fun. You can introduce these activities and lead them the first time. After children understand the activity they can set it up and play by themselves, taking turns as the leader. Some examples of skill-building activities appear on the next page.

Skill-Building Activities[5]

Stepping Out

Ages/Players: 5 to 6 years, one at a time   **Equipment:** 27 egg cartons
Skill: Balancing, tiptoeing   **Location:** Indoors

Use the egg cartons to make two rows of squares, with five squares in each row. The rows are connected with no space between them. Children take off their shoes and take turns tiptoeing one foot at a time through each square without touching the egg cartons.

Underhand Knockdown

Ages/Players: 8 to 12 years, one at a time   **Equipment:** Foam ball, five egg cartons, table
Skill: Throwing at a target   **Location:** Indoors

Stack the egg cartons on the table. The first child stands about ten feet away from the table and throws the ball underhand trying to hit the stack. After all children have had a turn, they move back two feet and repeat the activity. The throw is considered successful if any of the egg cartons fall down.

Nerve Ball

Ages/Players: 8 to 12 years, one at a time   **Equipment:** Foam ball
Skill: Catching   **Location:** Outdoors or indoors (gym)

One child stands with back turned, 15 to 20 feet away from the rest of the players standing in a line. The first player in line throws the ball towards the "catcher's" back, yelling "ball" as he or she releases it. This is the cue for the child to turn around, catch the ball, run it back to the next child in line, and go to the end of the line. The child who threw the ball takes the place of the "catcher" and the next child in line throws the ball. Children can repeat the activity until all have had one or more turns in each position. An alternative is to have a staff member throw the ball while the children take turns as the "catcher."

Dribble About

Ages/Players: 10 to 12 years, one at a time   **Equipment:** Basketball/utility ball, egg cartons
Skill: Dribbling   **Location:** Outdoors or indoors (gym)

Set up egg cartons in two parallel lines about ten feet apart, with about five feet between each carton. Children dribble the ball in a zigzag motion around and between the egg cartons.

---

[5] Based with permission on Linda Ouellete and James Parcelli, *Games Kids Play* (Fairfax, VA: Fairfax County Office for Children, 1981).

Movement Stations[6]

Children can also use movement stations to develop and improve specific skills, such as jumping, hopping, throwing, and catching. Each station includes (1) instructions printed on a large poster board and (2) whatever equipment might be needed. To meet the needs of children at different stages of development, the movement stations should address a variety of skill levels. Children can select which activities to do and perform them at their own pace. New challenges can be added as children develop new skills.

You can set up movement stations in a gym or other large room. For some stations, you need to make a line on the floor with masking tape (or another tape that is easily removed). The children can help you set up the stations, or you can do so before they arrive. When you introduce the stations, "walk" the children through the instructions for each one. Ask for volunteers to demonstrate the different movements. You can offer encouragement, explain instructions that might be confusing, and remind children to drink plenty of water when they are exercising. Some children may want to keep track of their progress. You can provide stop watches, yardsticks, and paper and pencil so they can keep individual exercise diaries.

Descriptions of eight movement stations follow. They should be set up as an optional activity for children who are interested in participating.

---

[6] Based with permission on materials developed by the Fairfax County Office for Children, Fairfax, VA.

Movement Stations

1. Jumping

- Jump high, clap hands over head, land on feet with knees bent.
- Jump high, clap hands behind back.
- Jump high, clap hands over head, then behind back.
- Jump high, clap hands under one leg.
- Jump and turn halfway around.
- Jump and make a full turn before landing.
- Jump and click heels in the air.
- Jump as high as you can, as far as you can, and as quietly as you can.
- Jump backward.

2. Moving Your Body

- Make yourself as big as you can.
- Make yourself as small as you can.
- Make yourself as wide as you can.
- Make yourself as long as you can.
- Make your body as straight as you can.
- Make your body as curvy as you can.
- Walk on the line (taped to the floor) with your hands out for balance.
- Walk on the line without using your hands for balance.
- Walk the line backward with your hands out for balance.
- Hop from one end of the line to the other.
- Touch your nose with your left hand while grabbing your left ear with your right hand.
- Touch your nose with your right hand while grabbing your right ear with your left hand.

3. Throwing and Catching Bean Bags

- Throw the bean bag in the air and catch it with both hands, ten times.
- Throw the bean bag in the air and catch it with your right hand, five times.
- Throw the bean bag in the air and catch it with your left hand, five times.
- Throw the bean bag from one hand to the other, from left to right over your head.
- Throw the bean bag in the air; jump to catch it with two hands; then with one hand.
- Throw the bean bag in the air and clap your hands three times before catching it.
- Throw the bean bag in the air and turn all the way around before catching it.
- Stand with the bean bag balanced on one foot; try the other foot.
- Hop around with the bean bag balanced on one foot; try the other foot.

4. Using Hula Hoops

- Put the hoop over your head with hands at your sides; shake the hoop down over your body to the floor.
- Place the hoop on your right arm and make big circles with your arm; repeat with your left arm.
- Hold the hoop with two hands close to the floor; jump into the hoop with both feet and lift it over your head.
- Place the hoop over your right ankle; balance with the hoop off the floor while counting to ten. Repeat with your left ankle.
- Place the hoop over your right ankle, toe pointing up, hands on hips. While balancing, twirl the hoop. Repeat with your left ankle.
- Place the hoop on the floor and stand inside; jump out of the hoop and back inside, each time leaving the hoop at a different place.
- Stand in the center of the hoop, jump up and click your heels, and land in the center of the hoop, five times.
- Stand in the hoop and do ten jumping jacks without touching the sides.

5. Throwing and Catching Balls

- Hold the ball in both hands, throw it in the air and catch it.
- Hold the ball in your left hand, throw it in the air and catch it. Repeat with right hand.
- Throw the ball in the air, clap hands, then catch it.
- Throw the ball at the wall; catch it on its rebound before it hits the ground.
- Throw the ball at the wall, let it bounce once, then catch it.
- Throw the ball at the wall, turn around, and catch the ball on the first bounce.
- Dribble the ball with your right hand. Repeat with your left hand.
- Dribble the ball balancing on one foot. Repeat with the other foot.
- Dribble the ball down the line (taped on the floor) and back.
- Sit down, legs spread apart, and dribble the ball in between legs.
- Lie down on your back, throw the ball up in the air, and catch it.

6. Throwing and Catching Balloons

- Keep the balloon in the air with these parts of your body:

left hand	right hand	both hands
head	nose	shoulders
elbows	hips	knees
feet	back	stomach

- Sit down and keep the balloon in the air using just your hands, feet, head.
- Lying down, keep the balloon in the air using just your hands, feet, head.
- Kick the balloon from Point A to Point B (marked on the floor).
- Blow the balloon from A to B. Push it with your head from A to B.

7. Hopping

- Hop on both feet ten times.
- Hop on your left foot ten times, then your right foot ten times.
- Hop in a circle three times.
- Hop on both feet down the line (taped to the floor) and back.
- Hop on your left foot down the line, then come back hopping on the right foot.
- Hop on both feet, clapping each time your feet hit the ground.
- Hop on both feet sideways to the left, then back to the right.
- Hop on both feet while bouncing a ball in front of you.
- Hop on both feet backward down the line and back.
- Write your name on the floor by hopping out the letters.
- Hop as fast as you can, as slowly as you can, and as quietly as you can.

8. Jump Roping

- Spread the rope in a line on the floor; walk along the rope and back.
- Walk along the rope and back by sideways steps.
- Stand facing the rope and jump forward and backward over the rope.
- Stand beside the rope; jump back and forth over the rope until you get to the end.
- Pick up the rope, then jump rope ten times.
- Jump rope with your left foot only, ten times.
- Jump rope with your right foot only, ten times.
- Jump rope as fast as you can.
- Jump rope down the line (on the floor) and back.
- Jump rope with a friend as many times as you can.

Applying Your Knowledge

In this learning activity you focus on a child who is sometimes reluctant to participate in physical activities. Ask the child if he or she would be willing to keep a fitness record for three days; then develop a plan for participating in physical activities. Explain you will keep your own fitness record and develop a plan, too. Give the child a copy of the example that follows before you begin. Read the example together to make sure the child understands how to record his or her physical activities.

Begin by recording your fitness activities for three days. At the end of the third day, meet with the child to discuss your fitness records. You and the child answer the questions provided, then develop fitness plans to be carried out over the next week.

At the end of the week meet with the child to discuss what happened.

There are blank forms for both you and the child.

Child's Individual Fitness Record and Plan
(Example)

Name: _Mark_   **Age:** _8 years_   **Date:** _October 12-14_

Fitness Record

Record your physical activities for each day.

Day One

Climbed on jungle gym, played catch with Jason, had P.E. at school.

Day Two

Jogged around the field five times with the Jogging Club.

Day Three

Played dodge ball.

Review your fitness record. What have you learned about yourself?

I don't like organized games very much. I'm not very good at sports. I like the Jogging Club.

Fitness Plan

List some physical activities you could do at home:

Take my dog for longer walks.

Ride my bike.

Rollerblade.

List some physical activities you could do at school:

Join in games at recess.

List some physical activities you could do at the program:

Continue jogging but do it more often.

Try the movement stations to see if I like them.

Participate in the soccer clinic, maybe start playing in soccer games.

Try out your plans for a week. Then meet with your fitness partner to discuss what happened.

Staff Member's Fitness Record and Plan
(Example)

Name: _Ms. Jenssen_　　　　　　　　**Date:** _October 12-14_

Fitness Record

Record your physical activities for each day.

Day One

Used my 20-minute workout video at home.

Day Two

Jogged with the Jogging Club.

Day Three

Played games with the children.

Review your fitness record. What have you learned about yourself?

I like getting up early to use the 20-minute workout video. It gives me extra energy.

Fitness Plan

List some physical activities you could do at home:

Use the 20 minute workout video every other day.

Walk rather than using my car whenever I can.

List some physical activities you could do at the program:

Continue leading and participating in the children's physical activities.

Try out your plans for a week. Then meet with your fitness partner to discuss what happened.

What Happened?

Child: *Mark*

The soccer clinic was a lot of fun. I am going to start playing soccer.

I didn't really like the movement stations. I didn't understand the directions.

I've been jogging almost every day. I feel great.

Staff member: *Ms. Jenssen*

I've been keeping up with my fitness plans, too. And I feel great, just like Mark does!

Plan for Encouraging Physical Development

The program can provide more clinics such as the soccer clinic where children can learn the rules and basic skills used for a sport.

Mark can ask a staff member to show him how to use the movement stations. I will rewrite the instructions to make sure they are clear.

Staff can continue encouraging Mark and noting his efforts.

Mark would like to try the 20-minute workout video. I said I would bring it in so he can watch it. If he is interested, I will help him start an Aerobics Club.

Child's Individual Fitness Record and Plan

Name: _____ Age: _____ Date: _____

Fitness Record

Record your physical activities for each day.

Day One

_____

_____

_____

_____

_____

_____

Day Two

_____

_____

_____

_____

_____

_____

Day Three

_____

_____

_____

_____

_____

_____

Review your fitness record. What have you learned about yourself?

_____

_____

_____

Fitness Plan

List some physical activities you could do at home:

_____

_____

_____

List some physical activities you could do at school:

_____

_____

_____

List some physical activities you could do at the program:

_____

_____

_____

Try out your plans for a week. Then meet with your fitness partner to discuss what happened.

Staff Member's Fitness Record and Plan

Name: _____ Date: _____

Fitness Record

Record your physical activities for each day.

Day One

_____
_____
_____
_____
_____
_____

Day Two

_____
_____
_____
_____
_____
_____

Day Three

_____
_____
_____
_____
_____
_____

Review your fitness record. What have you learned about yourself?

_____
_____
_____

Fitness Plan

List some physical activities you could do at home:

_____

_____

_____

List some physical activities you could do at the program:

_____

_____

_____

Try out your plans for a week. Then meet with your fitness partner to discuss what happened.

What Happened?

Child: _____

_____

_____

_____

_____

Staff member: _____

_____

_____

_____

_____

Plan for Encouraging Physical Development

_____

_____

_____

_____

_____

_____

_____

_____

_____

_____

Discuss this activity with your trainer and with your colleagues.

Learning Activity IV.
Using the Environment to Encourage Fine Motor Skills

IN THIS ACTIVITY YOU WILL LEARN TO:

- provide materials in each interest area that allow children to use fine motor skills; and

- review the program's materials to make sure they challenge and encourage children to further develop their fine motor skills.

Materials in each interest area can encourage children to use their fine motor skills.

In the school-age years children use their fine motor skills in many different ways—at home as they get dressed or comb their hair; at school as they write, draw, use computers, or conduct a science experiment; and while participating in a variety of activities at the school-age program. Many interest areas can give children opportunities to use their fine motor skills.

The types of materials you provide will vary according to the ages of the children in your program and their strengths, needs, and interests. Children who have had many opportunities to use their small muscles can usually have success with more challenging learning materials and equipment than can children with limited experiences. It is important to observe children using the materials so you will know when it is time to offer more challenging items and activities.

Applying Your Knowledge

In this learning activity you focus on how the environment provides opportunities for children to develop and practice fine motor skills. The chart on the following pages lists examples of how children use fine motor skills in the different interest areas. (See Module 3, Program Environment, for a discussion of interest areas.) As you review the chart, add more examples of ways in which the interest areas in your program can offer children opportunities to use their fine motor skills.

Using Fine Motor Skills

Interest Area	What Children Can Do
Quiet Area	*Draw and write with pencils, pens, and crayons* *Use a computer keyboard and mouse* *Turn pages of a magazine or book*
Dramatic Play Area	*Make puppets* *Put on costumes* *Use props*
Arts and Crafts Area	*Thread needles* *Use calligraphy pens* *Mold clay*
Sand and Water Table Area	*Pour water or sand through a funnel into a container* *Use a baster or eye dropper* *Tie the strings on a waterproof apron*

Using Fine Motor Skills
(continued)

Interest Area	What Children Can Do
Science and Nature Area	*Use tools to take apart a clock* *Hold a hand lens over a leaf* *Pour food into pet dishes*
Woodworking Area	*Hang tools on a pegboard* *Glue a dowel into a hole* *Use a ruler to measure a board*
Music Area	*Put a tape in the player* *Pluck a ukulele* *Shake a tambourine*
Blocks and Construction Area	*Build with Lincoln Logs* *Take apart Legos* *Tape fabric to a table to make a house*

Using Fine Motor Skills
(continued)

Interest Area	What Children Can Do
Board and Table Games Area	*Play pick-up sticks* *Do a puzzle* *Play checkers*
Math Area	*Make a design with pegs on a pegboard* *Use a calculator* *Write math problems*
Outdoors	*Draw hopscotch squares* *Paint at an easel* *Make snowballs*

Discuss this activity with your trainer.

Learning Activity V.
Helping Children Develop Positive Self-Concepts Through Physical Development

---

IN THIS ACTIVITY YOU WILL LEARN TO:

* recognize how physical development helps children develop socially and emotionally; and

* interact with children in ways that encourage a positive self-concept.

Physical development plays an important role in helping children feel good about themselves. When a child learns to pitch a ball, jump a distance, or build a geodesic dome with straws, the sense of accomplishment is enormous. The pride that comes from mastering physical skills helps children feel good about themselves. This sense of confidence and competence leads to emotional security and a willingness to risk learning difficult cognitive tasks. Thus, physical development affects children's growth in all areas and situations.

Encouraging Positive Self-Concepts Through Interactions With Children

Most children will eventually develop physical skills on their own; however, they may not feel proud of their accomplishments if they receive no encouragement or support for their efforts. This is especially true if children are slower to develop than their peers or feel pressure from adults. Your encouragement is therefore crucial to ensuring a sense of success. Here are some ways to provide encouragement. Add your own suggestion in the space provided.

Review for children how to do an activity right before they try it. "Before you do your long jump, swing your arms back and forth and bend your knees up and down. Imagine yourself in flight. Take a deep breath and jump as far as you can."

Verbally reassure a child who is reluctant or frightened. "I know you had a nasty fall last week when you were roller skating. Even though you were wearing safety equipment, it was scary. When you're ready to try again, would you like me to help you get started?"

Praise a child for trying something new. "I watched you hang upside down on the monkey bars today. Was that the first time you let go and hung by your legs?"

Suggest how a child can overcome an obstacle. "Before you cut out the eyes on your mask, put the bag on and ask a friend to mark where the holes for your eyes need to be."

_____

_____

_____

_____

When encouraging children, be sure to let them know you are praising them for their efforts—not how they stack up next to other children or standards. "I was watching you do handstands, today. You've really learned to keep your legs steady and straight." Children need to be made to feel important in their own right, not for meeting set measures of success. As always, it's important to be genuine in your praise. If praise comes too often and is vague, it loses its value. On the other hand, sincere praise can make a child feel good and try harder.

Playing Cooperative Games[7]

Playing cooperative games is another way children can develop positive self-concepts through physical activities. When children play cooperative games, everybody works together, everybody wins, and nobody loses. Children can play with rather than against each other. They don't worry about how well they will perform and they don't worry about failing. Instead, children focus on having fun during the game.

There are four essential elements to cooperative games:

Cooperation. Children learn to share, empathize, pay attention to each other's feelings, and work together toward a common end.

Acceptance. Each child has a meaningful role within the game and is partially responsible for the success of the group.

Involvement. Children feel a sense of belonging, contribution, and satisfaction because they are part of the action.

---

[7] Based with permission on Terry Orlick, _Cooperative Sports and Games Book_ (NY: Pantheon Books, 1978).

Fun. Children are free to have a good time without fear of failure or rejection. No matter what their skill level, they can enjoy the game and feel good about their involvement.

Try these cooperative games with children ages 5 to 7.

The following are examples of cooperative games children ages 5 to 7 usually enjoy.

Cooperative Musical Hula Hoops. This game is a variation of musical chairs. Have several children lay some hoops on the floor. When everyone is ready, turn on a music tape. Stop the music and ask children to hurry to get inside a hoop. Every time the music stops, a hoop is removed. The children have to work together to find room in the remaining hoops for everyone.

As an alternative, pairs of children can stand in a hoop, each holding up half of the hoop at waist level. As the music plays, the pairs of children skip around the room wearing their hoops. Each pair has to move in the same direction and at the same pace. When the music stops, two pairs have to combine in a single hoop. Turn on the music again. Next time it stops, the groups of four have to combine so there will be eight children per hoop. This involves lots of wiggling and giggling.

Big Turtle. Picture seven or eight children on their hands and knees under a "shell" trying to move in one direction. You're watching the game Big Turtle! Use a gym mat, large sheet of cardboard, or blanket as the shell. The children have to work together to get going in the same direction. An added challenge is to try to get the turtle over a mountain (a bench) or through an obstacle course (large cardboard boxes) without losing their shell.

Wagon Wheels. Have seven or eight children face each other and join hands to make a circle—this is the wagon wheel. Have the wheel move as a circle around the walls of the gym. As the wheel spins, two to three children at a time will have their backs touching the wall. Children can put the wagon wheel in reverse, change the speed limit, or become a hubcap. To do this, one child lets go and begins turning inside the circle. As he or she turns, the others follow. The circle keeps coiling until everyone still holding hands is wrapped into a human hub.

Big Snake. For this game, each child needs a partner. One child lies down on her stomach. Her partner lies down behind her and holds her ankles, making a two-person snake. Each snake slithers to another snake and joins together to make a four-person snake, then an eight-person snake. Snakes can try to turn over without coming apart or to move though obstacles.

Toesies. Partners lie on their backs or stomachs on the floor, touching feet to feet. They then try to roll across the floor keeping toes touched throughout. Variations include touching one foot or the other, touching feet while sitting, or touching feet with legs criss-crossed.

Grasshopper. Have eight to ten children stand around the edges of a blanket. Place a beach ball (the grasshopper) in the center of the blanket. Ask the children to pick up the blanket and try to make the grasshopper hop high in the air and back on the blanket without falling on the floor. A variation is to cut a hole in the blanket big enough for the ball to fall through. Ask the children if they can get the ball to pass through the hole or jump into the air and go through the hole.

The following are examples of cooperative games children ages 8 and up usually enjoy. They are also fun to play at family picnics or other events.

Try these cooperative games with children ages 8 and up.

Long, Long Jump. The objective of this game is for a group of children to jump collectively as far as possible. The first child begins at the starting line and makes a jump. The next player begins to jump where the other child landed. This game can be played indoors or outdoors, backward or forward, standing or running, hopping, skipping, or jumping. Each group can try to exceed the previous record set by an earlier group.

Collective Blanketball. Have children form two teams of eight to ten each. Spread out two blankets, one for each team. Have each team grasp the edges of its blanket. Place a beach ball in the middle of one blanket. To warm up, children can toss the ball into the air and catch it again or roll it around the inside edges of the blanket. Children can then pass the ball back and forward by tossing it in unison toward the receiving team. An alternative is to toss the ball straight up in the air so the other team has to run together to catch it. You can also use two balls—each team tosses their ball at the same time to the other team.

All-On-One-Side Volleyball. This version of volleyball is played with all the players (four to five children) on one side using a balloon or beach ball instead of a volleyball. A player volleys the ball to a teammate, then goes under the net to other side. The next player does the same thing. The last player to touch the ball taps it over the net and then scoots under. The object is to get all the players on the other side as many times as possible during the game.

Collective Stone. In this game there are no losers, just players involved in batting, fielding, and scoring. First, spread four or five bases on a field or floor. One person starts at home plate and propels (kicks, bats, or throws) an object (ball, puck, beanbag, Frisbee, or water balloon) into the field of play. This player then runs around the bases as quickly as possible. Players have to circle around each base, but they don't have to touch them. The fielders try to retrieve the object. The player who retrieves the object has to pass it to all the other fielders. When the last fielder gets the object, he or she yells "stone." The person who propelled the object must stop immediately (stone cold), even if between bases. Runners who have been "stoned" can continue around the bases after the next person up propels an object. Every time someone completes a circuit around the bases, they score. The game continues until the collective score equals the number of players—this should mean everyone has scored.

Players can vary the distance between bases and the number of bases to reflect their skill levels and the number of children playing. Fielders can all run to the object and quickly pass it to one another; stay in position with the closest person getting the object and throwing it to another; all run to the object, form a line, and pass the object under their legs; or make up another interesting way to play the game.

Shake the Snake. In this game, half the players are shakers and half stompers. Shakers hold eight-foot ropes between their thumbs and first fingers. They wiggle the rope so the end drags along the floor as they are running across the floor or field. Stompers try to step on the rope, thereby pulling it from the shaker's fingers. Once a stomper succeeds, the stomper and the shaker reverse roles. If the group is an uneven number, there can be more stompers than shakers.

You can adapt familiar games to make them cooperative.

Introduce children to these variations on popular games.

- Play softball by pitching to your own team, allowing unlimited pitches in which to hit the ball, and allowing every batter to have a turn at bat in every inning. This makes the game interesting for all the players and ensures every player will get a hit.

- Play basketball with no foul shots. You can also require that the ball be passed and touched by all members on the team before shooting. Foul shots slow down the game, so eliminating them makes the game more active. Having all players touch the ball encourages teamwork and cooperation.

- Play volleyball by rotating servers to the other team, allowing players to touch the net, and allowing players to hit the ball twice in a row. This makes it easier for younger children to play along with older ones.

- Play soccer in the "all score" version—everyone has to make a goal before the team can win. This encourages children to involve all players in the action.

- Play any game by rotating the positions. This allows all players to have a turn at different positions and encourages greater skill development. (If you're always positioned out in right field, you're not likely to have too many opportunities to learn to catch a ball.)

Applying Your Knowledge

In this learning activity you select a cooperative game to introduce to children in your program. You can focus on one age group or try a game with a mixed age group. Introduce the game, watch the children play, and write down what happened on the form provided. Begin by reading the example on the next page.

Playing a Cooperative Game
(Example)

Age Group: _Mostly 6- and 7-year olds_   **Date:** _February 8_

Game: _Big Turtle_   **Setting:** _Gymnasium_

How did you introduce the game?

I described the game, then I asked for two volunteers to demonstrate. Nicky and Erica said they would try it. I had them get down on their hands and knees and placed a large sheet of cardboard on top of them. They tried moving across the gym. Nicky said, "This is fun." Erica just giggled.

What did the children do?

The rest of the kids wanted a turn, so we started over with everyone under the cardboard. I said "Ready, set, go!" Some tried moving forward, some backward. Nicky suggested they all try going forward toward the bleachers. They had a hard time moving without the board falling off. Several times I heard children saying, "Slow down, you're making it fall off." The children on the sides reached up to steady the cardboard.

How did this game encourage self-esteem?

When they got to the bleachers, they all stood up and shouted, "We did it!" I could tell they all felt good about working together. They immediately wanted to do it again. Francie asked to be in the front. She said, "I'm not very big, so I make a good turtle head. I'll let everyone know when we're heading the wrong way."

Would you play this same game again? What changes would you make?

I asked the children if they would like to play again. Most said yes. Next time we could set up some obstacles or use the timer to see how long it takes to get from one point to another.

Playing a Cooperative Game

Age Group: _____   Date: _____

Game: _____   Setting: _____

How did you introduce the game?

_____

_____

_____

_____

What did the children do?

_____

_____

_____

_____

_____

_____

_____

_____

_____

How did this game encourage self-esteem?

_____

_____

_____

_____

Would you play this same game again? What changes would you make?

_____

_____

_____

Review your responses with your trainer. See the Bibliography for resources on cooperative games.

SUMMARIZING YOUR PROGRESS

You have now completed all the learning activities for this module. Whether you are an experienced school-age staff member or a new one, this module has probably helped you develop new skills for promoting children's physical development. Before you go on, take a few minutes to review your responses to the pre-training assessment for this module. Write a summary of what you learned, and list the skills you developed or improved.

_____

_____

_____

_____

_____

_____

_____

_____

_____

_____

_____

_____

_____

_____

If there are topics you would like to know more about, you will find recommended readings listed in the Orientation.

Your final step in this module is to complete the knowledge and competency assessments. Let your trainer know when you are ready to schedule the assessments. After you have successfully completed them, you will be ready to start a new module. Congratulations on your progress so far, and good luck with your next module.

ANSWER SHEETS

Promoting Children's Physical Development

<table>
<tr>
<td>

1. **What did Mr. Brody do to encourage the children's physical development?**

   a. He suggested the children bring up their idea for a sock hop at the next group meeting.

   b. He asked Sandra if her mother might be willing to teach the children some dances.

   c. He helped Sandra get her knitting back on the needles.

2. **Why did Mr. Brody suggest the children bring up their idea at the next group meeting?**

   a. He wanted to encourage the children to make their own plans for the sock hop.

   b. He knew more children needed to be involved to make the sock hop successful.

</td>
<td>

Reinforcing and Encouraging Physical Development Through an Appropriate Environment, Activities, and Interactions

</td>
</tr>
<tr>
<td>

1. **Why did Ms. Tunis set up the movement stations?**

   a. The movement stations can help children practice specific skills.

   b. Children can use the movement stations independently according to their own needs and interests.

2. **How did Ms. Tunis support Renaldo's development of gross motor skills?**

   a. She suggested movement stations that would be good for developing skills used in basketball.

   b. She sincerely complimented him on his ball-handling skills.

   c. She suggested he take a break and get a drink of water so he wouldn't get overheated.

</td>
<td>

Providing Equipment and Opportunities for Gross Motor Development

</td>
</tr>
</table>

Providing Equipment and Opportunities for Fine Motor Development

1. How did Mr. Shepard accommodate the different skill levels of the children?

   He suggested a similar game that could be played by children who might not be ready to play regular jacks.

2. How did Mr. Shepard encourage the fine motor development of Charles and Dana?

   a. He stepped in to suggest a game they might enjoy.

   b. He taught them how to play the game.

   c. He stepped back to let them play the game by themselves.

GLOSSARY

Eye-hand coordination   The ability to direct finger, hand, and wrist movements to accomplish a fine motor task—for example, fitting a piece in a puzzle or threading a needle.

Fine motor skills   Movements that involve the use of small muscles of the body, hands, and wrists—for example, picking up shells in the science area or cutting with a pair of scissors.

Gross motor skills   Movements that involve the use of large muscles of the body, the entire body, or large parts of the body—for example, running, cycling, or climbing.

Physical development   The gradual gaining of control over large and small muscles.

Sensory awareness   The gaining of information through sight, sound, touch, taste, and smell—for example, smelling spices or turning in the direction of a voice.

Module 5:

COGNITIVE

OVERVIEW

GUIDING SCHOOL-AGE CHILDREN'S COGNITIVE DEVELOPMENT INVOLVES:

- creating a varied environment that encourages children to experiment and make discoveries;

- interacting with children in ways that build on their natural curiosity; and

- providing opportunities for children to use their growing skills.

Cognitive development is the process of learning to think and to reason. We have learned a great deal about children's cognitive development from the work of Jean Piaget, Lev Vygotsky, and Howard Gardner.

Piaget defined the stages of thinking that children progress through from birth to maturity. Through his research, he noticed children think differently at each stage of development. For example, Piaget noticed young preschoolers think that a tall, thin glass can hold more water than a short, wide one—even when they see identical amounts of water poured into both glasses. This is because young children tend to focus on one feature of an object at a time—in this case, the height of the glass and not its width. By about age 6 or 7, though, children come to understand that the amount of water in both types of glasses is the same. This understanding comes when children are old enough to be able to think more abstractly and after they have had many experiences with water and other liquids. It is through their interactions with real objects and materials, according to Piaget, that children grow cognitively.

Piaget taught us that children think differently from adults.

Vygotsky's theories show us children learn best through social interactions with other children and adults; children need adults and "competent peers" to support their initial learning. Competent peers are children who already know what is being learned. Vygotsky compares this support to the scaffolding placed around new buildings as they are erected. This scaffolding provides a framework in which children can use their cognitive skills on their own. Vygotsky sees the role of adults as facilitators and guides, rather than as transmitters of knowledge.

Vygotsky explained how adults facilitate and guide children's learning.

Gardner defined eight types of intelligence.

Howard Gardner's research on how humans learn to think has led to an expanded definition of intelligence as more than just verbal and math skills. Each child's abilities are unique, and may be described in terms of potential for achievement in eight areas. These areas, or multiple intelligences, are described by Gardner as follows:[1]

1. **Logical**—analysis and mathematical reasoning. Children who have strong potential in this area might be outstanding chess players, solve difficult brain teasers, or easily calculate how to double a recipe or how much string is needed to set up a loom.

2. **Linguistic**—appreciating the rhythms and meanings of words and using language well. Children who have strong potential in this area might write poems and plays, develop large vocabularies, or read a wide variety of books.

3. **Musical**—appreciating different forms of music and producing and appreciating rhythm, pitch, and timbre. Children who have strong potential in this area might easily recognize the instruments in a piece of music, sing in harmony with others, or enjoy many kinds of music, from classical to popular.

4. **Spatial**—accurately seeing the physical world and being able to understand and make changes in it, as in the visual arts. Children who have strong potential in this area might construct complex block structures, plan and create three-dimensional structures, or paint an elaborate mural.

5. **Bodily Kinesthetic**—using the whole body, including both fine and gross motor skills to solve problems and create products. Children who have strong potential in this area might excel in dance or gymnastics, take apart and rebuild a radio or clock, or invent a squirrel-proof birdfeeder.

6. **Interpersonal**—understanding and responding appropriately to the moods, temperaments, motivations, and desires of other people. Children who have strong potential in this area might mediate conflicts between other children, show a younger child how to do something, or organize the group to perform a talent show.

7. **Intrapersonal**—knowing one's strengths, weaknesses, desires, and intelligences, and using the knowledge productively. Children who have a strong potential in this area might write an autobiography, set and pursue long term goals, or give advice to a friend on how to handle a difficult personal problem.

---

[1] Howard Gardner, *Multiple Intelligences: The Theory in Practice* (New York: Basic Books, 1993) as described in *Building the Primary Classroom*, Toni S. Bickart, Judy R. Jablon, and Diane Trister Dodge (Portsmouth, NH: Heinemann and Washington, DC: Teaching Strategies, Inc., 1999), p. 27.

8. Naturalist—being able to distinguish among, classify, and use environmental features. Children who have strong potential in this area might collect and organize things found in nature, memorize and talk about the detailed characteristics of cars and other items, or plan, plant, and care for the school-age program's vegetable garden.

Gardner's work shows the importance of getting to know each child's strengths. Instead of asking "How smart is this child?" you should ask "How is this child smart?" Use the answer to the second question to plan activities and experiences that will inspire a child.

Thus, to combine and summarize the work of Piaget, Vygotsky, and Gardner, children develop cognitive skills by continually exploring and investigating everything around them. They want to know how magnets work, what causes lightning, and why the days get shorter in winter. They are constantly investigating and solving problems, continually on a quest for answers to the questions that sprout from their minds.

Children's cognitive development is not merely the sum of what they know. Equally important is how children approach learning and thinking. Children need self-confidence and skills to explore, try out ideas, make mistakes, solve problems, and take on new challenges. Helping children develop and use their cognitive skills is an important part of your job. If you help children to see themselves as good learners, you will help them succeed in school and in life.

Most children are eager to explore the world around them and find out how things work. They want to explore the things they see in the world around them. You can build on this natural curiosity to guide children's cognitive development. First, you can create an environment that encourages children to experiment and make discoveries. Second, you can ask questions and talk with children in ways that build on their natural curiosity. Third, you can provide opportunities for children to use their growing skills.

Listed on the following page are examples of how school-age staff demonstrate their competence in guiding children's cognitive development.

It's important to know each child's strengths.

Self-confidence is an important part of cognitive development.

Creating an Interesting and Varied Environment That Encourages Children to Experiment and Make Discoveries

Supply materials that enable children to pursue and develop special talents for example, in art, design, music, athletics, science, and the culinary arts. "Denise, the calligraphy pens we ordered have arrived. Would you like to use them after school?"

Offer children space and time to develop and carry out their plans. "Jacques, you and Kendrick have been making some interesting structures out of Legos lately. Would you like to draw up some plans for building your own Legoland? We could set aside part of the construction area just for you two."

Create discovery boxes on topics such as magnets, static electricity, solar energy, and weather for children to use on their own or in small groups. "Ellen and Casey, now you are experts on solar energy, can you tell us how we're going to keep our houses warm in the future?"

Offer a wide range of books and magazines that reflect children's diverse interests and vary these resources to match children's changing interests and growing skills. "Laura if you want to know which dinosaurs were meat-eaters, you can look it up in the new dinosaur book in our library."

Provide open-ended materials that children can explore and use in many different ways. "Kara, I've noticed you like taking things apart. Someone gave us an old radio. Since it doesn't work any more, you could take it apart to see what's inside."

Provide materials that help children learn to classify, sequence, and understand cause and effect. "John, tell me about your experiment growing onions. Why do you think these three plants look so different from each other?"

Interacting With Children in Ways That Build on Their Natural Curiosity

Accept and respect children's ideas, suggestions, and solutions. "Devorah, that was a great idea to draw a picture of the rug you want to weave before you set up the loom. You were able to set aside enough yarn in the colors you need to carry out your plans."

Ask recall questions to help children describe what they already know, remember past events, and understand how what happened in the past relates to what's happening now. "Remember when we tried to grow tomatoes earlier this year and they all got big black spots? We looked it up and the gardening guide said something was missing from our soil. What do we need to add to the soil this year so the tomatoes will be healthy and edible?"

Ask questions to help children think about cause and effect or to make predictions (convergent). "So, you think there are 100 marbles in the jar because you counted the ones you could see on the top (10), then multiplied by how many layers (10) you think are in the jar. Without counting the marbles, what other ways could you estimate the number?"

Ask questions that encourage children to come up with several possible ideas or solutions (divergent). "I've noticed the prop boxes aren't used very often. Can you think of some themes for new prop boxes or some things to add to the ones we have to make them more interesting?"

Ask questions that encourage children to make a judgment (evaluative). "What would you do if you saw a friend do something dangerous?"

Expose children to new information, ideas, concepts, and experiences. "The city has a new recycling law and we need to begin separating our recyclable paper, plastic, and metal materials and containers. How can we make sure we know what's recyclable and remember to put them in the right bin?"

Talk to and question children about what they are observing and learning. "You're right Tim, geese flew over our playground every day this week. Where do you think they're going?"

Encourage children to make decisions and solve their own problems without adult assistance. "Sammy and Hannah, I'm sure you can work out a way to share the stethoscope in the health clinic prop box so you can both have a good time."

Providing Opportunities for Children to Use Their Growing Skills

Encourage children's emerging sense of humor by suggesting they write and share riddles, jokes, and limericks. "Pedro, you've written a lot of funny limericks. Would you like to type them up on the computer and make a book? "

Involve children in planning and evaluating the program's routines and activities. "It's time to develop the menus for next month's snack. You can either come to the meeting this afternoon or write down your suggestions and put them in the box."

Plan activities that allow children to explore natural science and the outdoor environment. "The Nature Club will meet on Tuesday afternoon. We're going on a swamp walk, so wear your boots. We'll bring along a tape player to record swamp sounds."

Provide opportunities for children to participate in and learn about the real world—locally, within the state, nationally, or internationally. "The skits you made up were really funny. Would you like to perform them for hospitalized children?"

Follow a schedule that allows children to choose what they want to do and provides sufficient time for their long-term projects. "Emily has been keeping a weather journal of the temperature highs and lows, precipitation (rain and snow), and barometric pressure. Each day she notes how sunny or cloudy it is and predicts what it will be like the next day."

Involve children in setting rules and establishing procedures for the program's operations. "Now that the warmer weather is here children can choose to play outdoors during the free choice periods. We need a system for keeping track of who's inside and who's outdoors. Do you have any suggestions?"

Allow children plenty of time to talk to each other and to the staff. "You two don't have to stop your conversation but when you're through, could you help us get ready to go outside?"

Provide opportunities for children to demonstrate their growing cognitive skills and apply them to new situations. "Laura and Hank, you've been reading lots of books about dinosaurs. What are some ways you could share what you learned with the rest of us?"

Introduce children to the steps in problem solving. "Polly, now that you've made your prediction, conducted your experiment, and observed the results, what are your conclusions?"

Provide children with opportunities to learn in ways that match their learning style. "David, I know you enjoy talking things through. Why don't you record the story about the tournament using the tape recorder and then type it up for the newspaper?"

Guiding Children's Cognitive Development

In the following situations, school-age staff are guiding children's cognitive development. As you read each one, think about what the staff are doing and why. Then answer the questions that follow.

Rita comes bounding into the program calling, "Victor, Victor, I got a letter from my pen pal, just like you said I would!" Mr. Crain looks up from his Parcheesi game and says, "I'm over here. Come tell me all about it." "Well," starts an out-of-breath Rita, "her name is Katerina and she's 11, too, and she has two brothers, one older and one younger, and she lives in a small apartment in Moscow and she wants to be a doctor and she was thrilled to hear from me." Mr. Crain smiles, "She sounds very similar to a girl I know." "Yeah," responds Rita. "I couldn't believe it. Maybe she wants to be a pediatrician too." "What else did she tell you about her life in Russia?" asks Mr. Crain. "She said she has to wear lots of sweaters to keep warm in their apartment—they don't have much heat. She goes to an all-girls school, but she likes a boy who lives next door and is friends with her brother." Mr. Crain smiles as he listens, then adds, "Have you written back already? It would be just like you to sit down and respond immediately so you could get another letter from Katerina as quickly as possible." "Not yet," laughs Rita. "I'll write to her this afternoon. Maybe when Jocelyn and Danica see my letter they'll want to get their own pen pals." "Sounds like a good plan," says Mr. Crain. "I'll post the address for the pen pal organization that pairs American children with children from other countries on the bulletin board."

Creating an Interesting and Varied Environment That Encourages Children to Experiment and Make Discoveries

1. How did Mr. Crain encourage Rita to experiment and make discoveries?

_____

_____

_____

2. What did Rita learn from becoming a pen pal?

_____

_____

_____

Interacting With Children in Ways That Build on Their Natural Curiosity

Seven-year-old Samantha recently went with her family to a planetarium. In discussing the visit with Ms. Williams, she blurts out, "I know why the stars shine at night. It's because we live inside the earth. When it's dark inside the earth, it's light outside. When we look out through the holes in the earth, we see the light of the stars." Ms. Williams immediately realizes Samantha has pieced together information about day and night and how light is viewed and then developed her own explanation about the stars. She holds back the temptation to provide Samantha with a "correct" explanation, and instead says, "That's a very interesting theory. Let's dig some holes in the ground so that we can see how your theory works."

1. Why did Ms. Williams not just give Samantha the correct facts?

_____

_____

_____

2. How did Ms. Williams encourage Samantha to think through her theory?

_____

_____

_____

Ten-year-old Brian was so excited about a recent camping trip that he decided to publish a book about it. For the last three days, after snack and a turn around the track with the Running Club, he diligently typed his story on the computer. Now that he's ready to illustrate his story, Brian seems troubled. Despite Ms. Saavedra's encouragement, Brian is dead set against using hand-drawn pictures. Even though he thinks his pictures look "okay," he says they will take away from the professional look of his story. "I wish there was some way I could draw on the computer screen," says Brian. "Then my drawings would look as good as my writing." "Well there is a way," says Ms. Saavedra. "Here are two drawing programs for the computer. You can experiment with them and see which looks the most professional to you. Both of the programs have built-in tutorials to help you use them. Plus, the users' manuals are in the library if you need them." After spending half an hour playing with the programs, Brian selects one that is object-oriented. By piecing together objects of differing shapes, sizes, and colors, Brian is able to create illustrations. Six illustrations later, Brian declares, "My book is finished."

Providing Opportunities for Children to Use Their Growing Skills

1. How did Ms. Saavedra provide an opportunity for Brian to use his skills?

_____

_____

_____

3. How did Ms. Saavedra support Brian's mastery of new skills and concepts?

_____

_____

_____

Compare your answers with those on the answer sheet at the end of this module. If your answers are different, discuss them with your trainer. There can be more than one good answer.

Your Own Experiences with Learning

Learning is a lifelong experience.

Cognitive development continues throughout life. People don't stop learning when they leave school; they continue to refine their thinking and reasoning skills. You probably know people you feel are good learners and thinkers. Most likely, in many situations you think of yourself as a good learner. People who have confidence in their ability to learn generally have some of the following characteristics.

- They are not afraid to accept a challenge. "I don't know the answer but I'll find out."

- When they confront a problem, they don't give up if they can't resolve it right away. They try to figure out what to do. "I'm going to ask Mary's parents if anything is happening at home that might explain why she's suddenly become so aggressive."

- They are curious and interested in learning new things. "I hear that book is really interesting. I'd like to read it when you're finished."

- They are creative thinkers—they can look at something and see lots of possibilities. "I think that if I work a few extra hours on the weekend, I'll be able to take that class on Friday night."

- They speak up and say what they think. "I'm not sure I agree with you. Here's what I see happening."

We aren't all intelligent in the same ways.

We don't all have the same abilities, nor do we need to. An auto mechanic knows a lot about the parts of a car, what makes it go, and how to fix it. When there's a problem, the mechanic tries to figure out the cause. If you know very little about how a car operates, this doesn't make you less smart. You know other things the mechanic doesn't know. What's important is whether we each have the knowledge and skills to function in our lives.

Many factors affect our ability to learn something new. Most important is whether the new information is useful to us. If we can see a way to use what we are learning, we are likely to be more interested in putting forth the effort. It helps if the new information is related either to something we already know about or know how to do—or to something we've wanted to know for some time.

Each of us has a different style or way of learning that works best for us. Some need to read over directions and think about them for a while. Others prefer to watch someone else demonstrate a task, or need to hear directions explained a couple of times.

As an adult you are probably aware of what helps you learn a new skill or new idea. Think of a time recently when you were in a learning situation—for instance, learning to swim, taking an adult education course, or going through these modules. List some factors that helped you to learn in that situation.

Learning style affects what we learn.

_____

_____

_____

_____

_____

_____

_____

_____

Some factors that affect our ability to learn relate to the instructor or to the material itself: how the information is presented, how it is organized, and whether it is on our level. Our readiness to learn is also affected by how we feel at the time. If we are tired, distracted, uncomfortable, or unsure of what is expected of us, we are less likely to learn.

Many factors can affect our ability to learn.

This training program is designed to help you learn new concepts and skills and feel good about yourself as a learner. The training design includes a number of strategies to make it a positive learning experience:

• The information is organized into individual modules so you won't be overwhelmed with too much information at once.

• All the modules relate to your work and should be immediately useful.

• There are many examples within each module to help you understand the content.

• Answer sheets, a colleague, or your trainer can give you feedback.

• You receive your own set of materials to keep as an ongoing reference on the job.

• You complete many of the learning activities with the children in your program.

As you enhance your skills and knowledge in ways that make you feel confident, you will be able to do the same thing for children. Like you, children learn best when they are interested in and ready to receive new information. They like to try out new ideas and discover what works and what doesn't on their own. As you go through these modules, you will try out many ideas and discover for yourself what approaches work best for you and for the children in your program.

When you have finished this overview section, you should complete the pre-training assessment. Refer to the glossary at the end of this module for definitions of the terms used.

PRE-TRAINING ASSESSMENT

Listed below are the skills school-age staff use to guide children's cognitive development. Think about whether you do these things regularly, sometimes, or not enough. Place a check in one of the columns on the right for each skill listed. Then discuss your answers with your trainer.

Creating an Interesting and Varied Environment That Encourages Children to Experiment and Make Discoveries

	I Do This		
	Regularly	Sometimes	Not Enough
1. Supplying materials that allow children to pursue and develop special talents.	☐	☐	☐
2. Offering children space and time to develop and carry out their plans.	☐	☐	☐
3. Creating discovery boxes on topics such as magnets, static electricity, solar energy, and weather.	☐	☐	☐
4. Offering a wide range of books and magazines that reflect children's diverse interests.	☐	☐	☐
5. Providing open-ended materials that children can explore and use in many different ways.	☐	☐	☐
6. Providing materials that help children learn to classify, sequence, and understand cause and effect.	☐	☐	☐

Interacting With Children in Ways That Build on Their Natural Curiosity

7. Accepting and respecting children's ideas, suggestions, and solutions.	☐	☐	☐
8. Asking recall questions to help children describe what they know, remember the past, and relate the past to the present.	☐	☐	☐
9. Asking convergent questions to help children think about cause and effect or to make predictions.	☐	☐	☐
10. Asking divergent questions so children can think of several possible ideas or solutions.	☐	☐	☐
11. Asking evaluative questions so children learn to make judgments.	☐	☐	☐

Interacting With Children in Ways That Build on Their Natural Curiosity (continued)

	I Do This		
	Regularly	Sometimes	Not Enough
12. Exposing children to new information, ideas, concepts, and experiences.	☐	☐	☐
13. Talking to and questioning children about what they are observing and learning.	☐	☐	☐
14. Encouraging children to make decisions and solve problems on their own, without adult assistance.	☐	☐	☐

Providing Opportunities for Children to Use Their Growing Skills

	Regularly	Sometimes	Not Enough
15. Encouraging children's emerging sense of humor by suggesting they write and share riddles, jokes, and limericks.	☐	☐	☐
16. Involving children in planning and evaluating the program's routines and activities.	☐	☐	☐
17. Planning activities that allow children to explore natural science and the outdoor environment.	☐	☐	☐
18. Providing opportunities for children to participate in and learn about the real world.	☐	☐	☐
19. Following a schedule that allows children to choose what they want to do and provides enough time for long-term projects.	☐	☐	☐
20. Involving children in setting rules and establishing procedures for the program's operations.	☐	☐	☐
21. Allowing children plenty of time to talk to each other and to the staff.	☐	☐	☐
22. Providing opportunities for children to demonstrate their growing cognitive skills and apply them to new situations.	☐	☐	☐

Providing Opportunities for Children to Use Their Growing Skills (continued)	**I Do This**		
	Regularly	Sometimes	Not Enough

23. Introducing children to the steps in problem solving ☐ ☐ ☐

24. Providing opportunities for children to learn in ways that match their learning styles. ☐ ☐ ☐

Review your responses, then list three to five skills you would like to improve or topics you would like to learn more about. When you finish this module, you can list examples of your new or improved knowledge and skills.

_____

_____

_____

_____

_____

Begin the learning activities for Module 5, Cognitive.

LEARNING ACTIVITIES

Learning Activity I.
Using Your Knowledge of Child Development to Guide Cognitive Development

---

IN THIS ACTIVITY YOU WILL LEARN TO:

- recognize some typical thinking and reasoning behaviors of school-age children; and

- use what you know about school-age children to guide their cognitive development.

During the school-age years children begin to think in ways that are familiar to us as adults. They start to think and reason logically about objects and people in their environment. School-age children can readily order and organize things by size, color, volume, or tone. They understand substances remain the same even when their shape or physical arrangement changes. For example, they are no longer confused when a ball of clay is rolled into a long, snake shape. They realize that both shapes contain the same amount of clay.

In the school-age years, children's thinking begins to resemble that of adults.

School-age children are developing an appreciation of rules—in games, sports, clubs, and life—and typically they take great satisfaction in following rules to the letter. By about age 8 or 9, most children can differentiate between right and wrong. For the majority of children this means things are either "right" or "wrong" and there are no "gray" areas open to interpretation. Something is either "right" or it's not.

Older school-age children are able to think abstractly. This is quite a leap in learning from the preschooler who must see everything in concrete terms in order to learn. School-age children are now able to approach problems systematically. They are willing to consider a wide array of solutions to a problem before settling on an answer. They are comfortable using trial and error to solve problems. By the onset of adolescence, most children have become mature thinkers.

During these years, children increasingly focus on the skills they need for school and life. They enjoy working on real projects and making things. Some older children like competing—with other children and against themselves. Unlike younger children who are more interested in the process of creating rather than a finished product, most school-age children take deep satisfaction in seeing a project through to completion.

School-age children need the support and guidance of caring adults.

It's important to keep in mind that although children this age are capable, they are still children. They may not need guidance and attention to the same degree younger children do, but they need the support of caring adults. You can help school-age children develop and enhance their cognitive skills by providing a challenging environment and serving as their resource and guide.

Applying Your Knowledge

The charts which follow list some typical behaviors of children at ages 5 to 7, 8 to 10, and 11 to 12. Included are behaviors relevant to cognitive development. The right column asks you to identify ways staff can use this information to guide cognitive development. Try to think of as many examples as you can. As you work through the module, you will learn new strategies, and you can add them to the charts. You are not expected to think of all the examples at one time. If you need help getting started, turn to the completed charts at the end of the module. By the time you complete all the learning activities, you will find you have learned many ways to guide children's cognitive development.

> As you complete the charts that follow, keep in mind that many of the examples of children's behavior and staff responses apply to more than one age group. Developmentally appropriate programs are based on a knowledge of child development and are responsive to children's individual strengths, needs, and interests. Therefore, it is important to observe children regularly and to use what you learn to individualize the program.

Understanding and Responding to 5- to 7-Year-Old Children

What 5- to 7-Year-Old Children are Like	How Staff Can Use This Information to Guide Cognitive Development
They are eager to learn the answers to "why" questions.	*Respect children's questions. Help them predict answers to their questions and test them out. Offer answers to stretch their thinking.*
They like to take on responsibility.	
They are developing an understanding of time, but the concepts of past and future are still vague.	
They are curious and want to explore many things.	
They express their thoughts and feelings—typically in great and vivid detail.	
They read and write simple words, sentences, and texts.	
They are beginning to understand number concepts and relationships but still need experiences with real objects to fully grasp them.	

Understanding and Responding to 8- to 10-Year-Old Children

What 8- to 10-Year-Old Children are Like	How Staff Can Use This Information to Guide Cognitive Development
They like to collect and catalogue "things" such as coins, baseball cards, and rocks.	*Provide space and time for children to create displays of their collections. Use nature walks and field trips as opportunities to plan new collections. Share your own collections, for example, owls collected on trips to other countries.*
They are intrigued by how things relate to one another.	
They understand explanations and rules and enjoy following rules to the letter.	
They may be critical of their own performance and may need help sorting out realistic goals from unrealistic ones.	
They make step-by-step plans and carry them out.	
They work on projects over a long period of time.	
They vary greatly in academic abilities and interests.	
They ask many questions and want thoughtful answers in return.	

Understanding and Responding to 11- to 12-Year-Old Children

What 11- to 12-Year-Old Children are Like	How Staff Can Use This Information to Guide Cognitive Development
They typically can think in abstract terms.	*Talk with children about current events and social issues such as recycling. Encourage children to make predictions about the future. If children are interested, help them organize a Futurists Club to learn more about what people think the world will be like when they are grownups.*
They are increasingly skilled in reading and writing.	
They use a systematic approach to solve problems.	
They add, subtract, multiply, and divide with growing skill.	
They are serious about working and learning.	
They show proficiency in particular skills and talents.	
They can appreciate other points of view.	

When you have completed as much as you can of these charts, discuss your answers with your trainer. As you do the rest of the learning activities, you can refer back to the charts and add more examples of how school-age staff guide children's cognitive development.

Learning Activity II.
Helping Children Understand Their World

IN THIS ACTIVITY YOU WILL LEARN TO:

- observe how school-age children make sense of the world; and

- support children's cognitive growth throughout the learning cycle.

School-age children gradually learn to accept the expectations and standards of society.

Children have an inborn desire to make sense of the world in which they live. They first gain understanding by making sense of their own experiences. These personal interpretations give way to shared understandings of what they know and believe and how it fits into the way other people think. Consider this example. At age 7, Sarah writes stories using invented spelling. As she is exposed to books and print, she begins to modify the personal system she uses for spelling by incorporating "correct" spelling and grammar she has seen and heard repeatedly through books and in her classroom into her writing. Eventually Sarah uses conventional rules of spelling and grammar rather than her own system. This cycle of learning is a natural process which occurs over and over during one's lifetime. It takes place whenever we acquire a new skill or understanding.

The learning cycle includes four stages.

As described by Bredekamp and Rosegrant,[2] the learning cycle takes place in four stages:

1. Awareness. In this first stage of the learning cycle, we experience the skill or concept in a broad, general way.

> Matt watches children playing computer games, including one he has never tried. On several occasions he stands behind a group of children playing labyrinth and maze games. At this stage he is becoming aware of what it is he would like to learn.

2. Exploration. In this second stage we try to figure out the components of what it is we want to learn. Through observation and active use of all our senses we construct our own personal meanings.

---

[2] Based on Sue Bredekamp and Teresa Rosegrant (Eds.), *Reaching Potentials: Appropriate Curriculum and Assessment for Young Children* (Washington, DC: National Association for the Education of Young Children, 1992), pp. 32–34.

When no one else is at the computer, Matt tries playing the computer game on his own. Using the maze, he experiments with the cursor. Several times he causes the program to crash. Matt concludes the key to winning at the games is speed; he must move quickly or the programs will crash.

3. Inquiry. In the third stage, we compare the personal meanings we have developed with those held by others. In this stage we learn to adapt what we think to fit societal conventions.

Matt asks some of the more experienced players if he can sit with them as they play. Keith responds to Matt's request and explains the strategies he uses. Matt asks Keith a number of questions. Keith responds both verbally and by demonstration. By watching Keith, Matt learns the program does not crash easily; Matt was making it crash by clicking on the mouse inappropriately. Matt also realizes succeeding at these games relies more on planning than it does on speed. Matt plays along with Keith. Then he plays on his own using the strategies he learned from Keith and others he developed based on what Keith had shown him.

4. Utilization. In this last stage, we apply what we've learned to real life situations.

Matt confidently plays computer games on his own or with other children. He especially enjoys playing with Keith, who no longer needs to serve as a mentor. Matt is excited with his new proficiency and eagerly joins the Computer Games Club.

You can promote children's learning of both skills and knowledge by knowing these stages of the learning cycle and helping children progress through them.

Here are some strategies you might use to support children throughout the learning cycle:

Try these suggestions.

At the **awareness** stage, you can:

- establish interest areas and provide materials in response to children's skills, needs, and interests;

- introduce new materials and props;

- invite guest speakers and parents to discuss new ideas and concepts;

- pose problems for children to solve; and

- show interest in and enthusiasm for children's ideas.

At the **exploration** stage, you can:

* encourage active investigation and use of the environment;
* follow a schedule that allows children to choose what they want to do and what materials they want to use;
* extend children's imaginative and dramatic play;
* describe for children what they are doing;
* ask open-ended questions that encourage exploration and discovery;
* have children reflect on their activities and relate these to past experiences; and
* respect children's mistakes and help them learn from them.

At the **inquiry** stage, you can:

* focus children's attention on certain details or aspects of an object, topic, or idea;
* ask open-ended questions that focus children's attention on key characteristics or relationships;
* provide information upon request;
* expose children to accepted standards and beliefs;
* help children compare and contrast; and
* help children generalize and make connections.

At the **utilization** stage, you can:

* help children apply knowledge and skills to new situations;
* provide meaningful ways for children to apply their learning; and
* assist children in formulating new hypotheses (predictions about what might be the answer to a question or problem).

The learning cycle repeats itself.

Once children pass through the learning cycle, it begins again. With their newly acquired skills or knowledge, children are exposed to new skills and new knowledge; they enter the awareness stage again. For example, after Matt learned to play the labyrinth and maze games he became aware of other computer games and wanted to learn to play them. Learning is a dynamic process which, hopefully, never ends.

Applying Your Knowledge

In this learning activity you complete observations of three children in your program: one age 5 to 7, one 8 to 10, and one 11 or 12. If you work with only one age group or do not have a full span of ages enrolled, conduct three representative observations. Observe each child as he or she works on an activity or interacts with another child or an adult. (Conducting and recording observations is covered in Module 12, Program Management. Refer to this module if you need to review this skill.)

As you complete your observations, ask yourself, "In what stage of the learning cycle is this child?" Then review your observation notes and complete the observation summary forms. It may take you a week or longer to finish your observations. Two examples are provided. A sample blank form follow the examples.

Observation Summary:
Supporting Cognitive Growth Throughout the Learning Cycle
(Example: 5- to 7-year-old)

Child: _Toni_   **Age:** _5 1/2 years_   **Date:** _June 8_

Briefly describe what you observed:

Toni and a group of children were feeding the fish in our aquarium. One child observed the water line in the tank was much lower than it was several weeks ago. The group agreed this was true. Toni offered an explanation: "The fish are drinking the water!"

In what stage of the learning cycle is this child? How do you know?

I think Toni is in the exploration stage. Based on her observations, she came up with an amusing—but logical —explanation for her observations.

What can you do to support this child's cognitive growth?

I thought Toni might learn from setting up an experiment to test her hypothesis that the fish are drinking the water. To do this, we decided to fill up a second tank, the same size as our aquarium. The second tank has no fish. Using a grease pencil, Toni marked the water level in both tanks. She'll check the water level of both tanks each day. She's sure the water in the second tank will not go down. I can't wait to see her reactions as the experiment progresses.

(Example: 8- to 10-year-old)

Child: _Seth_   **Age:** _12 years_   **Date:** _June 9_

Briefly describe what you observed:

Seth is very interested in baseball cards. This afternoon he went through his cards, dividing them into three piles. I couldn't figure out what criteria he was using to sort his cards—they weren't grouped by teams, make of card, year, or anything I could think of. I asked Seth to tell me how he was sorting the cards. He said he was putting the cards into piles according to how much he thinks they are worth—one pile was for players he thought might someday get into the Hall of Fame, another was for cards in mint condition, and the third was for rookies with uncertain futures.

In what stage of the learning cycle is this child? How do you know?

Seth is able to categorize using abstract concepts—the potential value of the cards. This is an advanced way of thinking. It depends on making predictions about how much the cards will be worth in the future. I would say he is definitely in the utilization stage.

What can you do to support this child's cognitive growth?

I plan to build on Seth's interest in making money from his baseball cards by going to the library and checking out the latest issue of Becket's baseball card magazine which will give him information on the current value of his cards. I'll also suggest he make some graphs and bar charts on the computer to illustrate the value of his collection. He could then use his graphs and charts to help him decide whether to hold, sell, or trade specific cards. I'll ask him if he'd like to sponsor a card show. He and other interested children could swap cards and share their collections.

Observation Summary:
Supporting Cognitive Growth Throughout the Learning Cycle

Child: _____   Age: _____   Date: _____

Briefly describe what you observed:

_____

_____

_____

_____

_____

_____

_____

_____

In what stage of the learning cycle is this child? How do you know?

_____

_____

_____

What can you do to support this child's cognitive growth?

_____

_____

_____

_____

_____

_____

_____

_____

Use this form to document your observations. Make as many copies of it as you need. When you have completed three observations, discuss them with your trainer and your colleagues. Plan ways to continue supporting children's cognitive development.

Learning Activity III.
Asking Questions To Promote Children's Thinking Skills

IN THIS ACTIVITY YOU WILL LEARN TO:

- recognize the skills children use in learning; and

- ask questions that help children expand their thinking skills.

Children need to feel good about learning.

There is an endless amount of information school-age children can learn. As important as what children learn, however, is whether they are "learning how to learn" and whether they feel good about their ability to learn. Some of the thinking skills children develop and use throughout their lives are described below along with ideas you can use to help children become "good" learners.

Children use their senses to identify characteristics.

During the awareness and exploration stages of learning (described in the previous learning activity) children use their senses—touching, seeing, hearing, smelling, and tasting—to learn about concepts and ideas. They learn to give labels to the characteristics they notice—for example, stiff or flexible, magenta or lime, cloudy or clear, and sour or sweet. You can help children become aware of the characteristics of things around them by asking questions such as the following:

> "How would you describe the way these different types of sandpaper feel?"

> "What does the smell of the vanilla in this jar remind you of?"

> "What makes this screwdriver different from the other one?"

Children use classification skills to make sense of the world.

Children use classification skills to make sense of the world. They sort objects, people, events, and ideas into groups according to traits they have in common. Here are some questions that help children develop their classifying skills:

> "How could you arrange our books so other children can find what they need?"

> "How can you group the sports equipment so it's easy to get out and put away?"

"How will you decide what to put in each discovery box?"

"Your graphs compare how many boys versus girls are in the program. What are some other ways to describe the children in the program?"

School-age children like to compare themselves with their peers. This interest can be used to enhance their classification skills. You can encourage children to conduct surveys and organize the information into graphs—for example, favorite clothes, birthplaces, "pet peeves," or favorite vegetable. This type of activity can help children learn how people are alike and different, an important step in learning to appreciate and value each other.

Sequencing is the ability to put things in a certain order. For example, a time sequence would be first, next, last; a sequence of sizes would be small, medium, and large; sequences in sounds might go from loudest to most quiet; and color shades could go from darkest to lightest. Sequencing is also an important part of the math and reading skills children develop during the school-age years. Here are some questions that help children develop their sequencing skills:

Sequencing helps children in math and reading.

"What happened first in the story? Then what happened? What happened at the end?"

"You're making an interesting pattern with your beads—two green; two purple; red, yellow, blue; two purple, two green. If you keep using this sequence, how many sets of this pattern will it take to complete your bracelet?"

"How should we arrange these drums so that they go from the lowest sound to the highest?"

School-age children are constantly trying to figure out why something happened or what is going to happen next. For example, if a child notices the leaves are starting to fall, she might announce the weather's going to turn cold soon. This child remembers from past years falling leaves marked the end of warm weather and the beginning of colder days. Another child might notice the plants in the window are drooping. He knows from past experience the plants need water. The last time the plants were this droopy they almost died. As children develop a more refined understanding of cause and effect, their abilities to make accurate predictions also expand. By the school-age years, making predictions is an active part of most children's approach to problem solving. Scientists call this "formulating hypotheses." To help children learn to make predictions, ask questions such as these:

Understanding cause and effect leads to predicting outcomes.

"Where should you put the cheese in the maze to help our pet mouse, Mickey, learn the new route?"

"What do you suppose would happen if we didn't have any rules in our program?"

"Last time you made a lanyard with four colors, it took two yards of each color. How much gimp will you need now, if you're only using three colors?

Ask open-ended questions to encourage children's thinking.

Open-ended questions have many possible answers. They encourage children to think of lots of possible answers and they stimulate further thinking. There are four types of questions you can include in your everyday conversations with children.

Recall questions ask children to describe what they already know: "What do you already know about a swamp?" or "What happened to the black stallion in the book you just finished reading?"

Convergent questions ask about cause and effect or ask a child to make a prediction: "Based on this cover, what type of music do you think will be on this CD?" "How might Roger feel if you used the wood he put aside for his project ?"

Divergent questions require a child to come up with possible ideas and solutions: "What are some ways we can use the *National Geographic* magazines Jose's father gave us?" or "What jobs should we add to the list after we set up the new terrarium?"

Evaluative questions ask a child to make a judgment: "What would you do if you got lost on a field trip?" or "What would you do if you saw some friends smoking?"

Applying Your Knowledge

This learning activity will help you become more aware of how children develop thinking skills. During the next week, keep notes on the times you see children demonstrating thinking skills and what you say to promote thinking and learning. Try to use all four questioning techniques. The sample chart that follows will give you an idea of how to do yours. You can keep a small note pad or index cards handy to jot down your observations as they occur. Review the example; then complete the blank chart with your own observations.

Promoting Children's Thinking
(Example)

Dates: _March 5-9_

Thinking Skill	What the Child Did	What I Said To Promote Thinking
Noticing characteristics of things	_Emilio (7 years) carried a tray of marbles and a magnifying glass to the table. He sat down to examine the marbles._	_"How are these marbles the same? different?"_ _"What can you discover using the magnifying glass?"_
Classifying	_Lisa (11 years) announced she was going to clean up the collage supplies. She took the containers off the shelf and placed them on the table._	_"What's your plan for organizing the supplies?"_ _"Yes, I'd agree it makes sense to separate the different kinds of fabric. How will you decide what goes together?"_ _"That's a good idea. Sorting by type of fabric—cotton, wool, felt, corduroy—will make it easier for children to find what they want."_
Sequencing	_Dean and Chaundra (8 years) came in from the playground with a pile of leaves they collected. They spread them out on a table and examined them._	_"It looks like you have a lot of different leaves. Can you put them in order by size and type?"_ _"After you order them by size and type would you like to find out what kind of trees they came from? There are some books about trees in the library area."_
Understanding cause and effect	_Janice (5 years) is working with some older children making paper maché masks. Each child has made a bowl of paste using wheat flour and water. Janice's paste is much thinner than the other children's. It's making the paper soggy. She sees the others aren't having this problem. She asks if she can use someone else's paste._	_"You could probably use someone else's paste, but let's try to find out how to fix yours."_ _"What could you do to make it less runny?"_ _"That might make it thicker. You could add more wheat flour and see what happens."_

Promoting Children's Thinking

Dates: _____

Thinking Skill	What the Child Did	What I Said To Promote Thinking
Noticing characteristics of things		
Classifying		

Promoting Children's Thinking
(continued)

Thinking Skill	What the Child Did	What I Said To Promote Thinking
Sequencing		
Understanding cause and effect		

Discuss your observations and use of questioning with your trainer.

Learning Activity IV.
Using the Physical Environment to Promote Cognitive Development

---

IN THIS ACTIVITY YOU WILL LEARN TO:

- use the environment to help children develop cognitively; and

- provide materials that invite children to explore and question.

A well-planned environment supports cognitive development.

As discussed in Module 3, Program Environment, the environment of your program sets the stage for learning. A well-planned environment is one filled with challenging and interesting materials and equipment, and with a layout and schedule that encourage children to make choices.

The environment can offer many opportunities for children to observe and explore concepts, relationships, and ideas. Therefore, it is important to think carefully about the materials and equipment you select. Materials should reflect the skills and interests of the children in the program. Children grow and change each day, so you and your colleagues will want to review your observation notes to assess the appropriateness of what's on hand and decide when changes are needed. Keep in mind the seven areas of intelligence identified by Howard Gardner: logical, linguistic, musical, spatial, bodily kinesthetic, interpersonal, and intrapersonal. Include equipment and materials that enable you to allow children to build on their strengths.

The environment should respond to children's basic intellectual needs.

Consider these basic intellectual needs of school-age children when equipping your environment:[3]

Children like to focus on reality. Most school-age children like to participate in activities rooted in what they see, hear, and know. Using prop boxes to explore adult roles, painting pictures, participating in group meetings, and writing letters to the newspaper in support of recycling help children represent and share what they have learned.

---

[3] Based on Judith Bender, Barbara Elder, and Charles Flatter, *Half a Childhood: Time for School-Age Care* (Nashville, TN: School Age NOTES, 1984), p. 48.

Children like to demonstrate their increasing cognitive abilities. The school-age years are the years of industry. Children like working on projects, and they like demonstrating their newly acquired reading, writing, and math abilities. Long-term projects such as building a paper maché model of Mount Rushmore or creating a display related to a hobby or special skill address this need.

Children's natural curiosity stimulates their learning. They are natural decision makers and problem solvers and rarely tire of opportunities to do either. Involving children in setting program rules and establishing procedures for using new equipment address this need.

Children find humor makes learning fun. Most children have a well-developed sense of humor and irony and most love word play, magic, and just plain silliness. Participating in Joke or Magic Clubs, writing short stories, and making up and performing skits address this need.

Applying Your Knowledge

In this learning activity you focus on how the materials used by children in different interest areas encourage cognitive growth. The chart that follows lists, for each interest area, examples of materials typically found there, followed by an explanation of how they encourage children's cognitive growth. For each interest area, add three more examples of materials found there and an explanation of how they support and encourage cognitive growth.

Using The Environment to Encourage Cognitive Growth

Quiet Area

Magazines, books, and reference materials (build on curiosity, stimulate reading ability and pleasure, compare what is thought to be real with what is accepted by society)

Computer with age-appropriate software (use thinking skills such as sorting, classifying, patterning, cause and effect, problem solving; enhance creativity)

Writing materials such as pencils, pens, markers, calligraphy pens, ruled and blank papers (express ideas and creativity, develop linguistic skills)

1. _____

_____

2. _____

_____

3. _____

_____

Dramatic Play Area

Prop boxes related to specific cultures or eras in history such as ancient Greece (compare different cultures and times, solve problems unique to the cultures or eras, develop empathy and understanding of others)

Costumes (express creativity and humor, try on new roles)

Theme-related prop boxes such as an inventor box (make predictions, develop thinking skills such as problem solving, express creativity)

1. _____

_____

2. _____

_____

3. _____

_____

Drawing and painting materials (express creativity, learn cause and effect, develop planning skills)

Sculpting and constructing materials (develop problem-solving skills, a sense of balance, and aesthetic appreciation)

Weaving and stitchery (develop patterning and sequencing skills, promote special talents)

Arts and Crafts Area

1. _____

_____

2. _____

_____

3. _____

_____

Soap flakes and dyes (observe changes in properties, solve problems, make predictions)

Bubble making prop box (develop creativity, observe changes in volume and physical states, make predictions)

Funnels and containers (observe changes in texture and volume, make comparisons, solve problems, make predictions)

Sand and Water Area

1. _____

_____

2. _____

_____

3. _____

_____

Science and Nature Area

Reference books, charts, and posters (generalize and develop personal understanding of conventionally accepted knowledge)

Old clocks, radios, and machines with mallets and tools for taking things apart (investigate how things work, make predictions, test theories, learn cause and effect) Tape measures, rulers, yardsticks, scales, and timers (take measurements before and after experiments, use when making comparisons, examine the properties of objects)

1. _____

_____

2. _____

_____

3. _____

_____

Woodworking Area

Variety of woods, nails and screws, and hammers and screwdrivers (compare properties, make predictions, understand cause and effect)

Books and kits for projects (promote special talents, present standard carpentry techniques, demonstrate basic principles of physics)

Assorted scraps, bottle caps, fish line (use creativity, develop aesthetic sense, solve problems)

1. _____

_____

2. _____

_____

3. _____

CDs, tapes, and players (appreciate differences in pitch, timbre, and mood; appreciate cultural diversity; experience storytelling and oral expression)

Variety of musical instruments (appreciate differences in pitch, timbre, and tempo; appreciate cultural diversity; understand cause and effect, express creativity)

Scarves to use in movement (increase awareness of body movements, express creativity)

Music Area

1. _____

_____

2. _____

_____

3. _____

_____

Hardwood unit blocks (explore math principles such as proportion and equivalence, understand cause and effect, solve problems)

Large hollow blocks (understand volume, proportion and balance, make and test hypotheses)

People, animal, and transportation props (engage in dramatic play, develop evaluative thinking skills)

Blocks and Construction Area

1. _____

_____

2. _____

_____

3. _____

_____

Board and Table Games Area

Books of crossword puzzles, brainteasers, and word games (use and expand vocabularies, develop problem-solving skills)

Materials to make new games (enhance creativity, encourage problem-solving skills, test cause and effect)

Jigsaw puzzles (solve problems, notice characteristics)

1. _____

_____

2. _____

_____

3. _____

_____

Math Area

Geoboards (develop thinking skills such as classifying, patterning, and problem solving; notice characteristics)

Rulers and tapes (measure, generalize and compare what is thought to be real with what is accepted by society, compare, sequence)

Calculators (generalize and compare what is thought to be real with what is accepted by society, develop functional math skills, make and test predictions)

1. _____

_____

2. _____

_____

3. _____

_____

Garden (learn cause and effect, experiment with light, learn about nutrition, classify)

Outdoors

Colored chalk (express creativity, understand spatial relationships, develop aesthetic appreciation)

Equipment for organized sports (understand rules, learn about cause and effect, make predictions)

1. _____

_____

2. _____

_____

3. _____

_____

Discuss your answers with your trainer and your colleagues. Share your suggestions for additional materials and resources for the program with your supervisor.

Learning Activity V.
Helping Children Learn to Solve Problems

IN THIS ACTIVITY YOU WILL LEARN TO:

- help children develop problem-solving skills; and

- plan and offer activities that encourage children to think and solve problems.

Problem solving is the process of thinking through a problem, coming up with possible solutions, and trying them out. School-age children typically enjoy experimenting and testing out hypotheses. They make wonderful detectives—they're always on the lookout for clues and solutions. In fact, reading mystery books is a favorite pastime for many school-age children.

Problem solving allows children to be responsible for their own learning.

Children solve problems every day—at school, at home, in the community, in sports activities, in their relationships with other children and adults, and in their activities at the school-age program. The ability to solve problems in everyday situations helps children feel competent and self-assured. By actively seeking answers to questions that interest them, children are learning how to be learners and taking responsibility for their own learning.

If you show children you like to solve problems and learn about the world, they will soon pick up on your enthusiasm. Your positive attitude is very important. It is the first step.

Try these suggestions.

Here are some suggestions for helping children learn to solve problems.

Accept and respect whatever responses children give. Children are more likely to solve problems when they know all their ideas are accepted and valued. Let children know this is a safe place to take risks and make mistakes.

Offer many opportunities to practice problem solving. Provide materials such as puzzles, games, riddles, and rebuses. Encourage children to solve problems related to the program—for example, thinking of a way to serve snack so children can eat when they are hungry rather than at a specific time. Make solving problems fun and rewarding; encourage children to view problems as an opportunity to be creative.

Allow plenty of time for children to talk. Some children have trouble putting their thoughts into words or converting their ideas into a plan of action. It may take some time for them to express their ideas.

Give children a chance to work out their own problems rather than offering suggestions and solutions. If you do step in, offer only enough assistance to get the child back into action. When a solution doesn't work, help the child try other possibilities. Children may need opportunities to try and try again before they are successful. Let them know a solution that doesn't work isn't a failure; it's a step in problem solving.

Respond to children's questions by asking questions that further stimulate their thinking. "Why do you think it didn't work?" or "Who remembers what happened last time?"

Explain the reasons for what you are doing to solve a problem. For example, explain what you are doing to repair a tape player or why you are moving the aquarium away from the window during a winter cold spell. Think out loud as you solve problems so children will see this is a normal part of daily life.

Let children know you are there to support them as they solve problems. Your presence and attention as they work is an important source of support.

Encourage multiple solutions. This allows children to think of many new possibilities and options.

In addition to setting a tone that encourages problem solving, many school-age staff find it helpful to actually lay out the steps children can follow to solve a problem. These steps, known as the "scientific method," can be applied whenever there is a problem to solve. For example, Ms. Nunes realizes the children need to use some of their time at the program for homework because they are in scouts and on sports teams. The older children are complaining because it's so noisy they can't get their homework done. She helps the children arrive at a solution by following these steps:

Show children how to use the steps in the scientific method.

337

1. Gather information.

When asked to explain the situation, Gillian says, "The Drama Club holds meetings right next to the homework table. We asked them to move but they said they didn't have anywhere to go." Petra, a member of the Drama Club responds, "We don't want to be in their way, but we need a place to hold our club."

2. State the problem in clear, readily definable terms.

Some children need a quiet place where they can do their homework without distractions or interruptions. The Drama Club needs a place to hold their meetings.

3. Generate ideas to solve the problem.

Ms. Nunes invites the children to offer suggestions and asks Gillian to write them on the board:

a. Schedule one time for homework and another for Drama Club.

b. Move the club to a new location in the room or in the building.

c. Move the homework table to a new location in the room or in the building.

4. Evaluate the answers and select the "best" option.

The children discuss the three options and decide to try moving the club to a new location. Ms. Nunes says they might be able to use the gym for Drama Club. Sandy says, "If that doesn't work maybe we can hold our club in the board and table games area. We could move the table and chairs out of the way, then move them back after we are finished." Everyone agrees this is a good second choice if the gym is being used.

5. Test out the selected option.

> Ms. Nunes asks the building manager if the club can use the gym for their meetings twice a week. He agrees. The next day the Drama Club meets in its new location and the older children settle down to do their homework.

Problem solving helps children of all ages with academics and everyday life. Learning to solve problems helps them be better observers, first-rate scientists, and social mediators. Problem solving is a skill children can use throughout their lives.

Applying Your Knowledge

In this learning activity you help children develop problem-solving skills by focusing on three children—one aged 5 to 7, one 8 to 10, and one 11 or 12. For each child, state the problem, describe what he or she did, what you did, and your plans for the future. Begin by reviewing the examples, then select the three children you will observe.

Using the Scientific Method of Problem Solving
(Example: 5- to 7-year-old)

Child: _Scott_   **Age:** _5 1/2 years_   **Date:** _October 11_

State the problem:

Scott was getting very frustrated; all his block constructions were falling down. His face was flushed and he kept wiping his hair out of his face. From past experience, I could tell he was on the verge of kicking the blocks, so I quickly joined him. He needed help solving how to keep a tower from falling.

Possible solutions:

I had a quiet talk with Scott about what was going wrong. He was at a loss as to why all of the towers he built kept falling. I watched him build a tower so we could both see what was going wrong. After eight blocks, the tower fell.

I asked Scott to carefully observe with me what was taking place to see if we could figure out the problem. Scott suggested the floor might be crooked, the blocks might be too thin, or he might be hurrying too much to put the blocks on carefully.

Evaluation and testing:

I asked Scott to think of how he could test one of his theories. He decided the biggest problem was the size of the blocks. He gathered a great many blocks of different sizes. This time he started with a large block as the base. Gradually, he narrowed the blocks that were stacked. Using this approach he created an impressive tower of twelve blocks. Scott was mighty pleased with the results and with himself.

Reflections on the process:

I was as pleased as Scott was with the experiment. Another day I'll ask him if he wants to test some of his other theories to see if they, too, will produce positive results.

Using the Scientific Method of Problem Solving
(Example: 8- to 10-year-old)

Children: _Tawan, Sam, Eugene_   **Ages:** _9 and 10 years_   **Date:** _October 12_

State the problem:

A group of boys have been monopolizing the board and table games area. Even though we have rules about taking turns and rotating activities, they somehow manage to take over the area. The other children—especially the girls—have been complaining.

Possible solutions:

I asked the boys to meet with me to discuss the situation and think of ways to resolve it. I decided to try a conflict resolution technique that would involve them in developing a solution. I asked them to brainstorm some possible solutions, and Sam recorded everything they came up with. Their ideas ranged from banning girls from the area to finding floor space for them to play on.

Evaluation and testing:

After they had exhausted their ideas we went through the list together, eliminating the far-out ideas and expanding on the more reasonable solutions. The boys decided on a solution—they would rearrange the area to create floor space for playing games. This would free up the table for others.

Reflections on the process:

I was pleased the boys came up with their own solution rather than me having to impose rules on them. Working together, they came up with a solution that met the entire group's needs—not just their own. It's been a week now and the solution seems to be working. I now plan to regularly use conflict resolution techniques. Also, I will remind the children they can solve problems on their own without my help, starting by brainstorming solutions.

Using the Scientific Method of Problem Solving
(Example: 11- to 12-year-old)

Child: _Pete_   **Age:** _12 years_   **Date:** _October 13_

State the problem:

Pete, who is very health conscious, was quite distressed when his dentist told him he was not doing a good job of brushing the insides of his teeth.

Possible solutions:

Pete felt he could either brush his teeth for a longer period of time or get a more effective toothbrush. I encouraged Pete to try his hand at designing a new brush.

Evaluation and testing:

Pete thought brushing longer was a "fall back" option. He wanted to see if he could invent a more effective toothbrush, one that would reach the insides of his teeth. For several hours Pete was consumed with this task. When he showed me his finished design, I was amazed by his creativity: the top of the toothbrush handle forked out into a "y"—on both sides of the "y" there is a brush. The two brushes face each other to brush both sides of the teeth at the same time.

Reflections on the process:

Now Pete wants to develop a model of his invention. He's going to bring in some old toothbrushes from home and use the program's tools and materials. I think his idea is so good, I want to help him find out about getting a patent. I'm also going to urge him to enter competitions like Odyssey of the Mind.

Using the Scientific Method of Problem Solving
(5- to 7-year-old)

Child: _____   **Age:** _____   **Date:** _____

State the problem:

_____

_____

_____

_____

Possible solutions:

_____

_____

_____

_____

_____

_____

_____

_____

_____

Evaluation and testing:

_____

_____

_____

_____

Reflections on the process:

_____

_____

_____

_____

Developing Problem-Solving Skills
(8- to 10-year-old)

Child: _____   **Age:** _____   **Date:** _____

State the problem:

_____

_____

_____

_____

Possible solutions:

_____

_____

_____

_____

_____

_____

_____

_____

Evaluation and testing:

_____

_____

_____

_____

Reflections on the process:

_____

_____

_____

_____

Developing Problem-Solving Skills
(11- to 12-year-old)

Child: _____ **Age:** _____ **Date:** _____

State the problem:

_____

_____

_____

_____

Possible solutions:

_____

_____

_____

_____

_____

_____

_____

_____

Evaluation and testing:

_____

_____

_____

_____

Reflections on the process:

_____

_____

_____

_____

Discuss your responses with your trainer.

SUMMARIZING YOUR PROGRESS

You have now completed all the learning activities for this module. Whether you are an experienced school-age staff member or a new one, this module has probably helped you develop new skills for guiding children's cognitive development. Before you go on, take a few minutes to summarize what you've learned.

- Turn back to Learning Activity I, Using Your Knowledge of Child Development to Guide Cognitive Development, and add specific examples to the charts of what you have learned about guiding children's cognitive development. Compare your ideas to those in the completed charts at the end of the module.

- Next, review your responses to the pre-training assessment for this module. Write a summary of what you learned and list the skills you developed or improved.

_____

_____

_____

_____

_____

_____

_____

_____

_____

_____

_____

_____

_____

_____

_____

_____

If there are topics you would like to know more about, you will find recommended readings in the Orientation.

Your final step in this module is to complete the knowledge and competency assessments. Let your trainer know when you are ready to schedule the assessments. After you have successfully completed them, you will be ready to start a new module. Congratulations on your progress so far, and good luck with your next module.

ANSWER SHEETS

Guiding Children's Cognitive Development

1. How did Mr. Crain encourage Rita to experiment and make discoveries?

  a. He gave Rita the address of an organization that pairs American children with children in other countries so they can become pen pals.

  b. He listened to her as she told him what was in her letter.

  c. He let her know he knew of her goal—to become a doctor.

  d. He let her know he appreciated her interest and ability to get things done by teasing her about already having written back.

  e. He told her he would post the address in case her friends want to become pen pals, too.

2. What did Rita learn from becoming a pen pal?

  a. She learned about what she had in common with a girl from another country.

  b. She learned what everyday life was like in Russia.

  c. She learned to establish and continue a relationship.

Creating an Interesting and Varied Environment That Encourages Children to Experiment and Make Discoveries

1. Why did Ms. Williams not just give Samantha the correct facts?

  a. She knew Samantha was not yet ready to understand the abstract principles of physics that explain starlight.

  b. She knew it was more important for Samantha to come up with her own ideas about why the stars shine at night than for her to have the right answer.

  c. She didn't want to stifle Samantha's creativity.

Interacting With Children in Ways That Build on Their Natural Curiosity

2. How did Ms. Williams encourage Samantha to think through her theory?

a. She took Samantha's ideas seriously and decided to discuss the child's theory with her.

b. She offered to help Samantha dig holes in the ground and think through her theory.

Providing Opportunities for Children to Use Their Growing Skills

1. How did Ms. Saavedra provide an opportunity for Brian to use his skills?

a. She reinforced Brian's desire to do a professional job.

b. She let him select the drawing program he liked best.

c. She introduced him to computer drawing programs.

2. How did Ms. Saavedra support Brian's mastery of new skills and concepts?

a. She was available to work closely with him.

b. She allowed him to be in charge of his own learning by providing assistance when asked, rather than telling him what to do.

Understanding and Responding to 5- to 7-Year-Old Children

What 5-7 Year Old Children are Like	How Staff Can Use This Information to Guide Cognitive Development
They are eager to learn the answers to "why" questions.	*Respect children's questions. Help them predict answers to their questions and test them out. Offer answers to stretch their thinking.*
They like to take on responsibility.	*Ask for help doing program chores such as making snack or carrying equipment outdoors. Encourage children to help each other by explaining the rules for a game, demonstrating how to do a craft project, or showing how to feed the snake.*
They are developing an understanding of time, but the concepts of past and future are still vague.	*Ask recall questions such as "What happened yesterday?" so children can think about the past. Ask questions such as "What will we be doing next week?" to help them focus on the future. Use calendars to show when events took place or will occur. Have children keep a program scrap book with photos taken throughout the year and labels showing the date, names of people in the pictures, and a brief description (11-1-93, Sara and Ted, first snow).*
They are curious and want to explore many things.	*Regularly put out new and interesting materials to replace ones no longer being used and to respond to changing interests. Be flexible when children use materials in ways other than what you expected.*
They express their thoughts and feelings—typically in great and vivid detail.	*Encourage children to talk about home and school experiences. Ask lots of open-ended questions to stimulate discussions. Provide opportunities to participate in group meetings; otherwise older children may dominate. (Large programs may hold separate meetings for each age group.)*
They read and write simple words, sentences, and texts.	*Ask children to help make recipe cards, signs for the block area, or labels for the bulletin board. Provide a wide variety of books and magazines. Read to children (or enlist the aid of an older child)—perhaps a chapter a day from a book that is a little too difficult for them to read to themselves.*
They are beginning to understand number concepts and relationships but still need experiences with real objects to fully grasp them.	*Provide manipulatives—an abacus, geoboards, parquetry blocks—so children can explore number concepts and relationships. Encourage children to use math skills in program routines and activities—for example, figuring out how many children can be on each side in a ball game.*

Understanding and Responding to 8- to 10-Year-Old Children

What 8-10 Year Old Children are Like	How Staff Can Use This Information to Guide Cognitive Development
They like to collect and catalogue "things" such as coins, baseball cards, and rocks.	*Provide space and time for children to create displays of their collections. Use nature walks and field trips as opportunities to plan new collections. Share your own collections, for example, owls collected on trips to other countries.*
They are intrigued by how things relate to one another.	*Provide reference books and science activities related to children's interests. Interested children can make family trees.*
They understand explanations and rules and enjoy following rules to the letter.	*Provide materials children can use to make up their own games, complete with rules of play. Teach conflict resolution techniques and remind children to use them to solve their problems. To prevent disagreements, review the rules of new games so children will know what is or is not allowed in the game.*
They may be critical of their own performance and may need help sorting out realistic goals from unrealistic ones.	*Praise children's efforts and help them break down large tasks into smaller, more manageable pieces. Help children develop timelines and put them on a calendar so they can see how and when they will carry out their plans.*
They make step-by-step plans and carry them out.	*Help children write down the steps needed to carry out their plans (index cards work well)—for example, the steps needed to complete a recipe, do a woodworking project, conduct an experiment, establish a new club, or put on a gymnastics show.*
They work on projects over a long period of time.	*Allow children space and uninterrupted time for long-term projects such as weaving a wall hanging, making a drum, learning the steps to a complicated folk dance, or writing and illustrating a story.*
They vary greatly in academic abilities and interests.	*Provide a wide variety of open-ended materials that children can use in different ways, depending on their skills and interests. Allow children to choose what they want to use or do.*
They ask many questions and want thoughtful answers in return.	*Take the time to listen to children's questions. When you don't know an answer refer children to other resources such as reference books. Ask them to tell you what they find out. Ask children their opinions and share yours if asked to.*

Understanding and Responding to 11- to 12-Year-Old Children

What 11-12 Year Old Children are Like	How Staff Can Use This Information to Guide Cognitive Development
They typically think in abstract terms.	*Talk with children about current events and social issues such as recycling. Encourage children to make predictions about the future. If children are interested, help them organize a Futurists Club to learn more about what people think the world will be like when they are grownups.*
They are increasingly skilled in reading and writing.	*Include a wide range of reading materials at different levels, on different topics, and in different styles. Encourage children to write—newspapers, poems, plays, letters, skits—and share their writing with others. Introduce computer writing programs.*
They use a systematic approach to solve problems.	*Ask children to explain how they solved a problem so they can see how they used a systematic approach. Allow them to explore a number of alternative solutions to a problem. Help them weigh the pros and cons of each alternative, then select one or more to try.*
They add, subtract, multiply, and divide with growing skill.	*Encourage children to keep "stats" on professional teams over the season. They can calculate team and individual successes in points, assists, and fouls. Invite a stockbroker or financial advisor to speak about the stock market. If children are interested, help them organize an Investment Club—they can read about stocks, "purchase" some, and then watch them grow or decline in value over time.*
They are serious about working and learning.	*Show children you respect their work and want to learn from them. Acknowledge that their knowledge and intellectual skills are growing. In particular, let children know when they have more information about a topic than you do.*
They show proficiency in particular skills and talents.	*Provide a variety of outlets for children to share their skills and to perform. Plan talent shows, clubs, visits from professionals, displays of art and craft projects, and time for children to practice and continue building proficiency.*
They can appreciate other points of view.	*Encourage children to become pen pals with youngsters living in other countries or states. Use* Penpals for Kids *(www.kidspenpals.about.com/kids/kidspenpals). Remind them to use conflict resolution techniques to resolve their own disagreements.*

GLOSSARY

Abstract thinking	Thought that is based on ideas.
Cognitive development	Development of the expanding ability to think and reason.
Concept	An idea that combines details or several ideas in an organized way.
Conflict resolution	A systematic approach used to solve problems and disagreements.
Convergent question	A question that asks about the cause and affect of something and the possibility of what can happen.
Divergent question	A question that requires several ideas or solutions.
Evaluative question	A question that asks you to make a judgment.
Hypothesis	A prediction of the answer to a question or problem.
Multiple intelligences	A phrase coined by Howard Gardner to describe the many types of intelligence—logical, linguistic, musical, spatial, bodily kinesthetic, interpersonal, and intrapersonal.
Open-ended question	A question that can be answered in many ways rather than by "yes" or "no."
Problem solving	Thinking through a problem, coming up with one or several possible solutions, and trying out one or more of these.
Recall question	A question that asks you to describe or retell what you know.
Sequencing	Putting things or events in order.

Module 6:

COMMUNICATION

OVERVIEW

> ## PROMOTING CHILDREN'S COMMUNICATION SKILLS INVOLVES:
>
> - creating an interesting and varied environment that encourages children to develop and use communication skills;
>
> - interacting with children in ways that encourage them to express their ideas and feelings; and
>
> - providing opportunities for children to use their listening, speaking, reading, and writing skills.

Communication means expressing and sharing ideas, desires, and feelings with other people. The drive to communicate is strong. Newborns communicate their needs by crying. In a very short time, they can communicate joy by smiling and cooing when they see a familiar face. Older children and adults also convey messages through nonverbal communication. Gestures such as a wave or a shrug are readily understood by everyone. Facial expressions such as a smile or a frown communicate feelings as clearly as a pat on the back. We also communicate through images and pictures, which can represent ideas and feelings.

Communication is the expression of ideas, thoughts, and feelings to others.

Although all forms of communication—gestures, facial expressions, body language, touch, pictures—are important, language is the most critical; it is, therefore, the chief focus of this module. Language can be defined as a system of words and the rules for their use in speaking, reading, and writing. It is through language we communicate our feelings and ideas to others and interpret what others want to tell us.

The use of language is related to cognitive development. (See Module 5, Cognitive to learn about school-age children's cognitive development.) Learning language depends on a child's ever-growing ability to understand words and eventually to read and write them. Language skills, in turn, affect other areas of development. Social development, for example, is dependent on language. Children who have difficulty expressing themselves well are often less able to develop friendships. In addition, language is an important factor in emotional development. Children's self-esteem is enhanced by their growing ability to use words to express how they feel—to communicate their feelings accurately to others.

Language skills affect other areas of development.

Children are born with the natural desire to communicate. In just a few short years, they move from being nonverbal to speaking and understanding thousands of words, their meanings, and the rules for using them. By age 6, children have a working vocabulary of about 2,500 words. By the time they are 11 years old, children typically have a reading vocabulary of 50,000 words. This growth in language skills comes primarily from being around caring adults who talk to children and support their efforts to communicate.

School-age staff can promote communication in several ways. They can provide an environment that encourages children to develop and use communication skills. School-age staff can also interact with children in thoughtful ways that encourage them to express their ideas and feelings. And finally, staff can build into each day's activities opportunities for children to speak, listen, read, and write. Positive communication is the cornerstone of a quality program.

Listed below are examples of how school-age staff demonstrate their competence in promoting communication skills

Creating an Interesting and Varied Environment That Encourages Children to Develop and Use Communication Skills

Arrange the environment so there are places where children can work, play, and talk in small groups. "Nancy, I think the 'astronauts' in the dramatic play area might need some nourishment on their flight. Could you find out what they'd like for lunch besides Tang?"

Provide materials, time, and space for children to make up their own games and activities. "Today you will have plenty of time to work on the obstacle course you started yesterday."

Provide props, costumes, and other materials to encourage language development activities such as dramatic play, making up skits, and puppetry. "Dionne, the soap opera you and your friends are writing is hilarious. If you need any props, just let me know."

Stock the quiet area with materials that encourage writing such as pens, pencils, paper, book-binding materials, and a computer, if available. "Marisa, the computer is free now if you want to use it to write your story. If you use the computer, you can go back and make changes to make sure the story is just the way you want it."

Use printing rather than cursive writing on signs, bulletin boards, and other written materials directed at children. "Before posting this week's plan we always make sure all the words are printed and legible so even the youngest children can read some of them."

Include reading and writing materials in all interest areas, for example, pencils and paper in the science and nature area so children can record the results of their experiments. "Veronica, that's an interesting rock you found on our walk. If you want to identify it, there's a handbook on rocks and minerals in the science and nature area."

Provide (or arrange for use of) audio and video tape equipment so children can record their storytelling, plays, skits, and other creations. "Bradley, would you like to tape record the story you just told us about the baseball game. It was so funny, I think we would all enjoy hearing it again."

Designate the quiet area as a place where children can do homework, and respond to children's requests for assistance. "Tiffany, I'd be happy to quiz you on your spelling words. Spend some time going over them yourself, then let me know when you're ready for my help."

Include books, magazines, and reference materials in the quiet area in response to children's interests and expose them to new ideas and topics. Check frequently to see which materials are being used and which should be replaced. "So many of you are into collecting—baseball cards, Barbies, coins, stamps, caps—I thought you'd enjoy looking at some collector's magazines. These will tell you how much items are worth, where you can get things, and how to sell them. They'll be on the bottom shelf in the quiet area."

Ask open-ended questions to encourage children to think and express their ideas. "Valencia, the polymer clay necklaces you've been making are so festive. What do you do to the clay to make the colors so bright?"

Accept children's use of slang and popular expressions while serving as a model for standard use of language. When Zach tells you, "Like, I can't believe how cool this movie was I saw last week. The special effects were like so awesome," respond by saying, "It sounds like you really enjoyed yourself. Tell me about the special effects."

Support children's bilingualism by learning words in their native language and encouraging them to teach others. "Miguel, perhaps you would like to take the lead in putting out a Spanish edition of our newspaper."

Interacting With Children in Ways That Encourage Them to Express Their Ideas and Feelings

Remind children to review the rules before beginning a game or sport so all players can agree on how to play the game and keep score. "When we play 'wacky softball' everyone on the team has a turn at bat before the inning is over and we run around the bases backwards."

Show respect for children's ideas, even if they don't agree with your own. "Eduardo, I think you're right. Our recycling program probably could be more effective. Would you like to head a committee to look at how we might improve our efforts?"

Observe children's nonverbal cues (for example, body language, dramatic play, drawings, stories) and use the cues to ask questions about their ideas and feelings. "Maurice, your face is all flushed. Are you upset about what Nicky said? Is that what the look on your face means?"

Encourage children to read and write for pleasure, not only because they must complete assigned work. "Martha, this book has ten different short stories about horses. If you don't like the first one, you can try another one."

Help children find words to express their ideas and feelings. "Cara, it sounds like you are trying to help me make sure everyone follows the program's rules. You don't have to tell me when someone disobeys the rules. You can remind the person of the rule, then go back to what you were doing."

Providing Opportunities for Children to Use Their Listening, Speaking, Reading, and Writing Skills

Use group meetings as an opportunity for children to share their ideas, raise concerns, and discuss solutions. "Tonya, would you start off today's meeting by telling us about the Energy Conservation Challenge your class is sponsoring?"

Encourage children to share folklore, oral traditions, stories, songs, and books that reflect their family backgrounds. "Franny, could you teach us the Yiddish lullaby about the birds in the sky you were humming the other day?"

Help children plan and implement special interest clubs that use or explore communication skills, for example, publishing a newspaper, planting a garden, discussing favorite books, or learning about television production. "At today's first meeting of the Gardening Club we're going to tour the site, look at books about gardening and seed catalogs, and make a list of the seeds we'd like to purchase."

Offer materials and activities that respond to children's individual and developmental skills and interests. "Some of the third-graders are very excited about learning to write in cursive. Let's put out some lined paper and samples of cursive letters to help them practice."

Keep in touch with the elementary schools attended by children from the school-age program to find out what materials and activities the program could offer to build on or enrich the experiences offered in school. "Most of the children are in schools that use a writer's workshop model. Let's make sure we don't go around correcting everything they write since they're being encouraged to use invented spelling in the early grades."

Plan trips and special activities to expand children's language skills and interests. "You've been doing such a great job getting out our weekly newsletter, I thought you might enjoy taking a field trip to see how the city paper is written and delivered every day."

Build opportunities for children to develop and use communication skills into all program activities, not just those specifically related to reading, writing, listening, and speaking. "In yesterday's emergency drill some of you forgot our procedures. Jenny and Linda have made a chart to show everyone what to do and where to go in an emergency. They'll review the chart with you, then we'll post it next to the cubbies."

Promoting Children's Communication Skills

In the following situations, school-age staff are helping children develop communication skills. As you read them, think about what the staff are doing and why. Then answer the questions that follow.

Creating an Interesting and Varied Environment That Encourages Children to Develop and Use Communication Skills

As Ms. Alessi accompanies a group of children outdoors, she listens as eleven-year-old Jonathan enthusiastically reports on the trip his class made to the Museum of Natural History. Later that day, while Jonathan is working on a puzzle, she asks him about the field trip. "It sounds like you had a great class trip to the museum. Tell me more about what you saw." "You wouldn't believe all the dinosaur bones they had," Jonathan begins excitedly. "And whole skeletons. And wax models. There was an entire room with Tyrannosaurus and Brontosaurus and Diplodocus and Ornithopoda and Stegosaurus and Meglasaurus and Maurosaurus models walking around like they were still alive. It was awesome." "It sounds like the museum really made the dinosaur age come alive," says Ms. Alessi, matching Jonathan's enthusiasm. "You know," adds Jonathan, "sometimes I wish I lived back then so I would really know what it's like to have seen a dinosaur in the back yard." Ms. Alessi laughs at Jonathan's comment and then adds, "Actually, Jonathan, that's not a bad idea. You could write a story about what it would be like to be a boy living in the Dinosaur Age. I'm sure the children here and in your class at school would enjoy reading it. You can use the computer to make it look like a professional manuscript. We have several publishing software programs you can choose from. There are drawing materials and bookbinding supplies in the quiet area in case you decide to illustrate and bind your story into a book. And who knows—it might just become our next best seller!"

1. **How did Ms. Alessi build on Jonathan's interests to promote communication skills?**

_____

_____

_____

2. **In what ways did Ms. Alessi provide an environment that encouraged communication skills?**

_____

_____

_____

Seven-year-old Stuart loves to build with blocks—tall, elaborate constructions are his specialty. The last few days, Ms. Kearney has noticed Stuart has just been piling blocks atop each other without any clear design plan. She knows from talking with Stuart's mother that his father is away for a month on business. She thinks there might be some connection. Ms. Kearney goes over to the block area and kneels down beside Stuart. In a quiet voice she says, "Your block-building these past few days looks quite a bit different from the rocket launching pads and airports you usually build. These don't seem to have as much energy or excitement. Is that the way you're feeling?"

"I'm not feeling anything," Stuart replies. "Sometimes when we're sad it makes us feel kind of empty. Could that be what's going on? Is something making you sad?" asks Ms. Kearney. "Yeah," says Stuart. "My dad's gone and I miss him a lot." "I bet your dad misses you, too," says Ms. Kearney. "I have an idea. Would you like to write him a letter? I'm sure it would brighten his day to hear from you." Stuart nods. She walks Stuart over to the quiet area where there are lots of papers, pens, markers, and a computer. She asks Stuart what he'd like to use to write his letter and accompanies him as he chooses a pen and stationery. She asks, "Would you like to write your letter alone or shall I sit with you?" At his request, Ms. Kearney keeps him company while he writes the letter to his dad.

Interacting With Children in Ways That Encourage Them to Express Their Ideas and Feelings

1. **How did Ms. Kearney know something was bothering Stuart?**

_____

_____

_____

2. **How did Ms. Kearney help Stuart express his feelings and thoughts?**

_____

_____

_____

3. **What other questions might Ms. Kearney have asked to draw out Stuart?**

_____

_____

_____

Providing Opportunities for Children to Use Their Listening, Speaking, Reading, and Writing Skills

When Mr. Williams reviews the program's suggestion box he finds many ideas for activities. Several children want to write and share their stories, so he plans a Writer's Workshop. Members will learn about writing, then write and publish their stories in a journal. He asks, "What makes a good story?" "Something exciting happens," offers Derrick. "It makes you laugh," says Shantay. "It's unpredictable and it's fun," says Bob. "Okay," he says, "let's start with Bob's idea." He tells the children a story about his trip to Italy. "I was eager to try out my Italian skills, but I couldn't read the menu at the restaurant. When the waiter came, I tried making animal sounds to order pork chops. After eloquently going 'oink, oink' to the waiter, I felt sure savory pork chops would soon be mine. Unfortunately, the waiter thought 'oink' meant fried calves' brains. When my dinner came, I pretended it was just what I wanted."

Mr. Williams asks if anyone has a story in which something unpredictable happened to them, causing a funny turn of events. Bob and Morgan both share anecdotes. Then he asks, "Who remembers something scary that happened to them?" Ayeisha relates in great detail how she was awakened from sleep by an earthquake while visiting her dad in California.

Having set the stage, Mr. Williams says. "You all have stories to tell. Some are funny, some exciting, some scary. Some may be sad. What's important is they are your stories and will be interesting to read. I think we're ready to get started on our first issue. Let's include any story you think other children would like to read. We'll begin by discussing your ideas."

1. What did Mr. Williams do to interest the children in writing stories?

_____

_____

_____

2. How did the Writer's Workshop promote the children's language and literacy skills?

_____

_____

_____

Compare your answers with those on the answer sheet at the end of this module. If your answers are different, discuss them with your trainer. There can be more than one good answer.

Your Own Experiences with Communication

Communication skills are central to our ability to relate to others. Our relationships with colleagues, friends, and family members depend in large part on how well we understand and respond to what they have to say and how well they understand us.

To understand what others have to say, we need to do three things:

- receive the message;
- interpret the message; and
- send back an appropriate response.

Many factors influence how well we understand the communications we receive from others. These include how we are feeling at that moment, how well we know the persons communicating with us, and how carefully we listen. For example, suppose you've had a bad morning before coming to work. You are feeling overwhelmed. Your colleague greets you with the following statement:

"This storeroom is a mess! I can't find anything in it!"

You may interpret this message as a criticism and respond defensively: "When am I supposed to find the time to deal with the storeroom? I can hardly keep up with everything else I have to do!" Your colleague may be surprised by your response. She might herself react defensively: "Don't you think I'm just as busy as you are?" Neither of you meant to hurt the other's feelings, but that's exactly what happened.

On another day, when you are feeling more on top of things, you might interpret the message very differently. Your response might be something like this: "You're absolutely right. We've been so busy with other things, we never seem to get to the storeroom. Maybe we can ask some of the children to help us out." This time, the message was positively interpreted with respect for both parties.

In conveying our thoughts and feelings to others, we rely on our communication skills to get our messages across accurately. We send messages verbally (using words) and nonverbally (using gestures and body language). Verbal messages can be the clearest kind of message if we say what we mean.

Communication skills involve receiving and interpreting information.

Communication is both verbal and nonverbal.

"I'd like to do something about the storeroom. I can never find what I need. What do you think about asking some of the older children to help us out?"

"I'd love to go to a movie tonight. What time is best for you?"

Clarity is vital to communication.

But even verbal messages can be unclear if we fail to say what we really think and want. Using the same examples, we could say:

"What are we going to do about the storeroom?" (when we know very well what we think needs to be done).

"What do you feel like doing tonight?" (hoping the other person will want to go to a movie but remaining unclear about our own wishes).

Questions can clarify the sender's intent.

In addition to clearly sending messages, we need to receive them as they were intended. We can do this by probing the sender. Questions and statements that help to clarify the message include the following:

- Are you saying that . . .?
- Do you mean . . .?
- Do I understand correctly that . . .?
- It sounds like you want . . .

How do you rate your ability to communicate effectively?

	Regularly	Sometimes	Not Enough
I am able to state my ideas clearly	☐	☐	☐
I am able to express my feelings in words	☐	☐	☐
I say what I think	☐	☐	☐
If I'm not sure what someone means, I check out what I think was said	☐	☐	☐
I try to interpret nonverbal communication to help me better understand what someone is feeling	☐	☐	☐

Review your answers to this brief checklist. Are there any areas you would like to improve? As you go through this module, you may discover some strategies for improving your own communication skills.

When you have finished this overview section, you should complete the pre-training assessment. Refer to the glossary at the end of the module if you need definitions of the terms used.

PRE-TRAINING ASSESSMENT

Listed below are the skills school-age staff use to promote children's communication skills. Think about whether you do these things regularly, sometimes, or not enough. Place a check in one of the boxes on the right for each skill listed. Then discuss your answers with your trainer.

Creating an Interesting and Varied Environment That Encourages Children to Develop and Use Communication Skills

	I Do This		
	Regularly	Sometimes	Not Enough
1. Arranging the environment so there are places where children can work and play together in small groups.	☐	☐	☐
2. Providing materials, time, and space for children to make up their own games and activities.	☐	☐	☐
3. Providing props, costumes, and other materials that encourage language development activities such as, dramatic play, making up skits, and puppetry.	☐	☐	☐
4. Stocking the quiet area with materials that encourage writing such as pens, pencils, paper, book-binding materials, and a computer, if available.	☐	☐	☐
5. Using printing rather than cursive writing on signs, bulletin boards, and other written materials directed at children.	☐	☐	☐
6. Including reading and writing materials in all interest areas.	☐	☐	☐
7. Providing (or arranging for use of) audio and video tape equipment so children can record their plays, skits, storytelling, and other creations.	☐	☐	☐
8. Designating a quiet area as a place where children can do homework, and responding to children's requests for assistance.	☐	☐	☐
9. Including books, magazines, and reference materials in the quiet area in response to children's interests and expose them to new ideas and topics.	☐	☐	☐

Interacting With Children in Ways That Encourage Them to Express Their Ideas and Feelings	I Do This		
	Regularly	Sometimes	Not Enough
10. Asking open-ended questions to encourage children to think and express their ideas.	☐	☐	☐
11. Accepting children's use of slang and popular expressions while serving as a model for standard use of language.	☐	☐	☐
12. Supporting children's bilingualism through activities and interactions in the program.	☐	☐	☐
13. Reminding children to review the rules before beginning a game or sport so all players can agree on how to play the game and keep score.	☐	☐	☐
14. Showing respect for what children have to say.	☐	☐	☐
15. Observing children's nonverbal cues and using the cues to ask questions about their ideas and feelings.	☐	☐	☐
16. Encouraging children to read and write for pleasure, not only because they must complete assigned work.	☐	☐	☐
17. Helping children find words to express their ideas and feelings.	☐	☐	☐

Providing Opportunities for Children to Use Their Listening, Speaking, Reading, and Writing Skills	I Do This		
	Regularly	Sometimes	Not Enough
18. Using group meetings as opportunities for children to share their ideas, raise concerns, and discuss solutions.	☐	☐	☐
19. Encouraging children to share folklore, oral traditions, stories, songs, and books that reflect their family backgrounds.	☐	☐	☐

Providing Opportunities for Children to Use Their Listening, Speaking, Reading, and Writing Skills
(continued)

	I Do This		
	Regularly	Sometimes	Not Enough
20. Helping children plan and implement special interest clubs that use or explore communication skills.	☐	☐	☐
21. Offering materials and activities that respond to children's individual and developmental skills and interests.	☐	☐	☐
22. Keeping in touch with the elementary schools attended by children from the school-age program to find out what materials and activities the program could offer to build on or enrich the experiences offered in school.	☐	☐	☐
23. Planning trips and special activities to expand children's language skills and interests.	☐	☐	☐
24. Building opportunities for children to develop and use communication skills into all program activities, not just those specifically related to reading, writing, listening, and speaking.	☐	☐	☐

Review your responses, then list three to five skills you would like to improve or topics you would like to learn more about. When you finish this module, you can list examples of your new or improved knowledge and skills.

_____

_____

_____

_____

_____

_____

Begin the learning activities for Module 6, Communication.

LEARNING ACTIVITIES

Learning Activity I.
Using Your Knowledge of Child Development to Promote Communication Skills

---

IN THIS ACTIVITY YOU WILL LEARN TO:

- recognize typical behaviors of school-age children that are related to language development; and

- use what you know about school-age children to promote their communication.

The foundation for a child's ability to communicate is built early in life. Infants use different cries to communicate hunger, fatigue, or discomfort. In a remarkably short time, they recognize familiar voices, turning their heads and smiling in response. They understand words have meanings; they can point to their nose when an adult says, "Where's your nose?" They love to hear adults talk and sing to them and to hear the sounds they make repeated back to them.

Communication begins when infants learn to give and receive messages.

As in all areas of growth, children develop language at their own pace. Some say their first words before age one. Some hardly speak at all before age two. The average 18-month-old has a speaking vocabulary of at least 25 words; however, most toddlers understand far more spoken words than they can speak.

Children rapidly increase their vocabularies.

By the time they become preschoolers, most children have developed a wide range of skills in nonverbal and verbal language. They seem to learn new words every day. It is estimated preschoolers add 600 words to their speaking vocabulary every year from ages three through five.

During the school-age years, children learn to use language as a true tool of communication. While the rate of learning new words begins to taper off after the frantic rate of growth of the preschool years, children refine their skills rapidly. From ages 5 to 7, they increasingly use language to express themselves. This involves complex cognitive skills such as speaking to and with others about what they observe, struggling to find the appropriate words to describe their ideas, presenting evidence to support generalizations, and asking questions to learn more.

Younger school-age children are learning to use language to express their ideas.

Young school-age children are often nonstop talkers, engaging anyone who will listen in conversation. They may begin to use language aggressively—slang, mild profanity, and clichés tend to characterize their speech. Children this age may also show intolerance for those who speak with accents or speak a language different than theirs. On the positive side, they are beginning to use their language skills to cultivate friends, to socialize, and to critique their own behavior.

Young children are also interested in the meaning of language. The world of reading opens up great possibilities. They enjoy using their skills to read books, signs, instructions on the computer, and directions from a board game.

Language is used as a tool by 8- to 10-year-olds.

From ages 8 to 10, children become increasingly adept in their use of language. Children can express subtle emotions and think critically. There is a wide range of language skills in this age group. Some children are very fluent; others are developing language skills at a slower pace.

During these years, many children enjoy doing a great deal of socializing. A byproduct of these prolonged conversations may be the increased use of slang and profanity. Coded languages such as Pig Latin and secret passwords are also common.

Reading and writing are leisure activities.

Eight- to ten-year-olds are increasingly skilled in reading and writing, as well as oral language. For this age group, reading and writing become activities of choice, not just school work. Children seek out books and writing activities for pleasure.

From ages 11 to 12, children are able to use sophisticated grammar. Their use of compound and complex sentences, proper nouns, pronouns, and prepositions approaches that of adults. It is estimated their reading vocabulary stretches beyond 50,000 words—a far cry from the 25 spoken words a toddler knows.

Older school-age children use language to define their identity.

With this facility in language, older school-age children can use their language skills to achieve self-understanding. They continue spending a great deal of time talking to peers—at school, at the program, and over the phone. They never seem to run out of things to talk about. They use language to define themselves, their values, and the goals they want to pursue. In addition, slang and "fad" words may pepper their conversations. Some children use profanity, usually because they think it identifies them as a member of a particular peer group. The social connection they have with their peers looms all important in their lives.

Most children do not acquire all the sounds in the English language until age eight, and some speech errors could be caused by missing teeth or dental abnormalities. However, there may be children in your program with speech and language problems. Children who frequently mispronounce certain sounds or have difficulty understanding what is said to them, following directions, or expressing themselves, may have language delays. You can respond by giving them simple, one-step directions, and repeating them as necessary, modeling correct pronunciation of words, and introducing new vocabulary and a variety of language forms: stories, poetry, plays, songs. Discuss your observations with the child's parents. If they are already aware of the problem and working with the child's teacher and other professionals, you can coordinate your approach with that used at home and school. If they are not aware of the problem, encourage them to discuss your observations with the teacher and seek professional screening and assessment, if needed.

Stuttering is a common speech disorder, seen more frequently in boys than girls. If a child struggles to produce words, hesitates or repeats words or parts of words, observe the child more closely. Some repetition and hesitation is normal. However, if a child consistently and frequently seems to struggle with speaking, then the child may have a stuttering disorder. It is important not to add to any discomfort the child may already have about his stuttering. Don't interrupt or finish the child's sentences. Be patient and give the child as much time as needed to express himself. And, again, discuss your observations with the child's parents and coordinate the approaches you use to assist the child.

Work with parents to assist children with speech and language problems.

Applying Your Knowledge

The charts that follow list some typical behaviors of children at ages 5 to 7, 8 to 10, and 11 to 12. Included are behaviors relevant to communication skills. The right column asks you to identify ways staff can use this information to promote communication skills. Try to think of as many examples as you can. As you work through the module and learn new strategies, you can add them to the charts. You are not expected to think of all the examples at one time. If you need help getting started, turn to the completed charts at the end of the module. By the time you complete this module, you will find you have learned many ways to promote children's communication skills.

As you complete the charts that follow, keep in mind that many of the examples of children's behavior and staff responses apply to more than one age group. Developmentally appropriate programs are based on a knowledge of child development and are responsive to children's individual strengths, needs, and interests. Therefore, it is important to observe children regularly and to use what you learn to individualize the program.

Understanding and Responding to 5- to 7-Year-Old Children

What 5- to 7-Year-Old Children Are Like	How Staff Can Use This Information to Promote Communication Skills
They are interested in the meaning of words.	*Provide junior editions of dictionaries and encourage children to use them. Maintain a mystery word box to record and respond to children's questions.*
They ask seemingly endless questions.	
They enjoy engaging others in conversations.	
They like to provide rich details when describing things or events.	
They can be intolerant of people who speak with different accents or languages.	
They recognize grammatical mistakes.	

Understanding and Responding to 8- to 10-Year-Old Children

What 8- to 10-Year-Old Children Are Like	How Staff Can Use This Information to Promote Communication Skills
They often exaggerate, boast, and tell tall tales.	*Channel children's urges into storytelling activities. Share with them literature of this genre. Have an indoor or outdoor picnic at which children tell tall tales and ghost stories.*
Their language skills may vary greatly from those of their peers.	
They like to socialize with friends.	
They like coded languages and passwords.	
They can think critically.	
They can verbalize their ideas and feelings.	
They may begin to use slang and profanity.	

Understanding and Responding to 11- to 12-Year-Old Children

What 11- to 12-Year-Old Children Are Like	How Staff Can Use This Information to Promote Communication Skills
They often can speak with the fluency of adults.	*Provide lots of opportunities for children to develop and refine their speaking skills—for example, leading group meetings, putting on plays, expressing their ideas to others, describing an experiment, reciting poetry, and recording stories or poems on tape.*
They may question rules and beliefs they previously accepted.	
They may be self-centered and self-critical.	
They like to speak in complex sentences.	
They like thinking about abstract concepts.	
They use a lot of slang and "fad" words and sometimes use profanity as a way to identify with their peers.	

When you have completed as much as you can do of the charts, discuss your answers with your trainer. As you do the rest of the learning activities, you can refer back to the charts and add more examples of how school-age staff promote children's communication skills.

Learning Activity II.
Helping Children Develop Communication Skills[1]

IN THIS ACTIVITY YOU WILL LEARN TO:

- recognize the importance of all components of communication; and

- help children develop communication skills in each component area.

Children develop communication skills in four areas: listening, speaking, reading, and writing. Each area is vitally important. Children use these skills in their home life (taking a phone message for a parent), at school (to learn and complete assignments in almost every subject), at the program (to develop friendships), and in community activities (to learn and follow the rules of a sport or to work on scout badges). Mastering these skills allows children to be successful today and in their adult lives. You can encourage children to develop and use communication skills in every interest area and in every activity.

Listening

Listening involves hearing what is said and relating what is heard to personal knowledge. It can involve following directions, reflecting on what is heard, and paying attention. While children naturally develop listening skills throughout their lives, you can help children improve their listening competence.

One way you can help children improve their listening skills is to model them in your own conversations. For example, look directly at someone who is talking, give your undivided attention, comment on what was said, ask questions, facilitate discussions, and make sure each person who wishes to has an opportunity to speak. "I think I understand what you are telling me, Carolyn. The other children playing badminton want to keep score and you don't. Tell me some more about why you don't want to keep score. Then I can listen to the other children's point of view and try to help you and your friends solve the problem."

---

[1] Based on Toni S. Bickart, Judy R. Jablon, Diane Trister Dodge, *Building the Primary Classroom* (Washington, DC: Teaching Strategies, Inc., and Portsmouth, N.H.: Heinemann, 1999), pp. 263-275.

There are a number of strategies you can use to help children become better listeners. Here are some examples:

- Encourage children to participate in group discussions in which children speak one at a time. "I can see everyone has an idea for our Science Club fair. Ed, you can write them down as everyone take turns talking."

- Give oral directions that necessitate listening. Begin with one or two steps, then add more. "Marnie, when your group has finished making posters, please wipe off the tables and throw the trash in the outside bin."

- Have children face the person they are talking to and give their undivided attention to the conversation. "Mark, I'd really like to hear about your painting, but it's hard for me to hear because you keep turning around to look at the block builders. Try looking at me while you talk."

- Point out the differences in tone in spoken conversations. "Louise, I can tell you're excited about visiting your Grandma next week. You sound almost breathless. I really enjoyed hearing about the surprise photo album you made for her. Be sure to tell me exactly what she says and does when she opens the package."

- Play games such as "telephone" and teach children songs with choruses and different verses. "When we first learned to sing 'Stewball' everyone knew the chorus, but only a few of us could remember the words to all the verses. Now we sing out loud and clear for the chorus and the verses."

Speaking

Speaking skills develop hand in hand with listening skills. As children become better listeners, they develop more sophisticated speaking skills. They learn to convey ideas and questions in conversations, discussions, and presentations. Children may need your help to express their thoughts, organize their ideas, and learn more precise vocabulary words. Children who are encouraged to talk about their experiences and try out new words, find their enriched vocabulary can be empowering. For example:

Several children are discussing their field trip to a vegetable packing plant. Bernardo describes how the people worked together to pack the tomatoes. "You remember, they were all in a row and each person had a job to do and they did the job over and over again." "That's a perfect description," says Ms. Musen. "When people work like that they are working on an assembly line." Later that afternoon Bernardo is busily occupied in the block area constructing what looks like a factory. When Ms. Musen walks by she hears him tell another child, "Put these people in a row along that big block. They are going to work on an assembly line to get the peas and carrots to the city."

In addition, speaking also involves tone of voice. Think about how a simple word like "sure" can convey an entirely different meaning if it is said sarcastically rather than enthusiastically. You can encourage children to observe language and to reflect on the way words make them feel. Explain it's not just the words they choose, but how they say them that must be considered. Tone of voice and body language are important parts of communication.

You have many opportunities to promote children's speaking skills through nearly everything that happens in the program. In most cases, this happens indirectly, as children use interest areas, engage in activities, and make and carry out their plans.

Try these suggestions.

As you interact with children, you might:

- Encourage Jason and Theresa to state the rules for Chinese Checkers before beginning play;

- Ask Shantih to read aloud the minutes from the last meeting of the Magic Club;

- Adapt the group meeting agenda so Reynaldo can lead a discussion on the pros and cons of retiring some interest areas and offering new ones; and

- Spend one-on-one time with Brett so he can share his feelings about his mother's frequent hospital stays.

You can promote speaking skills by encouraging children to:

- Describe what they are thinking or feeling;

- Make up word games, riddles, and imaginary language;

- Share something they have written or an excerpt from a favorite author:

- Put on plays and skits;

- Participate in oratory contests and debates; and

- Talk to each other and to staff—in informal conversations and during club and group meetings, indoors and outdoors, on field trips and while at the program.

Reading is a complex process involving both the recognition and sound of letters and words and what they mean. Typically schools teach children to read using one of two approaches. The skills approach teaches children word attack skills, such as sounding out words by syllables. The whole language approach emphasizes learning to read and write throughout the curriculum. Instead of focusing just on the parts of language such as letter sounds or word recognition, children are encouraged to read and write as much as possible using the skills they have. In the process of reading and writing, children learn new skills and refine the ones they have. While the actual teaching of reading is the domain of the school, staff in school-age programs can support the process and help children become more confident readers.

It's important to understand what approach to reading the local school uses so that the program's activities support children appropriately. By treating reading as a natural and integral part of your program, you help children make reading a natural, integral part of their own lives.

Here are some things you might do to encourage children's enjoyment of reading.

Try these suggestions.

- Make print a natural part of the environment. When print is integrated into the program environment, children regard reading as a natural part of life. For example, label the activity areas, post weekly schedules, put up job charts that track children's responsibilities, provide message boards, showcase children's written work, and display children's signed art and architecture projects—including descriptions of the work in the "artist's" own words.

- Read aloud to children, either individually, in small groups, or to the full group. This is especially important for beginning readers, but older children may enjoy this activity as well. Older children may enjoy reading to younger ones.

  By hearing good books, children learn reading is both worthwhile and pleasurable. Reading aloud introduces children to different types of literature, expands their vocabularies, and lengthens their attention spans. It also provides children with models of different writing styles and familiarizes them with story structure. But most importantly, it creates an aura of comfort around language and reading.

- Choral readings are a wonderful way of making reading fun and giving children confidence. Favorite books—either in the form of "Big Books" or large print versions printed on flip chart paper are centrally displayed so all participants can see the print (and illustrations). Everyone reads together, allowing shy readers to be bolstered by the collective voice of the group. Particularly enjoyable are books with repetitive passages or "funny-sounding" names (such as Ricki-Tikki-Tavi in *The Jungle Book* by Rudyard Kipling), cumulative plots which build to a climax (such as "this is the cat that killed the rat that ate that malt that lay in the house that Jack built"), and rhymes (such as *Custard and Company* by Ogden Nash).

In addition to being fun and building confidence, shared reading experiences strengthen children's abilities to follow the printed word and increase the number of words they can recognize immediately by sight.

• Encourage children to read independently. As with most skills, practice with reading leads to proficiency. Provide a variety of reading materials that match children's skills and interests. Stock the quiet area with magazines, joke books, biographies, children's classics, sports books, how-to manuals, and books of lists and statistics. Children might make up an acronym to use as a sign for the area, for example DEAR (Drop Everything And Read) or SQUIRT (Special Quiet Uninterrupted Individual Reading Turf). Check this area regularly to make sure it is both appealing to children and stocked with books and magazines that reflect their current interests.

Writing

Like reading, writing is a skill that offers children many rewards. Most children have a natural desire to write. Even before they can read, young children make scribbled attempts at writing. As they become familiar with the alphabet, they start making recognizable letters. By the early school-age years, children begin to understand writing has to be organized on a page. They learn letters are not just randomly placed, but are grouped together to form words. As they grasp the connection between speech and writing children start to understand each letter represents a sound. At this stage they begin writing words, often "inventing" spelling according to the way a word sounds. With further exposure to reading and writing, children learn to use conventional spelling for their words.

It is likely that each child in the program has some level of writing ability. Most children below the ages of 8 or 9 years, use printing rather than cursive writing. Older school-age children (the exact age depends on when cursive writing is introduced in the elementary school curriculum) learn to use cursive writing. Some children are eager to practice and use "handwriting." Others, with less developed fine motor skills, may find it difficult to master this new form of writing. To promote children's printing or cursive writing skills it is important to know, first of all, what approach the local school is using in teaching writing and then, where each child is developmentally. For the younger children, model printed writing by forming letters according to accepted standards. For example, when making signs and labels, use capital and lower case letters rather than all capital letters. Use cursive writing with older children only. To find out the grade, style, and time of year at which cursive writing is introduced in your community, ask the principals at the schools attended by the children.

As with other forms of communication, an important way to support children's efforts to write is to serve as a role model. When children see you checking attendance, filling out forms, and posting notes on the message board, they observe writing serves a purpose. This, in turn motivates children to communicate in writing.

You can help children develop and refine their writing skills by offering meaningful writing opportunities. Here are some examples:

Try these suggestions.

- Encourage children to form a club to publish a newspaper or literary magazine.

- Sponsor a Writer's Workshop, as described earlier in this module.

- Encourage children to write short stories, poetry, plays, skits, and musicals they can perform for the group.

- Suggest children keep journals—to share or keep entirely private.

- Provide opportunities to research and write about topics of interest to them, featured in current events, or related to their school projects.

- Establish message boards children can use to write to each other.

- Provide information on organizations that match children with penpals from other countries or parts of the United States (see the list in the Orientation).

- Set up a graffiti board children can have fun with (remember to have the children establish rules for appropriate use of the board!).

- Make sure the quiet area has lots of papers, a variety of pens (including those used for calligraphy), and markers children can use for independent writing. There should be ample table space and comfortable, straight-back chairs to facilitate writing—although some children like to write on the floor using clipboards or another hard surface.

- Have children develop recipe cards for cooking and art materials (such as clay, paint, and wheat paste). Children can draw pictures, use photographs, or clip art to illustrate the text.

- Encourage children to develop and write up rules for games and sports activities that they then present to the group.

- Make it a practice to have children sign their art work. Have them provide titles and a narrative description similar to the way museums display this information.

- Establish an area where children can post their stories and poems for all to read and admire.

- Ask for "volunteers" to assist staff in writing-related tasks, such as taking phone messages.

- Stock the computer with creative writing programs of various difficulty levels.

- Provide tables in a quiet area where children can work on written homework assignments by themselves or with adult assistance.

- Put up a suggestion box so children can communicate their ideas to staff.

Applying Your Knowledge

In this learning activity you complete four observations, one for each area of communication—listening, speaking, reading, and writing. Observe one child age 5 to 7, one 8 to 10, and one 11 to 12. The fourth child may be any age. If you work with only one age group or do not have a full span of ages enrolled, conduct four representative observations. Then, review your observation notes and complete the observation summary forms. It may take a week or longer to finish your observations. Begin by reading the example that follows.

Supporting Children's Communication Skills: *Writing*

(Example)

Child: *Bethany*   **Age:** *5 1/2 years*   **Date:** *November 2*

Describe this child's writing skills:

Bethany can write her name and those of her family, including her dog Ben and her fish George and Babs. She signs her name to her artwork, but asks me to print descriptions of what she has made on the bottom of her drawings and paintings. She likes me to read them back to her at least three or four times.

What I did to support this child's development:

Bethany seems excited about her emerging writing skills. I think the best thing I can do to support her development is to provide her with new opportunities to try printing. I'm also going to involve her in writing the descriptions of her artwork, instead of doing it all myself. When she does write words, even if they are not spelled correctly, I will praise her and won't make any corrections because I don't want to discourage her enthusiasm.

What were the results?

I'm very pleased with Bethany's development. It's a pleasure to see how much satisfaction she takes in writing. Most of the time she writes the descriptions of her artwork herself rather than asking me to do it. She enjoys making letters (and many squiggles). She's very proud of what she does and points out each recognizable letter.

Since Bethany likes to cook, I thought it would be helpful to ask some of the older children to print words on the picture recipe cards. This has worked out great. Several times I found her copying the words on the cards. I also discovered these cards are teaching her to read. She can sight read many of the written words and match them to the pictures.

Supporting Children's Communication Skills: *Listening*

Child: _____ Age: _____ Date: _____

Describe this child's listening skills:

_____

_____

_____

What I did to support this child's development:

_____

_____

_____

What were the results?

_____

_____

_____

Supporting Children's Communication Skills: *Speaking*

Child: _____ Age: _____ Date: _____

Describe this child's speaking skills:

_____

_____

_____

What I did to support this child's development:

_____

_____

_____

What were the results?

_____

_____

_____

Supporting Children's Communication Skills: *Reading*

Child: _____ Age: _____ Date: _____

Describe this child's reading skills:

_____

_____

_____

What I did to support this child's development:

_____

_____

_____

What were the results?

_____

_____

_____

Supporting Children's Communication Skills: *Writing*

Child:_____ Age:_____ Date:_____

Describe this child's writing skills:

_____

_____

_____

What I did to support this child's development:

_____

_____

_____

What were the results?

_____

_____

_____

Discuss this activity with your trainer and your colleagues.

Learning Activity III.
Using the Physical Environment to Promote Communication Skills

---

IN THIS ACTIVITY YOU WILL LEARN TO:

- use the environment to help children develop communication skills; and
- provide materials that encourage children to use communication skills.

The environment lets children know that communication is valued.

The physical environment of a school-age program (see Module 3, Program Environment) lets children know that communication is valued. If there are few books and magazines or if there is no quiet place to do homework, children get the message this is not a place to be reading or writing. On the other hand, if there are tables for writing, a computer with interesting reading and writing software that can be individualized for differing skill levels, and a rich variety of books, magazines, and reference materials, children are encouraged to develop their reading and writing skills.

Children communicate freely in a supportive environment.

Setting up the environment to promote literacy is, indeed, one of the best strategies school-age staff can use to help children develop communication skills. First, you can create an environment that, by its design, lets children know they are free to communicate with one another. When children feel comfortable and relaxed, they are more willing to communicate their ideas and feelings. How you relate to each child—how easily each one learns you can be trusted—will influence their openness to listen and talk. When children learn you will accept them as they are, they are more likely to respond to your questions and to share their thoughts with you. Similarly, it's important to help children feel at ease with other children in the group. You've probably noticed the most verbal children are the ones who make friends easily. It's especially important to be aware of the shy children in the group. They may need your help to feel accepted by their peers and to learn how to communicate their ideas and feelings.

Try these suggestions.

Here are some specific ways to create an environment that encourages children to communicate.

Arrange the space so children can spend time in small groups. Conversations are more likely to occur when just a few children are present. Small tables where two to four children can play board games or put a model together serve this purpose well.

Create interesting prop boxes to enhance dramatic play. When children are fully involved in dramatic play, high levels of social interaction naturally take place. Props related to exploring space, running an animal hospital, or operating a park ranger station readily spur children to communicate with one another. (See Learning Activity II in Module 9: Social, for more information on prop boxes.)

Keep interesting things in the environment. Items such as mystery objects from nature, photographs depicting life in other countries, prints of famous paintings, and "beautiful junk" encourage children to explore, ask questions, talk about their ideas, and play with each other.

Plan group projects. These activities require children to plan and work together. Cooking activities or growing crystals, for example, foster verbal interaction.

Take trips and neighborhood walks. School-age children are ready to learn about the community beyond home, school, and the school-age program. Impromptu walks and planned field trips can expand children's experiences and give them new things to talk or write about.

Comfortable, quiet spaces invite children to read and write on their own. As important as it is to support group communication, it's also vital that children feel they have permission to be on their own. An inviting quiet area allows children to cozy up in an overstuffed pillow and read a novel or a joke book, sit at a computer and work through a creative story writing program, listen to a book on tape, do their assigned reading for school, write in a journal, or correspond with a penpal.

Children need quiet spaces for reading, writing, and listening.

Independent language and literacy experiences can also be encouraged throughout the room by the materials you provide. For example, you can include materials for making signs in the blocks and construction area. Index cards with directions for conducting simple experiments posted in the science area promote independent reading. Crossword puzzles and acrostics in the board and table games area also support independent activities.

Using print in meaningful ways throughout the environment can also contribute to a supportive environment. As noted in Learning Activity II, when children are exposed to print, they gain an appreciation for the usefulness of reading and writing in their daily lives. One of the most useful and natural ways to use print is as a management tool—attendance charts, job charts, schedules, program rules, and message boards, for example. You can also use

School-age staff can expose children to print in many aspects of the program.

print within each of the interest areas—as storage labels, as directions for using certain equipment, to enhance dramatic play environments, and to personalize work areas.

By using these techniques, you can make communication a natural part of children's activities. In an environment that facilitates literacy, children develop communication skills that will serve them throughout their lives.

Applying Your Knowledge

In this learning activity you focus on promoting children's communication skills in each interest area and outdoors. The chart that follows lists typical interest areas in school-age programs. For each one, list at least three suggested materials or design considerations to promote children's communication skills. Two examples are provided for each area.

Using The Environment To Promote Communication Skills

Quiet Area

Tables and comfortable chairs and floor space where children can read and write.

A computer with reading and writing software and documentation manuals. Software has varying difficulty levels so that gifted writers as well as children with language delays can work at their own pace: e.g., *Reader Rabbit* (The Learning Company), Mulliken *Storyteller* (Mulliken) and *Children's Writing and Publishing Center* (The Learning Company).

Dramatic Play Area

Books, magazines and newspapers.

Markers and writing materials for enhancing play themes: e.g., a medical office theme might include a receptionist's nameplate, message pads, a patient sign-in sheet, a monogrammed lab coat, forms, an appointment book, magazines, health care pamphlets, and phone books.

Arts and Crafts Area

Two-sided easels to encourage communication.

Recipes for making playdough, molding clay, goop (cornstarch and water), tempera, paint extender, chalk, paste, glue, and paper maché paste.

Sand and Water Area

Small tubs children can use in pairs, to facilitate dialogue.

Activity cards for making glycerin-based bubbles, performing water experiments with soap and dye, and casting sand prints with plaster.

Science and Nature

Reference books and activity cards with ideas for experiments.

Poster board and markers for charting scientific observations—for instance to graph the growth of plants, outline leaf shapes, or record changes in temperature.

Woodworking Area

Written (and illustrated) directions for carpentry projects.

Posted reminders for using tools safely.

Music Area

Words (or sheet music), librettos, and album notes for the CD's, albums, and tapes found in the area.

Blank note paper for children to write their own songs.

Materials for making signs to go with constructions.

Blueprints and instructions for constructing buildings, bridges, and other architectural projects.

Blocks and Construction Area

_____

_____

_____

Word games such as Scrabble, Boggle, and Pictionary, plus written rules for playing all games.

Tables and chairs arranged so children can play and discuss games in small groups.

Board and Table Games Area

_____

_____

_____

Math teasers and word problems.

Paper and pencils children can use to record calculations and measurements.

Math Area

_____

_____

_____

A quiet place where children can independently and privately read or write using books and magazines and a portable writing kit (a basket filled with paper and writing implements).

Score cards for recreational games, plus written rules for reference.

Outdoors

_____

_____

_____

Discuss your suggestions with your trainer and your colleagues.

Learning Activity IV.
Encouraging a Love of Reading

IN THIS ACTIVITY YOU WILL LEARN TO:

- choose books that children will find interesting and appealing; and
- help children become lifelong readers.

Staff who love reading can instill similar feelings in children.

One of the greatest gifts school-age staff can give children is the ability to enjoy reading. Reading experts believe a love for reading develops when children are regularly read to, when they are shown the delights of poetry, and when trusted adults share special books with them. Staff who genuinely enjoy reading, who like to tell stories, and who appreciate the rhythms and rhymes of poetry, are able to instill these same feelings in children. When you lovingly hold a book while reading with a child, share a tidbit from a story to excite a child's interests, repeat a particularly appealing description because you like the way the words sound, and read a story with great enthusiasm and expression, you convey how valuable and thrilling you think books are.

Books can offer children answers and comfort.

When children discover that the experiences of characters in books are similar to their own, they seek out books for answers and comfort. This is one reason why it is important to include books in the program that reflect the children's cultures and ethnic backgrounds. Once children have the opportunity to see themselves in books, they can also find links to their own experiences that depict cultural backgrounds different than their own. By seeing that people who look differently than they do can share similar feelings, they vicariously experience the lives of many different people. Books link children to the past and offer them hope for the future.

Select books based on children's reading skills and interests.

Selecting appropriate books for children ages 5 to 12 may seem like a difficult task. Reading skills obviously vary greatly. Most 5-year-olds are just on the verge of reading while many 12-year-olds have reading skills equal to adults. Moreover, children of different ages also vary in their individual reading skills. One 7-year-old reader may stumble through books, reading words aloud with no expression. Another may read with the ease of a 12-year-old, taking on different voices as she reads a story aloud. Yet the 7-year-old with advanced reading skills is probably interested in the same kinds of books as the less-skilled reader who is also age

7, rather than books about teenagers that might interest a 12-year-old. Probably the best way to select books is to ask children what they like to read now, and what books they enjoyed when they were younger. With limited resources you might need to be a selective consumer.

Young school-age children (5 to 7 years) enjoy many of the same books preschool children like. This is especially true of stories with humor or irony. Any of the picture books by Henry Allard about the silly Stupid family (*The Stupids Step Out, The Stupids Have A Ball),* for example, make many a 5- and 6-year-old double-over with laughter. Books known as "early readers" are especially appropriate for children in this age group who are beginning readers. These books are well-illustrated to help children make the transition from what they see to what the printed word says. They have chapters, like more advanced children's books. Many of these books are wonderful for shared reading experiences.

Picture books and "early readers" appeal to 5- to 7-year-olds.

Many children's classics are aimed at 8- to 10-year-old children. Adventure stories, mysteries, fairytales, folktales, and chapter books make appealing and exciting reading. You can read these books aloud to children in this age group. This is a highly effective way to motivate children to read for their own pleasure. The more they read, the better readers they will become.

Many classics are enjoyed by 8- to 10-year-olds.

Older school-age children (11 to 12 years) like reading about the teenagers they will soon be. Plots dealing with romance, family relationships, and school are appealing, as are biographies and stories of beloved animal pets like Lassie or Misty. As children become more confident readers, they prefer books that are mostly text. Illustrations interfere with the reading experience once children no longer need picture cues. Similarly, older and better readers prefer black-and-white illustrations over the more distracting color ones.

Older school-age children like reading about "real" people.

Most school librarians or the children's librarian at your local library will be happy to assist in selecting books. Look, too, for books that are previous winners of the John Newberry and Randolph Caldecott Medals. These medals are awarded annually by a committee of children's librarians to the author of the "most distinguished contribution to American literature" (Newberry) and to the artist of the "most distinguished picture book for children" (Caldecott). These books can be easily identified by the large metallic stickers on their jackets. The American Library Association's web site (www.ala.org) has lists of current and past award winners. Also, most newspapers publish a yearly or a twice-

Librarians and teachers can help select books.

yearly guide to children's books. These guides are particularly useful for keeping up with recent publications. It is also a good idea to find out what books children are reading at school. After the class has finished a book, it can be added to the program's library. Ask children for this information, or contact the teachers at the elementary school. Your outreach efforts will demonstrate the program's interest in establishing a partnership with the elementary school to support children's growth and learning.

Also, it's important to include books that build on field trips, clubs, or special activities offered in the program, and books that respond to problems experienced by children, such as moving to a new home or adjusting to divorce. Include some books of short stories as well. They tend to include fewer characters and simpler plots which make them more appealing to some children, particularly less skilled readers. Children may use short stories as the basis for developing skits and plays.

Provide a variety of general reference materials.

The program should also have some general reference materials of interest to school-age children of all ages, such as dictionaries (junior and more advanced editions), thesauruses, atlases, almanacs, and books of lists and facts like the *Guinness Book of World Records*, *Brown's Record Book of Weird and Wonderful Facts*, and *The Animals' Who's Who*. Also, provide nonfiction and "how to" books on a variety of subjects to build on children's experiences in different interest areas. For example, add books on inventions when children are busily engaged in their own experiments, books about dinosaurs when there is a flurry of interest in prehistoric times, and books on famous athletes for sports enthusiasts.

Consider these magazines and journals.

Magazines and special-interest journals provide reading materials that respond to children's interests and needs. Many can be purchased at bookstores, through subscriptions, or they may be available at the local library. The library will also have more information about each publication—the publisher and how to contact them. Some examples follow.

American Girl Magazine (www.americangirl.com) is popular with girls ages 6 and up. Published bimonthly, it features stories, plays, activities, instructions on making arts and crafts, and articles on different people from around the world.

Boy's Life (www.bsa.scouting.org), published by the Boy Scouts of America, is aimed at boys ages 7 to 17. Articles cover a wide range of topics of interest to both boys and girls.

Cobblestone: The History Magazine for Young Children (www.cobblestonepub.com) addresses a different historical theme in each issue. Children ages 9 to 14 will enjoy the articles, photographs, games, and activities.

Contact Kids (www.ctw.org), from the Children's Television Workshop, focuses on science, nature, and technology. Each issue includes stories, puzzles, mazes, and contests.

Cricket: The Magazine for Children (www.cricketmag.com) introduces children ages 6 to 12 to some of the best literature and art from all over the world.

Dolphin Log (www.dolphinlog.org) is published bimonthly by The Cousteau Society. It brings together science, history, and the arts as they relate to oceans, marine biology and ecology, natural history, and more.

National Geographic World (www.nationalgeographic.com/world) appeals to 8- to 14-year-olds. It includes fact-based stories on outdoor adventure, natural history, sports, games, and accomplishments of children.

Ranger Rick (www.nwf.org/rrick), a publication of the National Wildlife Federation, gives children ages 6 to 12 a greater understanding and appreciation for nature.

Sports Illustrated for Kids (www.sikids.com) is aimed at children ages 8 to 13 who are especially interested in sports. Athletic accomplishments of both professionals and amateurs are featured.

Stone Soup (www.stonesoup.com) includes stories, poems, and art created by children from around the world.

Zillions (www.zillionsedcenter.org) is a consumer-oriented publication for 8- to 14-year-olds. Readers learn to make informed decisions about purchases and to manage money responsibly.

Some newspapers and magazines distribute versions of their publications designed for children's use. Also, since most popular publications are written at the sixth to eighth grade reading level, older children may enjoy reading daily, weekly, or monthly newspapers and magazines. Newspapers and news magazines tend to include "all the news," some of which may be violent or upsetting. Ask parents which ones they think are appropriate to have on hand for their children.

Older children may enjoy newspapers and magazines.

Try these suggestions.

No matter what reading materials you select, be sure to provide children with both group and individual reading experiences, such as those described in Learning Activity II. In addition, here are some points to keep in mind:

- **Read aloud with children**. After children can read on their own, continue to read aloud to them. If you sense a child of any age could use some close "together" time, sharing a book or magazine in the quiet area might be just the answer. Children can get caught up in raucously chanting repetitive phrases and adding cumulative dialogue to stories read in a group. Books can also set the stage for interesting discussions and follow-up activities.

- **Encourage skilled readers to read to younger children**. Perhaps an arrangement could be made for the school-age children to read to young children at the local library or a nearby early childhood program.

- **Share the classic stories you enjoyed as a child**. They generally hold appeal for children of today as well. Younger school-age children will probably enjoy any of the *Winnie-the-Pooh* books by A. A. Milne or the series by Ruth Gannett that begins with *My Father's Dragon*. Other popular series include the *Chronicles of Narnia* by C.S. Lewis, which begins with *The Lion, the Witch, and the Wardrobe*. Don't forget some new "classics" such as Ann Cameron's *The Stories Julian Tells* for younger children and Scott O'Dell's *Island of the Blue Dolphins* for older children. Reading a chapter or two together at one sitting keeps children's attention and makes them look forward to continuing the book. You may need to keep a dictionary nearby to look up unfamiliar words—but this is part of the fun of reading classic literature.

- **Let children read to you as often as possible**. Beginning readers typically welcome a listening audience. Offer assistance when needed, but give beginning readers time to sound out letters and guess new words from their context. Even though it can try one's patience to wait for a child to say the appropriate word out loud, the more reading a child is able to do on his or her own, the more skilled a reader he or she will become.

- **Encourage children to regularly check books out of the library** so they can spend more time reading at their leisure. Also, let children know they don't have to finish a book if they don't like it. Stress reading is a pleasure, not a chore.

- **Be a role model**. If you let children know how much you enjoy reading, you send them the message reading is both pleasurable and something of value. You do this by asking children if they saw a particular article in the newspaper or by talking about the characters and plot of a book you just finished reading.

- **Play language and reading games**. Dorothy Rich, in the book *MegaSkills,* offers these suggestions:[2]

  > Make up rhyming riddles: "What rhymes with cat and is used with balls?"

  > Set up a mystery word box. Children can ask you to write down words they have no idea how to spell or define but appeal to them for some reason. They may be words a child has heard but doesn't know about (such as the Richter Scale) or funny sounding ones (such as onomatopoeia). As you print the word on an index card, discuss what the word means with the child and read it together. These mystery word cards can be stored in a file card box. These boxes become, in Rich's words, "a treasure house of favorite words."

  > Plan a scavenger hunt with clues based on rhymes or other word games.

Applying Your Knowledge

In this learning activity you focus on promoting the reading skills of one a child in your group. Think about what books the child is able to and interested in reading, then plan and implement a strategy for a shared reading experience. After trying out your idea, answer questions related to selecting and using a book with that child. Begin by reading the example that follows.

---

[2] Based on Dorothy Rich, *MegaSkills: How Families Can Help Children Succeed in School and Beyond* (Boston, MA: Houghton-Mifflin Company, 1988), pp. 160-164.

A Shared Reading Experience

(Example)

Child: _Marcus_   **Age:** _7 years_   **Date:** _February 5_

1. **List five books in the program's collection appropriate for this child's reading level.**

    Up North in Winter by Deborah Hartley   _Frog and Toad Together_ by Arnold Lobel
    In a Dark, Dark Room by Alvin Schwartz   _Green Eggs and Ham_ by Dr. Seuss
    The Shrinking of Treehorn by
        Florence Parry Heide

2. **List five books in the program's collection that reflect this child's interests and needs.**

    Dinnieabbiesister-r-r by Riki Levinson   _One At A Time_ by David McCord
    Danny and the Dinosaur by Syd Hoff   _Custard and Company_ by Ogden Nash
    The Book of Pigericks: Pig Limericks
        by Arnold Lobel

3. **Describe your strategy for sharing a book with this child and why you think it is appropriate.**

    Marcus loves word games, rhymes, and silly poems, so I asked the children's librarian to recommend some books. She recommended the work of David McCord because he "plays with words like toys." I plan to introduce Marcus to the poem Bananas and Cream from the anthology One At A Time. I decided to use this poem because it's a silly rhyme, it can be chanted out loud, and it's about bananas—three things Marcus adores.

4. **Describe what happened when you shared a book with this child.**

    I had Marcus read the poem to me. At first he stumbled, but as he got into the rhythm, his pace picked up. Next, I read the poem with Marcus, which he loved. He asked to read it together three more times. With each reading his voice got louder. I was worried we were getting too loud for the quiet area, so I suggested we take the book outside where we could recite the poem as loudly as we wished. Marcus liked this idea, so we went outside and chanted Bananas and Cream in the loudest speaking voices we had. Several other children came over to chant with us.

5. **What do you think the child got out of this activity?**

    Marcus found a poem he can chant with abandon. In fact, he's almost memorized the entire poem. He's declared McCord a "jammin" poet. His love of word play encourages him to read more—especially other lighthearted poems.

6. **How do you plan to build on this experience to further promote the child's reading experience?**

    I'm going to ask the librarian for other suggestions. I'm also going to encourage Marcus and some of the other children who share his interest in silly poems and limericks to hold a poetry reading, and perhaps write their own poems.

A Shared Reading Experience
(Example)

Child: _____ **Age:** _____ **Date:** _____

1. List five books in the program's collection appropriate for this child's reading level.

   _____   _____

   _____   _____

   _____   _____

2. List five books in the program's collection that reflect this child's interests and needs.

   _____   _____

   _____   _____

3. Describe your strategy for sharing a book with this child and why you think it is appropriate.

   _____   _____

   _____   _____

   _____   _____

4. Describe what happened when you shared a book with this child.

   _____   _____

   _____   _____

   _____   _____

5. What do you think the child got out of this activity?

   _____   _____

   _____   _____

   _____   _____

6. How do you plan to build on this experience to further promote the child's reading experience?

   _____   _____

   _____   _____

   _____   _____

Discuss this activity with your trainer and the child's parents.

Learning Activity V.
Helping Children Communicate Their Ideas and Feelings

IN THIS ACTIVITY YOU WILL LEARN TO:

- help children clarify their ideas and feelings; and
- interact with children in ways that encourage them to communicate their ideas and feelings.

Communicating ideas and feelings helps children feel in control of their lives.

The desire to share thoughts and feelings is a part of human nature for both children and adults. When Hannah's grandma died, she spent the afternoon huddled with her friends who listened and provided support. When Kyle won the third grade spelling bee he announced it at group meeting. When Laura had an idea for a story she spent the afternoon at the computer, then printed copies of her masterpiece for her friends and family. In fact, the National Council of Teachers of English and the International Reading Association have stated that the ability to communicate thoughts and feelings is a lifelong literacy goal.

Language and literacy skills provide the tools for communicating in close, personal ways. Children who can read and write about their experiences, express ideas clearly and listen to responses, usually feel more capable and in control of their lives.

Talk to children and encourage them to write.

Talking to children about what they are thinking and feeling is perhaps the best way to help them express their thoughts. Encouraging children to write down these thoughts enables children to see how much they really know. Asking children to continue writing even after they are convinced they have nothing more to say, encourages them to reflect further on their thoughts and feelings. When they write more, children think and learn more, as this example illustrates:

> After listening to some 9- and 10-year-olds argue about which baseball players to include on an all-star team, Ms. Hsiao suggests the children write about and explain their choices. She challenges them to support their choices by including each player's strengths and weaknesses. After writing a description of his ideal team, Pavel turns to Ms. Hsiao and says, "I know more about baseball than I thought I did!"

When children put their thoughts and feelings into words, they learn to make sense of the events affecting their lives. Sometimes they need adults to step in to prompt them to express their feelings. An example follows:

> Martin was about to move over 1,000 miles away. Mr. Thomas suggested he read a book about how a boy his age handled his family's move to a new community. Reading the book helped Martin understand his feelings about his family's upcoming move. He read and reread a passage in the book about what the boy was afraid of and found comfort in how the boy dealt with his fears. The book helped him articulate his own fears so the school-age staff and his family were able to help him get through this difficult time.

Through daily activities, the school-age program can encourage children to use their skills to share their ideas and thoughts with others. For example, the group meeting is an ideal format for using verbal skills to express and defend personal opinions. Providing a variety of writing materials encourages children to express their thoughts in writing. A schedule that allows ample time for free choice gives children time to develop close and supportive friendships.

Staff should also take advantage of snack and outdoor times to communicate with children one-on-one or in small groups. Private moments during the day lend themselves to sharing thoughts and feelings.

Another way to help children learn to communicate effectively is to make them aware of their own nonverbal behaviors. Like adults, school-age children use a variety of body language—slouching, averting eye contact, shrugging, drumming fingers, crossing arms-that unconsciously communicates messages to others. You can help children understand how these nonverbal gestures affect others and help them recognize when they are using them. This recognition and understanding allows children to think about and plan their nonverbal messages just as they think about their verbal ones. An example follows:

Help children notice and understand nonverbal behaviors.

> Mr. Prescott intervenes to help April, a very competitive athlete, understand the messages she communicates through her body language. "April, I've noticed you roll your eyes and turn your back when one of your teammates strikes out or misses a catch. The children recognize these gestures as signs you are disappointed with them. They feel angry and resentful

towards you, which leads to bickering and no one has fun playing the game." April responds, "That's exactly what I was thinking, but I didn't mean for the others to know what was on my mind. I didn't want to hurt their feelings." The next time a teammate strikes out April catches herself before she rolls her eyes. She relaxes and tries to focus on enjoying the game.

Teach children to use "I" messages to communicate their feelings.

Another important communication technique you can introduce to children is the use of "I" messages. Such messages begin with the word "I" and describe personal feelings: for example, you might say, "I feel angry when . . .," rather than "you make me feel . . ." They encourage the speaker to assume responsibility for his or her feelings rather than blaming someone else, and they defuse tense situations. If children use "I" messages when discussing a conflict, communication is likely to be more effective and lead to solutions that are mutually acceptable. It is easy to describe this technique, but very difficult to learn to use it consistently. Children will need many reminders from staff and from each other: "Use your 'I' messages." Children who master this technique will gain a valuable communication tool they can use in many situations and relationships throughout their lives.

Applying Your Knowledge

In this learning activity you focus on a child in your program who seems to have difficulty communicating his or her ideas and feelings. Describe the child's skills, then develop strategies for helping the child gain the skills needed to express him or herself. Begin by reviewing the example that follows.

Helping Children Communicate Their Ideas and Feelings
(Example)

Child: _Conrad_   **Age:** _9 years_   **Date:** _October 22_

Describe this child's communication skills:

> _Conrad is enthusiastic about many activities, but he shies away from reading and writing because he is not very skilled at either. Several of the children his age in the program are extremely adept readers and writers, which turns Conrad off to these activities even more. He does, however, like group story telling and participates in this activity._

What strategies can you use to help this child communicate his or her ideas and feelings? (State at least six.)

> _Regularly sit with and have private discussions with Conrad. I plan to use lots of open-ended questions that will encourage him to express himself._
>
> _Ask the children's librarian to suggest some books about children who have difficulty with school we can read together so Conrad doesn't feel so alone._
>
> _Encourage Conrad to participate more frequently in drama activities and perhaps to join the Drama Club._
>
> _Have Conrad dictate ideas and stories into a tape recorder which I'll then type up. Conrad doesn't know how to type. This way he'll get to see his thoughts in polished form. It will also let him know I value what he has to say._
>
> _Encourage Conrad to use the computer tutorial to learn to type._
>
> _Team Conrad (if he is interested) with a good writer to co-author a column for the newsletter._

Helping Children Communicate Their Ideas and Feelings
(Example)

Child: _____ **Age:** _____ **Date:** _____

Describe this child's communication skills:

_____

_____

_____

_____

What strategies can you use to help this child communicate his or her ideas and feelings? (State at least six.)

_____

_____

_____

_____

_____

_____

_____

_____

_____

_____

_____

_____

_____

_____

Discuss this activity with your trainer and colleagues who also work with this child.

SUMMARIZING YOUR PROGRESS

You have now completed all the learning activities for this module. Whether you are an experienced school-age staff member or a new one, this module has probably helped you develop new skills in promoting children's communication. Before you go on, take a few minutes to summarize what you've learned.

- Turn back to Learning Activity I, Using Your Knowledge of Child Development to Promote Communication Skills. Add specific examples to the charts of what you learned about promoting children's communication skills during the time you were working on this module. Compare your ideas to those in the completed charts at the end of the module.

- Next, review your responses to the pre-training assessment for this module. Write a summary of what you learned and list the skills you developed or improved.

_____

_____

_____

_____

_____

_____

_____

_____

_____

_____

_____

_____

_____

_____

_____

If there are topics you would like to know more about, you will find recommended readings listed in the Orientation.

Your final step in this module is to complete the knowledge and competency assessments. Let your trainer know when you are ready to schedule the assessments. After you have successfully completed them, you will be ready to start a new module. Congratulations on your progress so far, and good luck with your next module.

ANSWER SHEETS

Promoting Children's Communication

Creating an Interesting and Varied Environment That Encourages Children to Develop and Use Communication Skills

1. **How did Ms. Alessi build on Jonathan's interests to promote communication skills?**

   a. When she overheard him talking to his friend, she asked him for details about the trip to the museum.

   b. She enthusiastically responded to his comments about dinosaurs, letting him know she thought what he had to say was both important and interesting.

2. **In what ways did Ms. Alessi provide an environment that encouraged communication skills?**

   a. She suggested Jonathan use the computer and publishing software to write his story.

   b. She told him where he could find drawing and bookbinding supplies if he wanted to "publish" his story.

Interacting with Children in Ways That Encourage Them to Communicate Their Thoughts and Feelings

1. **How did Ms. Kearney know something was bothering Stuart?**

   a. Stuart's mother said her her husband was away on business for a month—so Ms. Kearney was on the lookout for any signs Stuart might be having problems.

   b. She observed a significant change in his block-building activity.

2. **How did Ms. Kearney help Stuart express his feelings and thoughts?**

   a. She engaged him in conversation.

   b. She compared the way his block structures looked to the way he might be feeling.

   c. She gave him words he could apply to his feelings.

   d. She suggested writing a letter to his father.

   e. She sat with him at his request.

3. **What other questions might Ms. Kearney have asked to draw out Stuart?**

> Many other questions are possible. They should encourage Stuart to express his feelings in words. Here are some examples:

a. "Is something going on today, Stuart? You didn't seem to be building in your usual spirited style."

b. "What special mood are you conveying through your building?"

c. "Is anything bothering you at home or at school? You haven't seemed your usual self these past few days?"

Providing Opportunities for Children to Use Their Listening, Speaking, Reading, and Writing Skills

1. **What did Mr. Williams do to interest the children in writing stories?**

a. He sponsored a Writer's Workshop.

b. He solicited the children's input.

c. He shared a personal story with the children.

d. He assured the children they all had something valuable to contribute.

2. **How did the Writer's Workshop promote the children's language and literacy skills?**

a. It focused children's thinking on the elements of a good story.

b. It showed children how to draw on their own experiences to tell a story.

c. It gave children a plan for selecting what they wanted to write about.

d. It gave children confidence in their ability to put together a literary journal.

Understanding and Responding to 5- to 7-Year-Old Children

What 5- to 7-Year-Old Children are Like	How Staff Can Use This Information to Promote Communication Skills
They are interested in the meaning of words.	*Provide junior editions of dictionaries and encourage children to use them. Maintain a mystery word box to record and respond to children's questions.*
They ask seemingly endless questions.	*Model good listening skills. Respond in ways that help children focus their thoughts.*
They enjoy engaging others in conversations.	*Provide space and opportunities for socializing; for example, while playing board and table games and during water play or dramatic play. Participate in conversations with children so they will learn to take turns talking and to respond to what others say.*
They like to provide rich details when describing things or events.	*Respond enthusiastically to children's descriptions so they know you appreciate their use of rich language. Show children how to use a thesaurus or a book of synonyms so they can find just the right adjectives or adverbs. Model expressive language: "The colors in Tad's shirt are so bright they're almost blinding."*
They can be intolerant of people who speak with different accents or languages.	*Use individual discussions and group meetings to emphasize the need to respect differences. Be sure the program includes a variety of multicultural and anti-bias materials that teach children respect for others.*
They recognize grammatical mistakes.	*Model correct standard grammar and praise children's efforts to correct themselves.*

Understanding and Responding to 8- to 10-Year-Old Children

What 8- to 10-Year-Old Children are Like	How Staff Can Use This Information to Promote Communication Skills
They often exaggerate, boast, and tell tall tales.	*Channel children's urges into storytelling activities. Share with literature of this genre. Have an indoor or outdoor picnic at which children tell tall tales and ghost stories.*
Their language skills may vary greatly from those of their peers.	*Individualize materials and activities to meet children's varying skills. Provide reading and writing materials and software that accommodate varied skill levels.*
They like to socialize with friends.	*Suggest children form clubs—newspaper, great books, autobiography—with children who have similar interests. Provide plenty of time in the schedule for free choice so children can interact with their friends.*
They like coded languages and passwords.	*Encourage children to use codes in making up games or developing a secret language they can teach others. Provide books and materials on secret codes used for espionage. Show children how to use invisible ink to write messages.*
They can think critically.	*Provide challenging problems children can solve on paper or on the computer or through experimentation. Reinforce the scientific method to solve problems. Involve children in planning program activities, selecting materials, resolving conflicts, and making rules. Use group meeting times as opportunities to discuss and analyze current issues.*
They can verbalize their ideas and feelings.	*Ask lots of open-ended questions to encourage children to express their thoughts and feelings. Suggest children keep daily journals. Encourage children to share their ideas with others. Teach children to be respectful while their peers are talking.*
They may begin to use slang and profanity.	*Involve children in setting program rules regarding use of language. For example, slang (if it's not about bodily functions or hurtful) is acceptable, but profanity is not.*

Understanding and Responding to 11- to 12-Year-Old Children

What 11- to 12-Year-Old Children are Like	How Staff Can Use This Information to Promote Communication Skills
They often can speak with the fluency of adults.	*Provide lots of opportunities for children to develop and refine their speaking skills—for example, leading group meetings, putting on plays, expressing their ideas to others, describing an experiment, reciting poetry, and recording stories or poems on tape.*
They may question rules and beliefs they previously accepted.	*Use group meetings as a time for open discussion of rules and beliefs. Encourage children to use conflict resolution techniques to resolve problems. Ask children to put their concerns in writing—for example, an explanation of why they think a rule is unfair along with a proposed alternative.*
They may be self-centered and self-critical.	*Accept this is normal for children at this stage of development. Encourage children to record their private thoughts in journals. Suggest they use the computer for writing so it is easier to make revisions.*
They like to speak in complex sentences.	*Encourage children's efforts without correcting their misuse of words. Expose them to books on tape and tapes of famous speeches such as Dr. Martin Luther King's "I Have a Dream" speech.*
They like thinking about abstract concepts.	*Encourage children to research or debate ideas related to topics such as freedom, bigotry, greed, or heroism. Sponsor a Debating Club and introduce children to some simple debating rules.*
They use a lot of slang and "fad" words and sometimes use profanity as a way to identify with their peers.	*Set and uphold clear standards for language use at the program—profanity is never appropriate. Accept children's use of slang and fad words, without using them yourself. Model standard use of language in conversations with children and adults. Introduce children to new vocabulary words that mean the same thing as the slang words.*

GLOSSARY

Communication	The act of expressing and sharing ideas, desires, and feelings.
Cumulative books	Those that build on the previous page's text by adding a new line to the repeated lines.
Language	A system of words and rules for their use in speaking, reading, and writing.
Literacy	A set of tools for communicating and learning, including listening, speaking, reading, and writing.
Nonverbal communication	The act of conveying feelings or ideas without using words.
Predictable books	Those with plots that are easy for readers to guess what will happen next.
Reading skills	Visual and perceptual skills needed to read, including following sequences from left to right and recognizing differences and similarities among things.
Repetitive books	Those that repeat certain words and phases.
Shared reading	A group reading experience resembling choral reading-everyone reads a story out loud together.
Skills approach	A method of teaching reading in which children use word attack skills as decoders.
Whole language	A method of teaching reading and writing which emphasizes reading, writing, and oral language across the curriculum, teaching skills in context rather than as isolated units of information.

NOTES

NOTES

NOTES

NOTES

NOTES

NOTES

NOTES

NOTES

NOTES

NOTES

NOTES

NOTES

NOTES